THE SPREAD OF THE RUSSIAN REVOLUTION

ESSAYS ON 1917

The Spread of the Russian Revolution

Essays on 1917

ROGER PETHYBRIDGE

MACMILLAN
ST. MARTIN'S PRESS

First published 1972 by
THE MACMILLAN PRESS LTD
London and Basingstoke
Associated companies in New York Toronto
Dublin Melbourne Johannesburg and Madras

SBN 333 13244 0

Library of Congress Catalogue Card Number 72–76589

Printed in Great Britain by
R. & R. CLARK LTD
Edinburgh

S. I. P.

In creative memory

Contents

Preface

The essays which follow are intended to serve as pointers to various aspects of the Russian revolution which have hitherto been somewhat neglected. The history of Soviet Russia in general as well as that of 1917 in particular has been viewed primarily in terms of the ruling few – their policies, power struggles and ideologies. Whilst this is an appropriate method for what has been an authoritarian system for most of the Soviet period, it is perhaps less pertinent to the situation in 1917, when even Lenin, who emerged as the most dominant political personality, was almost completely swept along by the revolutionary tide, which prohibited the establishment of any real authority at the helm of the state.

There is a need to break away from the conventional approach to 1917 in order to look in more detail at some of the broader social, economic and geographical factors which impinged upon the high political drama played out for the most part in Petrograd. Theodore Dan expressed a vital truth concerning the Russian revolution when he wrote 'In the conditions of the "freest" country, which was what, according to an expression in Lenin's *Theses*, the [February] revolution had made Russia, the attention of the labouring masses was less taken up than ever by questions of "politics". It was consumed more and more by those socio-economic disorders that were brought about by the constantly worsening wartime collapse.'[1] The Bolsheviks came to power eventually because Lenin grasped the fact that the vast majority of Russians were not enthralled by any political theory or personality, nor even by the attainment of their political rights, but rather by the hope of achieving certain

[1] Theodore Dan, *The Origins of Bolshevism* (London, 1964) pp. 405–6.

A 2

practical social and economic objectives. Lenin gave them
concrete form during the revolution: he put into the heads of
the factory proletariat the notion of 'workers' control', he excited the peasantry with a scheme for confiscating estates, and
delighted the war-weary soldiers with a campaign for an
immediate peace.

All the essays in this book deal in different ways with the
mutual interaction of the kaleidoscopic political changes at the
heart of the Russian state between February and October 1917,
and the social and economic disintegration of the nation as a
whole over the same period.

When a thoroughgoing political revolution occurs, as it did
in February 1917, the central *Government* changes almost at
once; but in the French and Russian revolutions, the two
greatest political changes in modern times, the sense of a new
social *community* grew at a much slower rate. In neither case did
it come into being at a given moment. It did not materialise
like magic on the Ninth Thermidor, 28 July 1794. Nor did it
descend on Russia in February 1917 in the way Kerensky thinks
it did: ' . . . all sectional, class and personal interests were set
aside, all differences forgotten . . . the February revolution was
unique in history in that all classes of society participated in it.
It was a moment which brought into being "my" Russia – an
ideal Russia which took the place of the Russia corrupted and
defiled by Rasputin and by the universally hated Monarchy.'[1]

The topics covered by the essays are distinct from each other.
It would not be possible to convert them into seriatim chapters
of a single book since this would mean forcing the varied
materials into artificially contrived channels. Nevertheless interesting relationships exist between the subjects dealt with here.
The first two essays are concerned with the communications
network in 1917. The railways, post and telegraph, and the
men who ran them, were of crucial importance since Russia is
the largest physical area in which a major revolution has ever
occurred. The English, American (confined to the eastern seaboard) and French revolutions were storms in a teacup by
comparison. In 1917 over 170 million people and an area even
vaster than the size of present-day Russia were involved. The
area of Russia straddled all Asia and half of Europe and in-

[1] *The Kerensky Memoirs* (London, 1966) p. 218.

cluded Finland, Poland and the Baltic states. The political
'centre' of this huge territory lay at its very edge. In spite of the
technological developments of the nineteenth century, Russia
was still a relatively static society by 1917, especially by other
European or North American standards.

It is well known to students of the Russian revolution that
the breakdown of the supply system was one of the most significant economic factors leading to the collapse of the Provisional
Government; yet the subject has not been examined in any
detail for the year 1917. This problem is treated in the third
essay, and it is hoped that the introductory section to the essay
on the railways may serve as a useful background to the supply
question as well. The dissemination of political news through
the rank-and-file of Russian society is considered in the essays
on the press and propaganda. The final essay is devoted to some
aspects of the relationship between Petrograd and the provinces that have received little attention so far in more general
accounts of the Russian revolution.

The sheer size of Russia and the peripheral location of her
political capital are two important geographical factors which
recur as background influences in all the essays. Another overriding influence which is prevalent throughout and which be-
comes even more powerful when considered in combination
with the size of Russia is the phenomenal speed at which the
revolution progressed. The situation changed radically from
day to day, necessitating constant fresh directives from the
Provisional Government and the Soviet to the nation. The
Provisional Government was eventually submerged in a flood
of business with which it could not possibly cope; and, what was
more dangerous, it did not keep in close enough contact with
the rapidly moving temper of the people. By October it was
out of touch in many ways.

The Russian revolution was certainly far more telescoped
than the French. 1788 witnessed the revolt of the French aristo-
cracy, but by 1790 Lafayette was still supreme. In Russia there
was no classic prelude during which the monarch quarrelled
openly with his nobles. The Tsar was removed from the stage
at the very outset in 1917. The rest of the Russian revolution
went at the same galloping pace. Whereas the Terror fell on
France late in 1793, it reached Russia by the autumn of 1918.

Shortly before 1917, a famous Russian revolutionary in exile in London, Ivan Maisky, told an English socialist the old fable of Ilya Murometz. Murometz was a giant of a man who sat in one place for thirty years without moving, but when he got up, he went so fast that no one could catch him. Maisky added, 'that is what will happen in my country when the hour of freedom from Tsarist tyranny strikes'.[1]

It would seem to be the natural tendency of revolutions to gather speed and political impetus. The fear of counter-revolution provides a powerful stimulus. In the case of Russia, another 'mighty accelerator', as Lenin put it, was the war. The economic disorder and moral distress caused by the unsuccessful war were foremost among the causes of the collapse of Tsarism, and the war did not end in February 1917. The French revolution broke out in peacetime, but in Russia the war continued to harass the Provisional Government, and incited political tempers to extremes, so that the pendulum of opinion swung violently from the centre to the left over a very short period.

[1] I. Maisky, *Journey into the Past* (London, 1962) p. 182.

Acknowledgements

I should like to thank the following persons for their advice: my colleagues in the Centre of Russian and East European Studies at the University College of Swansea and also Professor L. Schapiro, Professor G. Ionescu and Professor W. H. Greenleaf. I should like to express my gratitude to the library staffs of the University College of Swansea, Columbia University, New York, the Hoover Institution, Stanford, the Institute of Social History, Amsterdam, and the Lenin Library, Moscow. I am indebted to Mrs Beryl Langford, Miss Judith Hughes and Mrs Eileen Wimmers for their expert secretarial assistance. I also wish to acknowledge the permission of the editors of *Government and Opposition* and the *Russian Review* to reprint material in the text.

R. P.

1 The Railways

Comrades, railwaymen! The fate of the revolution
hangs on your decision. The future historian will
most likely say 'the railwaymen saved the revolution'
or 'the railwaymen ruined the revolution'.

From a speech at the Railwaymen's Union Conference.   October 29 1917

The political problems which involved Russia's railways in
1917 were predetermined to some extent by those economic
and geographical factors that had led to the building of the
railways in the first place and which continued to govern their
functions up to the revolution. In order to understand the
situation in 1917, we must look first at these factors. During the
years immediately before the downfall of the Tsarist regime,
two clearly defined periods emerge with regard to needs and
facilities in railway communications – the period of peace prior
to 1914, and the First World War.

THE PERIOD UP TO 1914

Russia's peacetime transport needs by the opening years of this
century were dictated mainly by the location of the labour force
and the regional pattern of natural resources in the widespread Empire. It was unfortunate for Russia, at first economically, and later, during the World War and the 1917 Revolution, from the political point of view also, that her population
and economic resources did not coincide geographically.

In the course of history settlers had accumulated within the
belt of the best arable soil in the country that stretches wide to

the north and south at the western frontier and tapers eastward to its limit around the Yenisei river. The emphasis on the west increased because the settled forest agriculture of European Russia encouraged the growth of markets there which could not flourish in the nomadic eastern regions. In more modern times these markets linked up closely with those of neighbouring European countries. The importance of Russia's trade and cultural ties with north-west Europe was symbolised by Peter the Great's new capital. Even by the start of the twentieth century, Moscow was the only big city in the Russian interior apart from a few large towns on the middle and lower Volga; but eighteen busy cities were situated round the edges of western Russia with large reserves of skilled manpower. Moreover those large population centres that lay outside the north and west clustered along the river systems and not as a rule where the rich economic resources were located.

The pattern of natural resources was quite different. The most important coalfields during the period before 1917 were in the Donets Basin at the south-east corner of European Russia. The potential of Siberian fields was far greater, but even by the mid-twentieth century, let alone by 1917, the centres of population did not correspond to these resources. St Petersburg relied heavily in peacetime on Polish and British coal. The distribution of iron ore conformed rather more to population centres. From the 1870s the iron and steel industry flourished in the eastern Ukraine, based on two east–west trunk railway lines, though it was more difficult to supply the larger cities in the north. At the turn of the century Russia was the world's leading producer of crude petroleum. For domestic consumption this commodity had to be transported from Baku up the Caspian and then along the sinuous length of the Volga to Russia's industrial cities. Grain from the southern black earth regions and cotton from Central Asia also filled the Volga with colourful water traffic in the continuous struggle to feed and clothe the north-west, and incidentally to use the same channel as an export route. Already by the end of our period the railways were fast taking over this river trade.

This brief summary shows that transport needs lay chiefly in moving commodities from the south and east to the more heavily populated north and west of European Russia. What part did the railways play in this compared with other forms of communication?

The answer is clear-cut – a role of overwhelming importance. In the first decades of this century the only rival to the railways as a means of communication was river transport, but this was hampered in several ways. The violent Russian climate alternately freezes, floods and dries up vast stretches of the river system. Also the great majority of rivers flow away from the centre of the Eurasian continent, with the regal exception of the Volga. Yet on the queen of Russian rivers it took about seven months for grain from the lower reaches to get to Moscow even after the introduction of steamships. According to the 1916 timetable, the passenger service from Nizhnii Novgorod to Astrakhan took five days on a so-called 'fast' boat, though it was undeniably cheap, costing only the equivalent of eighteen shillings third class.[1] By 1913 the waterborne traffic on the Rhine alone was nearly as great as that carried on all the rivers of Russia.

Maritime carriers for domestic purposes were of far less use than river craft. Apart from the inhospitable Aral Sea, all the seas open to Russia are peripheral and cut off from one another. The sea route from the Black Sea to Russia's eastern territories involves a voyage almost halfway round the world. Soviet Russia remains predominantly a land power, in spite of an intricate modern canal system.

Russian roads were undoubtedly among the worst in Europe. By 1914 there were no more than 16,200 miles of highways, of which only 3,200 were metalled. Most routes turned into a morass of mud in the spring. It was easier to travel in winter, on sleighs rather than on wheels. Even in summer the number of mechanised vehicles on the roads in 1913 was little more than 8,000, of which only 1,000 were motor lorries. Nearly all were imported from abroad.

The comparative importance of rail, water and road transport can be seen from the answers given to the following question put to 135 local delegates to the Second Congress of Soviets held in Petrograd at the time of the October coup: 'What steps has your Soviet taken to combat the breakdown in

[1] *Ukazatel' zheleznodorozhnykh, parokhodnykh i drugikh passazhirskikh soobshchenii pod redaktsii zheleznykh dorog: 1916 goda.*

transport?' All the answers mentioned the railways, but of the 135 only the representative of the Odessa Soviet alluded to river connections, and the road situation was ignored by all except the Soviet of the *guberniia* (province) of Kherson, which had appointed commissars to control the local highways. The rest of the delegates appeared to think only of railways. In the words of the Izhev Soviet delegate from the *guberniia* of Viatsk: 'There is no transport breakdown in our area, as there are no railways in our area.'[1]

The first Russian railway was built in 1837, not long after the early British lines. Twenty years later a ukase of Alexander II proclaimed 'We have long recognised that our fatherland, equipped by nature with abundant gifts but divided by huge spaces, especially needs suitable communications',[2] but railway expansion remained slow until near the end of the century. Then between 1890 and 1913 Russia became the fastest builder of railways in Europe, adding 31,000 kilometres to her system (Germany came second with 20,800 km.). Except for lines to the Far East, the basic network for European Russia had been completed by 1892. Three motives had inspired its layout: the economic need to link the north-west with the south and east; the need to connect the capital with the administrative centres; and the urge to improve national defences by building north–south arteries. After 1892 efforts were concentrated on filling out the main structure.

The new railways emphasised the importance of Moscow as the rail hub of Russia. Baedeker's *Russia* for 1912 listed nine mainline stations for the city. On the other hand many towns declined in significance. In the United States, another vast continent, new tracks were added to older river and lake transport systems, but the less fortunately disposed Russian water network was bypassed for the main part, and so were many of the old trading towns. New railways struck out boldly across the spaces of rural Russia.

Perhaps the most famous railway in the world is the Trans-Siberian, which was being used for through traffic along the 8,640 km. between Moscow and Vladivostok by 1905. It was built to protect recently acquired Far Eastern territories, to

[1] *Krasnyi Arkhiv*, vol. 84, question no. 14.
[2] *Polnoe sobranie zakonov, sobranie vtoroe*, item no. 31448.

open up Siberia as a useful source of raw materials and farming products and to encourage peasant migrants. This railway, unlike many others, did follow the old trade routes. It was a prestige concern for the whole nation. In 1900 Fabergé's workshop produced an exquisitely small working model of a Trans-Siberian train in gold and platinum for the diversion of the royal family.[1] Railway traffic increased rapidly in the period prior to 1914. Compared with 1898, the 1913 traffic (in ton/km.) was two and a half times greater, amounting to 98·6 billion.[2] Coal, cereals and timber made up almost half the freight load. The lines from the Donets Basin to the north and west carried much of the dense traffic.

So far no mention has been made of passenger traffic, which the layman thinks and hopes is of paramount importance in railway communications. In actual fact rail transport as a rule concentrates on a producer's rather than a consumer's service. In 1913, 244 million passengers travelled on the Russian railways; the average journey length was 120 kilometres.[3] Even before the World War and the 1917 revolution, passenger services were not well organised. Some trains were heavily overcrowded, others were always nearly empty. Small engines were set to draw heavy loads and passengers, and freight trains travelled at about the same speed to avoid the need for side-tracking on what were often single-track lines. As a result Russian trains were amongst the slowest in Europe. In 1905 the fastest train on the Nikolaev railway between St Petersburg and Moscow averaged only 35 m.p.h.[4]

Despite the development of Russian railways, the Empire contained a largely static society on the eve of the First World War. We have noted the geographical, climatic and transport factors that contributed to this. There were other reasons also. The reactionary Tsarist regime found it easier to enforce police control over a sluggish population. The social and legal ties of

[1] This object can be seen in the Kremlin Armoury Museum, together with an enamelled Easter egg on which is etched a map of Siberia and the route of the Trans-Siberian. The train fits into the Easter egg.

[2] S. Strumilin, *Statistichesko-ekonomicheskie ocherki* (Moscow, 1958) pp. 635–6.

[3] S. Danilov, *Ekonomika transporta* (Moscow, 1956) p. 74.

[4] *Ukazatel' zheleznodorozhnykh, parokhodnykh i drugikh passazhirskikh soobshchenii pod redaktsii zheleznykh dorog: 1916 goda.*

the agricultural commune bound the peasantry, forming four-fifths of the population, to the land, at least until Stolypin's agrarian reforms of 1906. The Government's internal passport system reinforced this tendency. The combined effect of all these factors may be seen by comparing the figure of 244 million passengers on Russian railways in 1913 with that of 1,021 million, excluding season-ticket holders, on the railways of England and Wales as early as 1901.[1] The immense disparity in size and population of the areas concerned should also be taken into account.

THE WAR: 1914–FEBRUARY 1917

Russia's peacetime transport needs were pressing enough; the advent of the war created entirely new demands. The available facilities did not expand accordingly. This discrepancy soon played a minor but nevertheless crucial role in causing those economic and political aggravations that were to lead to the revolution of February 1917 and later, in October of that year, to the fall of the Provisional Government. In the war, connections between bases and the front were urgently required. Arms, ammunition, food and clothes had to be supplied to the fifteen million troops called up during the war, who were scattered along immense land fronts. By the end of 1915 the Russians had already lost 4,360,000 men killed, wounded or taken prisoner. The railway lines were choked with replacements, men on leave, men sick or wounded and, as time went on, with an increasing number of deserters.

New facilities were provided to carry this traffic. The following table points undeniably to the hectic activity in railway building during the war until the year of the revolution.[2]

1911	1,309 km.	813 miles
1912	998 km.	620 miles
1913	1,165 km.	724 miles
1914	2,920 km.	1,814 miles
1915	2,979 km.	1,851 miles
1916	4,272 km.	2,654 miles
1917	995 km.	618 miles

[1] H. M. Ross, *British Railways* (London, 1904) p. 132.
[2] The figures are taken from H. Hunter, *Soviet Transportation Policy* (Cambridge, Mass., 1957) p. 11.

As late as 1917, a Five-Year Plan for future construction was outlined. Intense interest in prewar building was shown by the Germans, who realised that most of the new lines were for strategic purposes: their fears were expressed in the plethora of secret notes from German diplomatic sources in St Petersburg.[1] Russian military authorities like General Gurko on the other hand believed that the denser German railway network gave Germany a better chance of penetrating Russia's western fronts by surprise.[2]

The railway race did permit the Russian Government to transport an unprecedented volume of goods and men in 1915 and 1916. Up to 1917 operating income exceeded operating expenses, although the deficit in 1918 amounted to 8 million roubles.[3] But the increase in traffic volume during the first three years of the war cost the country great sacrifices that were to have more dire effects than a financial deficit. Railway construction before and during the war went on at the expense of other needs. When the Ministry of Ways and Communications asked the State Duma for 16,700 new freight trucks in 1914, funds were allocated for half that amount. Insufficient attention was paid to repairing rolling stock. The number of trucks in working order decreased from 539,549 in 1914 to 463,419 in 1916.[4]

The volume of military stores carried by the railway rose from 152 million puds (62 puds = 1 ton) in 1913 to 2,625 million puds in 1917, but over one-third fewer ordinary goods were being transported by the end of the same period.[5] As a result the European cities of Russia were already short of foodstuffs before the outbreak of the revolution. Moreover the railways themselves were deprived of fuel and vital machinery. This same narrow concentration on purely military needs also affected railway building. Too many tracks were laid in the western

---

[1] See the section *Eisenbahnen in Russland* in the Archives of the German Foreign Ministry.

[2] General B. Gurko, *Memories and Impressions of War and Revolution in Russia, 1914–1917* (London, 1918) pp. 4, 41.

[3] *Tekhnika i ekonomika putei soobshchenii* (Moscow, 1920).

[4] S. O. Zagorsky, *State Control of Industry in Russia during the War* (New Haven, Conn., 1928) pp. 46–51. The number of active engines went down from 20,071 at the end of 1914 to 9,201 in 1917.

[5] Ibid.

parts of the country. East of the line Petrograd–Moscow–Kharkov–Sebastopol low carrying capacities hindered the transport of goods to the west. Bottlenecks developed in the war on the routes from Siberia and the Donets Basin.

Very little could be done to relieve railway traffic by way of appealing to the Allies for supplies. On land the Central Powers blocked the way to the west. By sea Turkey closed the Straits to the south, whilst the German Navy and its minefields hedged off the Baltic as far north as the Åland Islands; Vladivostok in the east and Murmansk and Archangel in the north were accessible, but Vladivostok lay seven thousand miles from the western front along the largely single-track Trans-Siberian. The Murmansk railway was only completed in November 1916, and remained unreliable after that date. Railway connections with neighbouring Sweden were important as far as the Russian revolutionaries were concerned, but as Sweden was a neutral power she could be of no great help to the Russian Government. Mutual suspicion between the two countries accounted for the fact that the national lines were not quite connected at the frontier.[1] Russia was virtually isolated from her allies. As the war progressed, she was also cut off from parts of her own Empire, in industrial Poland and the Ukrainian bread-basket, as the result of foreign invaders. Despite railway building, the total length of the Russian network decreased in 1914 by 4,960 km. owing to the loss of territory.

The disorganisation of transport during the war years was due almost entirely to the inadequacy of the railways. Roads and waterways played a minor role, as in peacetime. The economic and technical conditions outlined above had a devastating effect on the morale and the political views of the Russian nation. The havoc caused by the dislocation of transport influenced men's opinions with regard to the Government. For all except those at the front, the disastrous course of the war was something one read about in the newspapers, but the ills caused by lack of transport were evident to the whole population throughout the length and breadth of Russia.

The military theatre remained the most important up to the February revolution, however. After all, until then the political fate of Russia depended on whether she won or lost the war.

[1] See M. Futrell, *The Northern Underground* (London, 1963) pp. 98–9.

The catastrophic state of the railways was rendered worse by the method of dividing administrative responsibility between the professional railway managers and the military authorities. The railway battalions controlled about one-third of the total network during the war. Responsibility was shared out on a line rather than a railway basis, so that business companies were split in two between the authorities. This artificial division between the front and the rear would have been difficult to deal with even if the two managements had agreed with each other. In fact they did not. Employees of the Ministry of Ways and Communications, used to long-established procedures, could not adapt themselves to the sudden and often inexperienced demands of the military commanders. In their desperate attempts to keep the front supplied with materials, the latter requisitioned empty goods trucks that should have been returned to the civil areas for shipping Donets coal or grain from the eastern provinces. The head of the Okhrana, which also had a hand in railway control through the agency of the railway police, was told that trains sent off to the Army in Warsaw were emptied, then shunted off into sidings and abandoned,[1] so that the depots must have looked like railway cemeteries. The police tried to mediate between the contesting authorities. Only in the winter of 1916–17 did one of the rivals take serious remedial action, when General Gurko urged the appointment of a Deputy Minister of Ways and Communications who would liaise with the Chief of Military Transport at Mogilev (Staff Headquarters).[2] In January 1917 all the railways were finally brought under the centralised control of the Ministry.

It was too late. The Russian fronts were now crippled by lack of supplies, and the first revolution in Petrograd was to be sparked off in the following month by embittered civilians waiting in the broad queues. The suspicion generated at the highest level between the civil and military leaders was to continue through the months of 1917, culminating in the Kornilov rebellion, which had a profound effect on the course of the revolution. The soldiers at the front blamed the Government in the rear, whereas civilian refugees from the western

[1] A. T. Vassiliev, *The Okhrana* (London, 1930) pp. 125–6.
[2] Gurko, op. cit., pp. 213–14.

provinces hated the military who excluded them from their special trains.[1]

Unrest spread to the civilian sector of the population. The most closely affected were the million railway workers, comprising the largest single labour group in pre-revolutionary Russia. Their combined influence had already played a significant part in the 1905 revolution. On 8 October 1905 the Union of Railwaymen had organised a nationwide strike, leading to a general strike which paralysed the country and was instrumental in forcing Nicholas II to issue the October Manifesto. In the years of renewed repression from 1907 the railway workers were relatively docile, but when they became politically active on a wide scale again in 1917, there is some evidence, though unfortunately not much, to show that individuals and undoubtedly local groups which took the lead in 1905 became prominent in the second revolution also. During the war their political activities were restricted, but they had growing evidence before 1917 of the Government's ineptitude. That is why the best amateur contributions to the illegal press of the Bolsheviks often came from railway workers,[2] and why Bolshevik cells survived from 1914 until February 1917 in Moscow railway depots.[3] Engine drivers brought in revolutionary literature from abroad via Finland to Petrograd, where railway workers stowed it away in their tool-boxes and carried it off with them.[4] The news of the February revolution passed quickly along the railway telegraph system. In his autobiography, Konstantin Paustovsky describes how he was caught by the revolution in an isolated country town where he had been sent by a Moscow paper to report on local reactions to the war news: 'Gifted orators sprang up overnight in tongue-tied Efremov. They were usually railwaymen.'[5]

The deficiencies of the railways as the main purveyor of news,

[1] The railway *Ukazatel'* for 1916, referred to above, lists many passenger trains reserved for military ranks only.

[2] I. Levitas *et al.*, *Revoliutsionnye podpol'nye tipografii v Rossii (1860–1917 gg.)* (Moscow, 1962) p. 336.

[3] *Zheleznodorozhniki i revoliutsiia: sbornik vospominanii i dokumentov o rabote zhelezno-dorozhnogo raiona Moskovskogo organizatsii R.K.P. sostavlenyi tt. Piatnitskim, Ziminym i Aronshtamom* (Moscow, 1923) p. 82.

[4] Futrell, op. cit., pp. 56–7.

[5] K. Paustovsky, *Slow Approach of Thunder* (London, 1965) p. 250.

food, material supplies and men had repercussions on the whole population of the country during the war, far beyond the military and railway employees. Not only were the towns affected, but the remote countryside also. Indeed, long before the war the expanding railway network had been the major factor in breaking down the economic self-sufficiency of the peasantry. The railways became the agent of revolution and unrest throughout the country in 1917; partly as a passive agent, owing to their gross inefficiency, and partly, through the intervention of the railwaymen, as an active instigator of political change. Already before and during the war years they were working in the way Count Witte, the chief architect of Russian industrialisation, had forecast in 1912: 'The railway is like a leaven, which creates a cultural fermentation among the population. Even if it passed through an absolutely wild people along its way, it would raise them in a short time to the level prerequisite for its operation.'[1]

FEBRUARY–OCTOBER 1917: THE BREAKDOWN OF TRANSPORT

In 1917 Russian transport facilities suffered an acute decline. At the same time new strains caused by the February revolution were superimposed on Russia's wartime needs: for it must be remembered that the war continued throughout the year. In terms of bald statistics railway construction dropped from 4,272 km. in 1916 to 995 km. in 1917. Freight trucks in working order went down from 463,419 to 174,346.[2] The number of available locomotives dropped sharply, as did their efficiency. It was estimated that whereas in April 1916 they were in use on average for 67 versts (one verst is equal to about two-thirds of a mile) per twenty-four hours, this figure decreased to 52 versts in April 1917.[3] The Provisional Government was continually reminded of the chaotic railway situation. On 26 May it issued strict measures for regulating the transport of passengers and

[1] S. Witte, *Konspekt lektsii o narodnom i gosudarstvennom khoziastve* (St Petersburg, 1912) p. 345.

[2] See Zagorsky, op. cit., pp. 46–51.

[3] A. Taniaiev, *Ocherki po istorii dvizheniia zheleznodorozhnykov v revoliutsii 1917 goda (fevral'–oktiabr')* (Moscow, 1925) p. 105.

freight,[1] and had already in April called in the services of the
American Stevens Commission, which sailed for Vladivostok
on 1 May. The Americans, whose job it was to restore the efficiency of Russia's railways, must have been daunted by the
sight of accumulated American stocks on the wharves. They
calculated that, owing to the gigantic bottleneck on the Trans-
Siberian at Tomsk, it would take the rest of 1917 and all 1918
to move them to European Russia. The main body of American
engineers did not arrive in Russia until December. The changed
political situation and the hopeless conditions in transport led
to their withdrawal to Japan after a three-day stay in Vladivostok.[2]

Among the many reasons for the final breakdown of the
railway system, the following may be considered the most important. In 1917 Russia went through two revolutionary upheavals in February and October, one attempted counter-
revolution by the military in August, and a whole series of
violent political tremors in the twin capitals of Petrograd and
Moscow. She was fighting a losing battle against the combined
forces of Germany, Austria and Turkey: on 21 August Riga,
Russia's most important trading centre on the Baltic after
Petrograd, fell to the Germans, and preparations were made to
evacuate Petrograd itself. From 24-26 September the whole of
the national railway network with the exception of some lines
was paralysed by a strike, and locally organised strikes continued to create havoc throughout October. Private anarchy
replaced public order in a country where for centuries strong
central rule had kept the impulsive character of the populace
firmly in check.

All over Russia the local population took the law into its
own hands. A well-wooded estate acquired by the Riazan'–
Ural railway line for fuel was felled by the local peasants for
their own use.[3] From another source we find that trouble arose
at another point on the same line, where

... the peasants forbade the contractor ... to fell timber.

[1] *Sobranie uzakonenii i rasporiazhenii pravitel'stva*, 1, 1, no. 711.
[2] G. F. Kennan, *Soviet-American Relations 1917–20*, vol. 1, *Russia Leaves the War* (London, 1956) pp. 284–7, 296–8.
[3] A. L. Sidorov *et al.* (eds), *Velikaia oktiabr'skaia sotsialisticheskaia revoliutsiia: revoliutsionnoe dvizhenie v Rossii v mae-iune 1917 g.* (Moscow, 1959) p. 400.

They paid no attention to any documents. The wood-merchant appealed to the commissar [the local agent of the Provisional Government] and armed with his sanction, resumed work. The peasants again obstructed him. He brought a detachment of soldiers from the Soviet garrison, who, he hoped, would persuade the peasants to let him finish his contract – again in vain. The only answer vouch-safed to him was: 'The wood will be ours; if you must have timber, cut it elsewhere'.[1]

The same bottleneck at Tomsk on the Trans-Siberian railway that cut off American supplies to western Russia was in part due to disorders at the Cheremkhovsky coalfields, which provided fuel for locomotives on the Tomsk stretch of the line. The miners took it into their heads that they should run the coalfields themselves. Coal supplies dwindled. Even the revolutionary district bureau of the East Siberian Soviet thought this was an irresponsible move:

... at the present time in conditions of capitalist society, when the workers lack any training for running such a complicated business on their own, this seizure has undesirable repercussions on the workers themselves, since it will undoubtedly lead to a complete breakdown and a work stoppage, causing unemployment and hunger amongst the workers. In view of the tremendous importance of the Cheremkhovsky fields in the defence of the country and the revolution, this act must not be allowed.[2]

Railway passengers adopted the same attitude. Refugees, troops and military deserters from the west, recent Siberian settlers returning from the east in quest of the gentry's fatter lands in Old Russia, aristocratic and bourgeois families fleeing from their estates and from the cities, crowded the trains to the limit of their capacity and beyond. Returning from the front to Petrograd in April (the journey took thirty hours), Bernard Pares arranged

to have a compartment reserved, but though it was locked

[1] C. E. Vulliamy (ed.), *The Red Archives* (London, 1929) p. 253.
[2] *Izvestiia ispolnitel'nogo komiteta obshchestvennykh organizatsii g. Irkutska*, no. 71, 3 June 1917.

it had been rushed before it reached the station; lots of people had keys of their own. We managed to keep one of the two berths, and I slept on the floor. . . . We could not possibly leave the compartment, and as it was there were several attempts to rush it in the course of the night. Now and then Keeble would open the door sharply and say: 'Angliiskii ofitser' which always had an effect. In the middle of the night I looked out into the corridor. It was a remarkable sight: innumerable passengers squatting on their haunches, half asleep: they looked like mushrooms.[1]

Just as the chaos on the railways contributed to the revolution of February 1917, so the further decline in their efficiency helped to push the political course of the revolution to the left between February and October, as impatience with the Provisional Government mounted. This Government inherited all the ills of the Russian transport system, both in peace and in war, and it would have been a miracle if any regime, even one far more decisive than the Provisional Government, could have improved transport facilities in a short time. There is no doubt that bad communications caused political problems for the leaders in Petrograd. Russia's 170 millions were affected. Some went short of food, as grain piled up in railway yards; some lost their jobs when raw materials were not delivered; others were starved of information in the form of newspapers and letters normally carried by the trains. Wild rumours spread, creating panic and disorder. Men on leave and hospital trains[2] took an eternity to get home, and every form of travel became a nightmare. Worst of all, the Russian war effort ground to a halt because soldiers could not shoot for lack of bullets or walk for lack of boots. All Russia was threatened.

The most dramatic political interventions in the revolution on the part of the railways were staged by the railway workers. They were an active force, uniquely equipped to make their influence felt in the political arena. Yet it could be argued that the involuntary collapse of the transport system had a more

[1] Sir Bernard Pares, *My Russian Memoirs* (London, 1931) pp. 420–1.
[2] The terrible conditions on hospital trains are described in Paustovsky, op. cit., chaps 9–11; working as an orderly behind the Rumanian front, he alone had to care for 40 wounded men and carry food to them through 47 carriage doors.

devastating effect on the population as a whole than anything done by active revolutionaries among the railway workers. The Bolsheviks flourished during 1917 on the increasingly extremist attitude in the country and took especial advantage of the chaotic conditions brought about by the breakdown in transport. Before turning to consider the role of the railwaymen in the revolution and the efforts of the various political parties to control them, it may be useful to assess the new needs in transport created by the revolutionary situation.

Russia was blessed, or cursed, with an enormous land empire, poor communications and a largely immobile population. Both the February revolution and the October coup originally broke out in Petrograd alone – a European city at the very edge of a land continent straddling Europe and Asia. It took literally months for them to take effect through the country as a whole. Obviously the new political leaders in February 1917 had to spread their control to the whole nation if they were to remain in power and stabilise the regime. The railways were the main channel. They carried news as fast as any other medium through the railway telegraph. They were needed to transport troops and agitators with newspapers and leaflets, and subsequently administrators, out to the provinces, and to bring in representatives and delegates to the capital for consultation. The Provisional Government was confronted by the left-wing Soviet of Workers' and Soldiers' Deputies which had the effrontery to meet in the same building in Petrograd, the Tauride Palace, and to issue its own orders, often in defiance of the other Government. Between February and October two Governments ruled, or rather failed to rule, Russia. They competed for the attention of the railway workers and officials. As the political temper of Petrograd moved to the left, the rivalry grew fiercer.

There is a Soviet propaganda film showing a map of Russia with illuminated lines radiating from the European cities of Russia to indicate how the February revolution spread round the country. In the overwhelming majority of cases, these lines coincide with the railways and do not penetrate much beyond their network. The dynamos of the revolution were Petrograd and Moscow, but the railway lines provided the electric current along which the revolution could spread. This phenomenon did not escape the notice of the civil and military authorities. The Provincial Section of the Provisional Government reported: 'Naturally the tidings [of the February revolution] first reached the large industrial centres (owing to their proximity to the railways . . .).'[1] The Supreme Commander of the Russian Army, General Alekseev, first felt the effect of the Petrograd Soviet's famous Order No. 1 issued on 1 March, along the railway lines. This revolutionary decree was to create havoc in Army ranks by providing for the election of committees of soldiers in all units. On 4 March, Alekseev telegraphed to the capital:

> It appears . . . that unruly bands from Petrograd, of a purely revolutionary character, which endeavour to disarm the gendarmes on the railways and which later on will undoubtedly try to seize power both on the railways and in the Army rear and probably will attempt to penetrate into the Army itself, have already made their appearance. Most drastic steps should be taken, by establishing observation posts in all the railway junctions and in the rear, and by having these stations garrisoned by reliable units under the command of firm officers.'[2]

The nearer the factory workers and peasants lived to the railway lines, the more restless they became. Reference has already been made to peasants interfering with the wood supply for the railways. There is evidence that peasants living near the lines were often those who first took to burning down the manor houses and confiscating the gentry's land.[3] No doubt they were influenced by the proximity of rural factories strung out along the railways. At the beginning of May we find the workers of a cotton mill near a line writing to the Moscow Soviet for political guidance: 'During the whole period since the overthrow of the autocratic Government and bloody Nicholas we have not had a single speaker here, and so we humbly request you to consider our position and to send us a speaker to organise us (a Social Democrat and a Bolshevik) and also a trade union organiser.'[4]

[1] Vulliamy, op. cit., p. 232.
[2] *Krasnyi Arkhiv*, vol. 5, p. 223.
[3] See Sidorov, op. cit. (*Aprel'skii krizis*), p. 668, for one among many examples of this.   [4] Ibid., p. 451.

THE RAILWAYMEN

So far, we have dealt almost exclusively with the impact which the breakdown of the transport system had on the economic and political life of the country. Technical factors, apolitical in themselves, came to affect politics. Now we turn to an examination of the economic and political demands put forward by the railwaymen. These demands impinged on high politics, as did also the action taken by the railway workers to lend weight to their arguments.

By October 1916 there were no less than 1,001,522 personnel employed on the Tsarist railways, as compared with 432,000 in 1898.[1] At the time of the 1905 revolution more than 700,000 railwaymen took part in the October general strike. Between the first Russian revolution and the start of the Great War, labour productivity on the railways improved so that it was found possible to reduce staff numbers from 844,000 in 1908 to 815,000 in 1913.[2] The figure soon crept up again, owing to the demands imposed on the railways by the war effort. The Russian railway industry was huge in size and geographical extent. It was also a highly complex industry. These features were reflected in its social composition. At the top of the hierarchy were the civil service employees in the administrative headquarters of the railway networks, and the owners and managers of the private companies. Next came the engineers, planners, statisticians and the less important office workers. These two groups represented between 16 and 17 per cent of all those engaged on the railways in 1917.[3]

Under this cumbersome bureaucracy worked many different kinds of employees. The gamut descended from skilled engine drivers and railway telegraph workers, conductors, points men, couplers, etc., to depot workers and porters. In 1905 a labourer at the Nikolaev station in Moscow earned 100 roubles a

[1] This figure is taken from a report by the division of statistics and cartography in the Ministry of Ways and Communications, quoted in *Rabochii klass i rabochee dvizhenie v Rossii v 1917 g.* (Moscow, 1964) p. 181 n. Figures for 1917 are quite unreliable, and even those for 1916 are probably not quite accurate. [2] Strumilin, op. cit., pp. 635–6.

[3] Compare Taniaev, op. cit., p. 3, who gives 16·8 per cent, and I. Pushkareva, in *Lenin i oktiabrskoe vooryzhennoe vosstanie v Petrodrade* (Moscow, 1964) p. 261, who puts the ratio at 'about 16 per cent'.

month.[1] At the bottom end of the scale we leave the proletariat altogether with the maintenance men, who were usually recruited from the local peasantry. Many of the less skilled among the so-called proletarian railwaymen had been born into the peasant class, but had won a place in the industry, often through the efforts of a *zemliak*, a fellow countryman from the same region. This social composition was not reflected in the first major railway conference of the revolution, convened in April 1917. Of the 212 delegates who filled in a questionnaire handed out at the meeting, three quarters belonged to the upper 16-17 per cent, so that the 83-84 per cent comprising the workers only had 25 per cent representation.[2] This discrepancy was not so much a result of political manoeuvring at this stage of the revolution as an indication of the low educational and political attainments of the mass of railway workers. On any railway system a good deal of ill-educated manual labour is involved. This was certainly the case on the highly inefficient Russian network. The railwaymen were not conscripted for military service after a disastrous period at the start of the war when the recruitment of thousands of skilled workshop men led to so many breakdowns that they were subsequently released. The railway workers' immunity in this respect had political repercussions. According to the orthodox Bolshevik accounts of the railways in the war, 'bourgeois' elements took jobs in order to avoid conscription: these same elements were also supposed to have wormed their way into the management of the railway unions. Soviet sources are never able to substantiate the second assertion, but there were some cases of middle-class persons taking on railway work to avoid being sent to the front.

These wide social rifts among the railway personnel produced many organisations with diverse economic and political demands in 1917. Whereas by 1918 over 40 per cent of all those employed in Russian industries were women who were rarely activists, they only made up 3 per cent of the railway workers. Working conditions also had their effect on railway politics. Nominally at least, wages rose quite fast in the period 1898–1913.[3] This may have had some influence on the rather slow

[1] Ia. Gordeenko, *Kurs zheleznykh dorog* (St Petersburg, 1906) Appendix.
[2] Taniaev, op. cit., pp. 22 ff.
[3] See Strumilin, op. cit., pp. 635–6.

initial reaction on the railways to the 1905 revolution. But after the start of the war, wages in other sectors of industry increased at a faster rate. About two-thirds of the railway employees who worked on state-owned lines relied on the Treasury for their pay, and the Treasury was in no position to be generous at that time. It has been calculated that the average railway worker's wage rose by 20-25 per cent in 1915 alone, but then the price level went up by 34 per cent in the same year.[1] On 3 February 1917, just before the revolution, the Tsarist Minister of Ways and Communications proposed a wage increase to the Council of Ministers, and his successor in the Provisional Government, N. V. Nekrasov, had to admit on 29 March that low wages impeded productivity.[2] Indeed not long before the war for every fifteen workers per kilometre of track in Russia there were about eight in France.[3] In the 1917 revolution the railwaymen sprang to life faster than in 1905. It seems reasonable to assume that the change in their economic situation since 1905 may have had something to do with this. Pay claims were put in very soon after February.

RAILWAY ORGANISATIONS IN 1917

The activities of the railwaymen in the 1905 revolution fore-shadowed their organisation in 1917, and so form a necessary prelude to this section. The first All-Russian Union of Railway Workers (Vserossiiskii Zheleznodorozhnyi Soiuz) had been formed at the Congress held in Moscow in April 1905. At the very start there occurred a split between left- and right-wing groups in the heterogeneous army of employees: a few railway lines dominated politically by the Social Democrats did not enter the union. Instead they set up rival bodies, in Trans-caucasia, the south-west, and also within the Moscow network. At the second Congress, held in July 1905, delegates from twenty lines decided to organise a strike in order to back their claim for better pay and working conditions, but not until 8 October were all the Moscow lines stopped. By the 16th the entire rail-way system of the Empire was at a standstill. The railway

---

[1] Taniaev, op. cit., p. 7.
[2] *Rech'*, 29 Mar. 1917.
[3] N. Vasiliev, *Transport Rossii v voine 1914–18 gg.* (Moscow, 1939) p. 15.

B

workers had shown the way in which they could control, or rather stifle, the country. No one could travel or get mail and newspapers. The railway telegraph was silent, and the union planned to close the General Telegraph Office in Moscow as well. Supplies ran short throughout Russia, and panic hoarding began.

Armed with such a powerful lever, the railwaymen submitted to the Government a list of demands which covered political as well as economic affairs. For instance the workers called for an All-Russian Constituent Assembly and an amnesty for political prisoners. The granting of a constitution by the Imperial Manifesto of 17 October was a concession to revolutionary Russia, and the general strike had been one of the chief means of wresting it from the Tsar. Left-wing influence in the Union of Railway Workers waned quickly after the suppression of the armed uprising in December 1905. Yet the Railway Union became the largest of the workers' organisations prior to 1917, embracing manual, clerical and administrative staff. The Union of Railway Workers in 1905 was not so united as the events of the mass October strike might suggest. It did not include all the railwaymen and could not control all its members. Attitudes varied according to the particular geographical region or occupation. Liberals, Socialist Revolutionaries, Mensheviks and Bolsheviks competed hotly for support. The latter were the main political influence on some Siberian lines, whilst the Mensheviks held sway in the Moscow workshops of the important Moscow–Brest line; Liberals controlled the higher employees, and so on. Geographical differences were recognised with the establishment of four regional centres at Moscow, Warsaw, Vilno and Saratov.

In this very brief survey of railway organisation in 1905, there is no mention of St Petersburg; the union meetings were held in Moscow, and the general strike spread from Moscow. In any history of the Russian railways the role of the older capital is paramount. This is because Moscow was the railway hub of the Empire. Most of the main lines radiated from there across Russia. The city housed the administrative headquarters of the railway network, as well as the main workshops of the nation.

Turning again to 1917, we shall see some of the characteristics of the 1905 railway organisation re-emerging after twelve years of dormancy. Given the proliferation of railway bodies in 1917, it might be useful to describe the moderates and the far left wing separately and then show how the organisations interacted. As a general rule, the moderate elements in Russian society were more active and vociferous from the February revolution up to the time of Kornilov's revolt at the end of August. The left wing, headed by the Bolsheviks, got off to a slower start, but increased rapidly in power after August. The meaning of 'moderate' in this context requires explanation. Before February 1917 the right wing consisted roughly of the Tsar, the majority of his advisers, most of the court, the nobility, the church, the police and sections of the government bureaucracy and the bourgeoisie. The February revolution set the political pendulum swinging rapidly to the left. What had been known as the liberal Progressive Bloc in the Fourth Duma now formed the conservative section in the new Provisional Government, which in turn represented the right in the Dual Government, with the Petrograd Soviet on the left. In 1917 the main body of the railwaymen adopted a political position mid-way between the Provisional Government and the more left-wing parties in the Soviet. A small minority supported the Bolsheviks on the extreme left.

On 28 February 1917 the Provisional Government appointed A. Bublikov, a transport engineer and a member of the Fourth Duma, as Commissar in charge of transport. Bublikov issued an immediate appeal to the railwaymen:

> The salvation of our native land now depends on you. Train schedules must be maintained without interruption and with twice as much energy. The country is expecting more than a fulfilment of duty on your part. It expects heroic deeds. The technical shortcomings and weaknesses of the Russian railway network must be compensated by dauntless energy, love for our native land, and awareness of the role of transport in war and in the planning and organisation of public services in the rear.[1]

Any signs of redoubled energy on the part of the railway

[1] *Izvestiia*, 28 Feb. 1917, p. 1. For more details of Bublikov's action and its great importance, see G. Katkov, *Russia 1917: The February Revolution* (London, 1967) pp. 380–2.

employees straight after the February revolution were not evident in tighter train schedules, but rather in the vigour with which the hated Tsarist railway police were thrown out of their jobs. Bublikov's suggestion that local railway committees be formed was taken up at once, so that by the time of the All-Russian Congress of Railwaymen convened in April it was clear from the questionnaires filled in by delegates that nearly all the lines had chosen committees. The railwaymen organised themselves by geographical location rather than by trades.

The organs of the moderate elements were the first to be established. On 8 March representatives from twenty-six railway lines, most of them privately owned, agreed to the formation of a Central Bureau for the Railway Union. It was this organ that called the April Congress which, as has been noted earlier, was dominated by the higher railway bureaucracy. The Congress proceeded to elect an All-Russian Executive Committee of Railway Workers, usually known by its abbreviated Russian title, Vikzhel. Vikzhel became the chief mouthpiece of the moderate section of the railwaymen. Initially it consisted of 15 members, 12 of whom were white-collar employees. Four were Mensheviks, 3 Socialist Revolutionaries, 4 Socialist-Populists, one a Ukrainian Independent and 3 belonged to no party.[1] At the second Railway Congress held from 15 July to 25 August in Moscow, Vikzhel was enlarged to include 40 members (14 Socialist Revolutionaries, 7 Mensheviks, 3 Socialist-Populists, 2 Mezhraionstsy, 2 Bolsheviks and one sympathiser, and 11 non-party representatives, many of whom supported the Kadets).[2] Their social composition was as follows: 12 senior administrative staff, 10 engineers and technicians, 3 lawyers, 2 doctors, 3 office workers, 2 engine crew and 8 clerical staff and workers.[3]

Thus Vikzhel's main support came from the middle and higher ranks of the railway employees, who were influenced by the two most important moderate revolutionary parties, the S.R.s and the Mensheviks. The Bolsheviks were an insignificant minority. Vikzhel conducted a running battle with the Pro-

[1] Taniaev, op. cit., p. 22.
[2] *Rabochii klass i rabochee dvizhenie v Rossii v 1917 g.*, p. 185 n. Taniaev's figures agree with this.
[3] See Taniaev, op. cit., p. 91.

visional Government over pay claims, but by the middle of August it was still sufficiently in sympathy with Kerensky to send a delegation to the Moscow State Conference which tried to rally the country behind the Provisional Government. As far as organisation was concerned, Vikzhel demanded the transfer of authority over the railways to the railway committees, whereas the Ministry of Ways and Communications under N. V. Nekrasov defended the principle of single authority. In its turn Vikzhel struggled against centrifugal tendencies in the union's railway administration. The statute drawn up at the second Congress represented a compromise between Vikzhel and the local All-Russian Congresses: individual railway lines could hold Congresses under Vikzhel's supervision at which their executive committees could be chosen.

The Railway Union was formed on regional lines and included the whole army of employees 'from the Minister to the train guard', as one of its enthusiastic Socialist Revolutionary supporters put it.[1] But it could not hope to contain the far left wing as the revolution continued on its course through 1917. At the end of June in Petrograd a separate Union of Railway Workers and Workshop Men was organised on class and occupational lines. Its members refused to pay 1 per cent of their wages as membership dues of the All-Russian Union. Even earlier, Bolshevik sympathisers from the railway workshops and depots had opted out of the All-Russian Union by joining the more radical trade unions of metalworkers and joiners. The workshops and depots included 35 per cent of the total railway labour force. Bolshevik cells existed in the depots and workshops of Moscow, Petrograd, Kiev, Kharkov, Saratov, Ekaterinburg and Krasnoiarsk shortly after February. Bolshevik influence grew because of the bad pay and work conditions in these two sectors, and also because of their close ties with the metal industry and the factory proletariat of the big cities.

On 10 July some of the Moscow railwaymen formed a parallel Union of Workers and Workshop Men which now included points men and lamp lighters as well. Whereas the Petrograd Presidium of the new union consisted of two Social Revolutionaries, one Mezhraionets and three Bolsheviks, the Moscow Presidium was entirely Bolshevik. The dominating influence

[1] *Zheleznodorozhniki i revolutsiia*, p. 25.

behind the organisation of the Moscow Union of Workers and Workshop Men appeared to be the railway Soviet of workers' deputies from the Moscow network. This body fought the issue through a plenary Moscow Soviet meeting in the teeth of bitter opposition from the Socialist Revolutionary faction, which believed that the new union would weaken the strength of the All-Russian Union. The original suggestion that Moscow should form the new union was passed to the Railway Soviet by the railway committee of the Bolshevik party organisation in Moscow. At this point we may take a closer look at the way in which these two bodies on the far left wing of railway politics functioned.

It was no coincidence that these two founts of Bolshevik influence were situated in Moscow, as were the offices of Vikzhel. Moscow's predominance over Petrograd in railway affairs repeated the pattern established in 1905. Both the Bolsheviks and Vikzhel strove to control the Russian network by sending agents and information out along the nine major lines radiating from Moscow to all points of the compass. Decisions taken in the offices, railway stations and workshops of Moscow could paralyse or quicken the nerve centre of this network. A few Bolshevik cells, like the one in the printing works of the Kursk railway line, already existed before the February revolution, but it was only after the downfall of the autocracy that formal links were set up between them under the supervision of the newly created railway committee of the Moscow Bolshevik party headquarters. This committee had official control over party activities up to the limit of the Moscow circle line, but in fact its influence eventually penetrated far beyond into the country at large. Immediately after the February revolution, however, the committee's influence was very weak. Years of political repression, combined with some measure of patriotic attention to duty in the early stages of the war, had discouraged the railway workers from advancing economic, let alone political, demands. Also Moscow shopkeepers had taken on railway jobs to avoid military service.[1] They were not likely to sympathise with Bolshevik aims, or even with the long-term aims of the professional railwaymen as a whole.

None of the three organisers of the railway committee was a

[1] Ibid. p. 6.

railway employee. They were all Bolsheviks from the Moscow party organ. Two of them, Piatnitsky and Aronshtam, only returned from exile after the February revolution. Zimin, the third, was thrown off the platform at a railwaymen's meeting on the occasion of Nekrasov's first visit to Moscow in his capacity as Minister of Ways and Communications shortly after the revolution. At its first plenary meeting[1] the group of railwaymen organised by the railway committee mustered approximately one hundred men, most of whom cannot have been Bolshevik party members, because the three organisers admit that at this time one party man had to supervise more than one of Moscow's railway lines.[2] From the end of April the group was represented on the Executive Committee of the Moscow Bolshevik party committee, ensuring close contact between the two bodies.

The railway Soviet attached to the Moscow Soviet escaped Bolshevik domination for a longer period than the railway committee. It was set up as a unique extra-territorial 'district' of the Moscow Soviet, and was palpable proof of the political influence of the railwaymen. Following on the February revolution railway workers in and around Moscow organised local committees. These bodies sent representatives to line committees, which in turn founded a network bureau of railway line committees. Armed with an overriding sense of their 'special caste, railway interests',[3] the well-organised workers pressed for and won separate representation in the Moscow Soviet. The main political force behind this new body were the Socialist Revolutionaries; but the first meetings of the railway Soviet in May revealed the vigorous methods used by the Bolshevik minority in an attempt to make up for lost time.

The initial election of deputies to the railway Soviet took place without the knowledge of the Bolshevik railway committee. Piatnitsky and Aronshtam arrived after the start, but managed to get in. This cannot have been difficult, because the first meeting was chaotic. There was no agenda, no presidium, not even a chairman. According to Zimin, Piatnitsky became

---

[1] The author has not been able to ascertain the exact date of this meeting, but it was almost certainly in March.

[2] *Zheleznodorozhniki i revolutsiia*, p. 6.

[3] Ibid., p. 53.

chairman during the first session at the suggestion of a workshop delegate from the northern line, which gave the Bolsheviks a better hearing than the other eight lines. Aronshtam disagrees, maintaining that this occurred at the second session, from 15 to 20 May.[1] In either case the Bolsheviks' shock tactics were remarkable. By the end of the second meeting Piatnitsky was in the chair and Aronshtam was secretary, although many Socialist Revolutionaries and Mensheviks were present. Aronshtam writes derisively that these two groups 'were merely strolling players, and it was obvious that they paid very little attention to the work of the district Soviet'.[2]

At first the Socialist Revolutionaries and Mensheviks seemed almost justified in their apathy. By the time of the Provisional Government's attempted suppression of the left wing in July, the railway Soviet had only fifteen members.[3] After July the Bolsheviks gained ground fast in all revolutionary organisations. Previously the railway committee of the Moscow Bolsheviks had only been able to assert effective influence over the workshop and depot workers, but after the July Days the railway Soviet managed to exert pressure on points men, conductors, couplers and even engine drivers and railway telegraph operators as well. At the end of August Bolshevik-inspired local Soviets in the suburbs of Moscow united with the extra-territorial railway Soviet in an abortive plot to oust the central Moscow Soviet, which refused to pass any resolution put forward by the Bolsheviks until 5 September. The industrial suburbs were naturally more left-wing than the middle-class quarters in the centre of the city. The railway Soviet survived until October 1918, when it was dissolved and its members integrated into the territorial district Soviets, which were now overloaded with the local supply and housing problems that harassed the new Bolshevik regime. The vision of workers' control soon faded after reaching its zenith in the late summer and autumn of 1917.

In Russia as a whole organisational ties between the Soviets and the railwaymen were fairly close by the time of the October revolution. Already in August the telegraph offices of the Moscow and Petrograd railway stations were secretly exchang-

[1] Ibid., p. 54.
[2] Ibid., p. 55.
[3] *Rabochii klass i rabochee dvizhenie v Rossii v 1917 g.*, p. 185.

ing the decisions of the Executive Committees of the two city Soviets.[1] At the Second Congress of Soviets held during the October coup, the delegates were asked in a questionnaire 'What connection does your Soviet have with the railwaymen?' In general the replies show that contact was good but of recent origin, usually dating from the time of the railway strike in September. The collaboration of the railwaymen was often contrasted with the cooler attitude of post and telegraph workers who had less radical views. It was the railwaymen who first approached the local Soviets and not vice versa. Despite the fact that in some cases one or two men spoke for five or six thousand railway workers, they were rarely elected to permanent representation on the Soviets.[2]

THE RAILWAYMEN'S ECONOMIC DEMANDS

Interaction and fatal conflict between Vikzhel and the All-Russian Railway Union on the political right and the Union of Workers and Workshop Men and the other Bolshevik-led organs on the left, came to a head only after the October coup. Trouble was brewing since February, however, as is apparent from the diverse nature of the railwaymen's economic demands and political action. The reasons for the railway workers' demands should be traced before we consider the nature of the demands themselves. Most of the negotiations with the Provisional Government between February and October 1917 centred on wage claims. The background to these claims has been outlined above.[3] All wages in Russian industry were pitifully low, and especially so on the railways, where they had fallen behind increases in other sectors after 1914. At the Railway Congress in April 1917, 36 per cent of the delegates had incomes of under 125 roubles a month, although three-quarters of the delegates came from the upper echelons of the railway employees.[4]

The prices spiral, which raced ahead of wage increases and

---

[1] Sidorov, *Revoliutsionnoe dvizhenie v Rossii posle sversheniia samoderzhaviia*, p. 508.
[2] *Krasnyi Arkhiv*, vol. 84, question no. 17.
[3] See pp. 18–19 above.
[4] Taniaev, op. cit., p. 27.

led to social unrest, was caused to a great extent by the technical troubles on the railway network, as contemporary observers pointed out. Since the trains were unable to carry sufficient supplies, traders were putting their prices up.[1] The general lack of supplies made the economic plight of the railway workers worse than it would have been otherwise. By 5 September *Izvestiia*, the press organ of the Petrograd Soviet, was reporting that 'only approximately 20–30 per cent of the normal orders of supplies are being delivered'. Just over a month later the journal *Novaia Zhizn'* ascribed the complete inefficiency of the Moscow railway network to the fact that 'engine crews do not turn up to work because they have no shoes'.[2] In December the chairman of Vikzhel announced in Moscow to assembled railway delegates:

> Our comrades from the provinces said that there are threats in the localities to break into trains carrying food supplies, because in the provinces food and other supplies for the railwaymen are extremely bad. Comrades who came to see us told us: 'The situation is such that we have to smash open the trucks, and we must even steal on occasions, but we cannot do otherwise.'[3]

Violent acts by the railwaymen must often have been incited by class hatred as well as by hunger and poverty. They were the best placed of all workers to see how grain stores stacked high at country stations were guarded against the hungry local population in the interests of 'bourgeois' speculators who waited in vain to ship to even worse-off areas in the hope of making a large profit. In the towns they were the first to notice that factories were no longer filling the goods yards with the articles they were supposed to be making. On 30 March the bureau of the Moscow railway network, the predecessor of the railway Soviet, issued a resolution demanding that 'measures be taken against sabotage by manufacturers and factory owners'.[4]

A railway worker did not need to have heard the Bolsheviks'

[1] Vasiliev, op. cit., p. 126.

[2] *Novaia Zhizn'* 14 Oct. 1917.

[3] From the stenographic record of the All-Russian Railway Congress of December 1917, quoted in Taniaev, op. cit., p. 102.

[4] Sidorov, op. cit., p. 578.

and Mensheviks' Marxist propaganda to realise that his economic interests were not the same as those of the middle classes.
The very few who did imbibe a little Marxism could find some
telling arguments. For instance, the Government after the
outbreak of the World War decided that more rolling stock was
needed, so the railway suppliers formed a cartel and refused to
provide engines and trucks until the Government raised its
offer price. Bolshevik party members and sympathisers who
knew anything at all about Lenin's writings on Imperialism
found ample support for Lenin's thesis in Russian railway
finance. In 1875, half the joint-stock capital and three-quarters
of railway bonds had been in foreign hands. After 1890 a large
proportion of investment was domestic, although in 1909 the
German Consulate-General in Petrograd noted with suspicion
that in strategic railway building 'English capital appears to
play a large part in all these undertakings'.[1]

Only occasionally, however, did concrete evidence of this
kind incite the railwaymen to take action. An isolated example
will suffice. In June a Belgian-owned electric railway between
Petrograd and Oranienbaum, a suburb to the west of the city,
decided to raise the fares. This directly affected many workers
in the industrial suburb of Peterhof which straddled the line.
The Soviet of the Peterhof district took immediate action: 'With
regard to the increase in travelling costs, the Soviet declares
that they must stay as they were for a period of three weeks,
until the question has been considered in more detail. In the
event that the management does not agree to these conditions,
the Soviet will ask its worker comrades to help it to bring the
local suburban railway under municipal control.'[2] The rest of
the document makes it clear that the employees on the line
objected particularly to the fact that foreign owners were raising
their prices in an attempt to exploit Russian workers.

The mounting grudges of the railwaymen were expressed in
organised claims for higher wages and better working conditions, but they got off to a slow start for several reasons. Just
before the February revolution the Tsarist Minister of Ways and

[1] Report of the German Consulate-General of 5 February 1909, in the
Section *Eisenbahnen in Russland* in the Archives of the German Foreign
Ministry.

[2] *Raionnye sovety Petrograda v 1917 g.*, vol. II (Moscow, 1965) p. 183.

Communications admitted that the railwaymen's pay was too low. After the revolution Nekrasov set up two successive government commissions to look into the matter. Neither took any positive action, but the conciliatory white-collar railway employees who ran the April Congress managed to stay the impatience of the lower ranks until May. They were no doubt encouraged to do this by the personal grants handed out to them by Nekrasov. Thus by May the railwaymen had not yet threatened to strike in support of their wage claims, as many other branches of industry had done. As a result the average wage of an unskilled factory worker was twice as high as that of a skilled workshop railwayman by May. But when some of the latter began to change their jobs, the Plekhanov commission announced the first round of wage increases. The railwaymen got rises of between 40 and 100 roubles per month, but as their special war bonus was cancelled at the same time, the increases were deceptive.

The workshop and depot men remained dissatisfied. On 12 May those on the Petrograd network arranged a meeting to decide on future action, and the Moscow workshops took similar steps. On 27 May the Petrograders decided by 40 votes to 3 to go on strike. In June isolated strikes of a very sporadic nature finally began. It is interesting to note that those lines which had been most active in 1905 touched off the spark again in 1917. They included the Moscow–Kazan' lines and sections of the Trans-Siberian.

At the start of May an editorial in the newspaper *Rabochaia Gazeta* had argued that whereas the railway strike had done the revolution of 1905 a great service, the situation was different in 1917. First, Russia was at war and, secondly, there had already been a successful revolution in February. A crippling nation-wide strike like that of 1905 might lose the war for Russia and undo the gains of the revolution. After the wage increases of 8 May, the Provisional Government advised the railwaymen to be patient until the Constituent Assembly, that universal panacea of Russia in travail, could look into their case. Vikzhel sent a circular to all railway lines in the form of a telegram advising against strike action, but the Petrograd Soviet disassociated itself from this opinion. The Provisional Government unexpectedly put up just the wages of workshop and depot men employed on the Moscow and Petrograd networks on 4 August. This was recognised by the engine drivers, stokers and greasers, who were in close touch with the workshop and depots, as an attempt to divide and rule. Drivers began to refuse to work, or else tried to transfer to better-paid work in the maintenance departments. Trained drivers had to be brought in from the fronts by the Government. The locomotive union went so far as to declare that it would go on strike on 20 August, but it faltered in the face of opposition from the All-Russian Union and Vikzhel.

The Provisional Government's constant prevarication on the question of wage increases was by no means entirely due to its hostility towards the railway workers. The truth is that it simply could not afford to raise their pay in 1917. In the words of one of the Ministers:

> since the revolution . . . the workers received an opportunity to demand better conditions for themselves, with respect both to working hours and to wages; but the workers' movement turned out to be much stronger and more widespread than our material resources could afford. A considerable part of the working class reasoned that since it was possible to make demands, and since these demands could be fulfilled, then it followed that they should be made and that they should be vast and significant in scope.[1]

It was estimated that employees on government railways were paid 540 million roubles more in 1917 than in 1916.[2] The temporary estimates of transport expenses as a whole for the period March–October 1917 amounted to 719·5 million roubles, but when extraordinary expenses were added, the total sum came to 2,560 million roubles.[3] The burden on the Treasury was crippling. When governmental purse strings were tightened, it was perhaps only natural that refusals to increase wages should be aimed primarily at the more militant campaigners for better conditions. In April we find the Tashkent workshops

---

[1] Speech by A. V. Peshekhonov, Minister of Food, reported in *Izvestiia*, 7 June 1917.
[2] *Ekonomicheskoe polozhenie Rossii nakanune velikoi oktiabr'skoi sotsialisticheskoi revoliutsii* (Moscow, 1957) vol. II, p. 377.
[3] Ibid., p. 385.

protesting against the refusal of the local railway director to pay Tashkent Soviet railway deputies their wages for March and April.[1]

Both sides taking part in the arguments showed considerable naïvety. In June a broadsheet issued by the railwaymen declared that as the Minister of Ways and Communications said there was no money left in the Treasury with which to supplement their pay, the only answer to the problem was for the railway workers to take over railway administration themselves; then 'we will work day and night and we will make money'.[2] For his part Nekrasov painted a glowing picture of what life would be like in the near future for railway employees, when he addressed them in July at the All-Russian Congress. He compared their future existence to that of British workers as it appeared to him in 1917: 'How happy the English worker must be. . . . I looked at workingmen's flats: workers have three rooms, a kitchen and a piano. Just imagine the spiritual satisfaction of a workman who comes home exhausted, takes a bath and then dines, whilst his children begin to play new piano pieces they have practised and to declaim verses.'[3] Only the aspidistra is missing.

Working conditions were certainly not idyllic for Russian railway employees in 1917. On average men in the telegraph, traction and traffic services were supposed to work a ten-hour day, and maintenance men and signalmen ten and a half hours.[4] In a Duma debate of 1908 it was revealed that in fact workers regularly put in sixteen hours a day; some engine drivers stayed on duty for twenty-four hours and above. The strain on labour increased enormously during the war. In 1917 the railway workers formed a common front with other industrial workers in the campaign for an eight-hour day. They were not in competition with them as was the case with pay increases. Factory workers from Yaroslavl' combined with railwaymen on the northern lines which ran through the town. Employees on the north-western line appealed to the Petrograd Soviet above the head of the local engineer in charge of them. They

[1] Sidorov, *Revoliutsionnoe dvizhenie v Rossii v aprele 1917. g.*, p. 434.
[2] *Mysl' zheleznodorozhika*, 17 June 1917.
[3] Quoted in Taniaev, op. cit., p. 85.
[4] I. Mikhailov, *Evoliutsiia russkogo transporta 1913–25* (Moscow, 1925) p. 26.

claimed that when he was questioned on the subject, the engineer replied, 'In March you're working ten hours a day, and in June you'll be working twelve'. To the Provisional Government's appeal for patriotic effort in wartime, these railwaymen answered with other workers, 'We agree to work even twelve hours a day, on condition that an eight-hour day is introduced and we are then paid for overtime'.[1] But where was the extra money to be found?

THE RAILWAYMEN'S POLITICAL ACTION

From February to October there were many examples of intrusion into high as well as local politics by the railwaymen. From the very start they were involved in crucial issues like the abdication of the Tsar. The February revolution found Niclolas II at Mogilev, the Army headquarters, 453 miles by rail to the south of Petrograd. Only dimly aware of the seriousness of the situation, he set out by train for the capital, but at least he took the precaution of travelling on the second of two trains. When Ezhov, the inspector of the Imperial trains who accompanied the Tsar, heard that the Nikolaev station in Petrograd was in the hands of revolutionary railwaymen and under the instructions of the Petrograd Soviet, he and others tried to prevail upon the Tsar to collect military reinforcements in Pskov before advancing to the capital[2] (General Ivanov's picked force sent by Nicholas to pacify Petrograd had moved independently, and in any case was unsuccessful, as Ivanov's troops went over to the side of the revolution). The Tsar decided to turn aside to Pskov, where there was a Hughes telegraph installation with a direct line to Petrograd. Inside the train he and his entourage had to rely mainly on oral reports. At Bologoe junction, the royal train got past the points just in time on its way to Pskov before the stationmaster received an order from the Petrograd Soviet to waylay it and dispatch it to the capital.

The royal train reached Dno, to which Nicholas had summoned Rodzianko, the President of the Duma. Rodzianko did

[1] Sidorov, *Revoliutsionnoe dvizhenie v Rossii posle scerzhenniia samoderzhaviia*, pp. 508-9.

[2] The account which follows is taken mainly from A. I. Spiridovich. *Velikaia voina i fevral' skaia revoliutsiia* (New York, 1962) pp. 225-45.

not appear. An eyewitness at a meeting of the Executive Committee of the Petrograd Soviet, N. Sukhanov, explains why: 'What had happened was that Rodzianko . . . was unable to comply, since the railway workers wouldn't give him a train without the Executive Committee's permission.'[1] Sukhanov put his view to the Executive Committee: 'Who can guarantee that the fate of the revolution does not depend on the decision whether to give Rodzianko a train? We must thank the railway workers for their correct understanding and conscientious performance of their duty towards the revolution, and refuse Rodzianko a train.'[2] This view prevailed, and it was the railwaymen who had inspired it. In the meantime the telegraph agencies as well as the railways had been taking action. General Alekseev, the Commander-in-Chief at Mogilev, was cut off from the Empress at Tsarskoe Selo, and even from Nicholas for a time. Alekseev was advised by Beliaev, the Tsarist Minister of War, to assert military control over the Russian railway system, but while Alekseev hesitated about acting on this advice, Commissar Bublikov in Petrograd was ordering the resumption of civilian rail traffic in the name of the Provisional Committee of the Duma.[3]

The Tsar's train got through to Pskov, but instead of finding support there he was confronted by a delegation from the Provisional Committee of the Duma, which persuaded him on 2 March to sign the act of abdication in favour of his brother, the Grand Duke Michael. This did not satisfy public opinion, nor the railwaymen, who once again took the first initiative. When the delegation returned to Petrograd, workshop men from the 'Warsaw' depot held up A. I. Guchkov, the Minister of War in the Provisional Government, and tried to seize the act of abdication from him.[4]

In the interval between the outbreak of the revolution and the founding of railway organisations, individual rail committees of the kind authorised by Bublikov had no qualms at all

[1] N. Sukhanov, *The Russian Revolution 1917* (London, 1935) pp. 108–9. Rodzianko also had his own reasons for not going to the Tsar. See Katkov, *Russia 1917: The February Revolution*, pp. 319–20.

[2] Ibid., p. 110.

[3] See above, p. 21.

[4] Iu. V. Lomonosov, *Vospominanie o martovskoi revoliutsii 1917 g.* (Berlin, 1921) p. 28.

about taking political action on a local level. Some of their demands were retrospective, as when workshop men on the Kazan' line in Moscow clamoured for the return of twenty-seven colleagues who had been shipped off to the front for going on strike prior to the February revolution.[1] Unrest spread out along the lines from the cities. On 10 April at another meeting held on the Moscow–Kazan' line, dissatisfied employees complained about the overbearing attitude of the railway Commissar sent out to them by the Provisional Government. When they failed to get an immediate reply to their requests, they dismissed the Commissar after four days and appointed a man of their own choosing. In the same period many factories on this line came under Bolshevik influence, and the peasants who lived near it began to seize the land at an early date.[2] The railwaymen did not hesitate to interfere with local politics outside their own domain. When, on 11 March, 500 out of 1,400 employees on the Rybinsk line to the north of Moscow wished to throw out of office the newly established local Soviet committee, a representative from the provincial section of the Moscow Soviet went there to restore order. He found he could do nothing but endorse their decision.[3]

All these examples illustrate disapproval of the new organs and advisers set up by the Dual Government, but of course most of the railwaymen's hatred was directed against the agents of the old regime. Some of the latter fully deserved their fate, like the engineer, Panov, who threatened to replace recalcitrant workers by Chinese labourers.[4] The rate at which officials were sacked was alarming: 'On the north-western railway line sixty-five men have been dismissed. . . . In the main workshops of the Nikolaev railway line – the most important in Russia – and the engine workshops only three foremen are left, all the others have been thrown out. . . . They are being replaced by assistants chosen directly by the shop workers themselves.'[5] In August it was calculated by the Minister of Ways and Communications

[1] Taniaev, op. cit., pp. 21–2.
[2] Sidorov, *Revoliutsionnoe dvizhenie v Rossii v aprele 1917 g.*, pp. 354–5, 453, 668.
[3] Sidorov, *Revoliutsionnoe dvizhenie v Rossi posle sverzheniia samoderzhavia*, p. 485.
[4] *Golos zheleznodorozhnika*, 8 June 1917.
[5] *Protocol of the All-Russian Conference of Social Workers*, Aug. 1917, p. 125.

that nine hundred such officials lost their jobs in the first four months of the revolution.[1] This number gives an indication of the activity of railway committees throughout the Empire, and also of the gross technical deficiencies that must have followed in the wake of these reprisals. In a decree of 7 June the Provisional Government vainly attempted to fill the gap by authorising the appointment of local public figures as Commissars for the state and private railways.[2]

The higher echelons of the railway administration did all they could to restrain this sort of action. After February they gave the railwaymen a free rein in organising supplies, welfare and educational activities, but tried to prevent them from intervening in staffing questions and problems of large-scale organisation. Nekrasov did what he could to support the higher officials. In a circular sent out in May he warned: ' . . . it is essential above all . . . that in each of these quarrels the committees have a strictly advisory role; in all instances the final decision lies with the authorities, and in the last resort with the Provisional Government.'[3]

Even the new central organs set up by the delegates of individual railway committees and lines found much of the infighting in the localities irresponsible and anarchic. Many of the violent demands sent up to the All-Russian Railway Union from lower levels were toned down. Dismissed officials were transferred to other lines, for their expert services were badly needed (a large number of them were engineers). The Central Committee of the Moscow–Kursk line tried to keep the situation under control by stipulating that candidates for posts had to be appointed with the approval of the Committee, and after being appointed they had to make regular reports to the Committee on their work.[4]

If the All-Russian Railway Union and Vikzhel considered some actions to be irresponsible, the middle- and upper-class shareholders on the Council of Private Railways (representing about one-third of the railway system) were far more critical, not only of the left-wing railway organs, but also of Nekrasov. During the period of reaction against the Bolsheviks in July,

[1] *Golos zheleznodorozhnika*, 10 Aug. 1917.
[2] *Sobranie uzakonenii i rasporazhenii pravitel'stva*, 1, 2, no. 1365.
[3] Quoted in Taniaev, op. cit.   [4] Ibid., p. 126.

interested circles managed to get Nekrasov replaced as Minister of Ways and Communications by P. P. Yurenev, a Kadet, who was less inclined to be conciliatory. Yurenev introduced new repressive measures: unruly local committees on state-owned lines had their pay stopped, individual railway workers were brought to trial, and military units were dispatched to deal with the more acute situations. Meanwhile the Council of Private Railways egged the new Minister on: 'In the place of the inadequate technical resources of the railway system you must substitute the superhuman efforts of each individual worker.'[1]

From the July Days in Petrograd until the end of August, the pendulum of revolutionary politics was swinging towards the right, culminating in the Kornilov affair from 27 to 30 August. General Kornilov had been made Commander-in-Chief of the Army on 18 July. He took ruthless steps to restore military discipline. He was hostile to all socialists, and he disliked Kerensky, now head of the Provisional Government. As early as 6 or 7 August 1917, he ordered troop units to concentrate near Petrograd, supposedly to protect the Government. On 10 August his proposal for military rule on the railways and in war industries was virtually bypassed by Kerensky. Kornilov next used the Moscow State Conference, held from 12 to 15 August, as a demonstration of right-wing hostility towards Kerensky and even more towards the Soviet. Backed by land-owners, financial magnates and political leaders of the pre-revolutionary Duma period, Kornilov issued a patriotic manifesto to the populace, and on 27 August dispatched troops to Petrograd in an attempt to overthrow the existing Government and set up a new one in which it appeared that he, Kerensky, and Savinkov, Assistant Minister of War, would form a triumvirate.

The railwaymen played a leading part in crushing Kornilov's intervention. The more left-wing elements among them were no doubt as willing to take action on their own initiative as they had been in the case of the Tsar's abdication, but in the Kornilov affair they were also spurred on from above in varying degrees by all political groups to the left of Kornilov. Kerensky

---

[1] Speech of a member of the Council in the *Protocol of the All-Russian Conference of Social Workers*, Aug. 1917, p. 98.

in the Provisional Government, the Executive Committee of the Petrograd Soviet, Vikzhel and the Bolsheviks all issued their separate instructions to the railways. In a last-minute bid to win the railway workers over to his side, Kornilov pretended to support the threatened strike of the engine drivers. 'Therefore Kerensky . . . took all steps for repelling Kornilov's forces', wrote Nekrasov, the ex-Minister of Ways and Communications. 'The order for halting the movement of echelons of Kornilov's troops by rail, signed by Kerensky, was transmitted to me by P. P. Yurenev, who had submitted his resignation the day before but had remained, together with other ministers, to attend to official duties.' All the Kadet ministers resigned with Yurenev from the Government, apparently hoping to cause its collapse. Two hours later Nekrasov was informed by telephone 'that the echelons were breaking through by force and that they could only be stopped by similar use of force. In order to accomplish this, it was necessary to dismantle the rails and arrange an artificial wreck. I informed Kerensky of this at once, and, without any hesitation, he issued an order to apply these heroic means.'[1] This was on 27 August.

On the same day, and before the arrival of the attacking forces, action was also taken through the Soviet and Vikzhel by moderate socialists and Bolsheviks who combined in a 'Committee for Struggle against Counter-Revolution'. At their orders, the railwaymen on the lines approaching Petrograd from the south and west put engines out of use, blocked the lines by upsetting trucks, tore up the rails and cut the telegraph wires. When Kornilov's troop trains drew up, they were pushed on to the wrong tracks and eventually brought to a halt. The soldiers lacked supplies for a march on foot and were therefore stranded. So was Kornilov, caught with a cold at Mogilev, whence he could not escape. In his own words, 'the railwaymen had received orders: I could not get a train that would take me to the environs of the capital. I would have been given a train at Mogilev, but I would have been arrested at Vitebsk.'[2]

Vikzhel sent a telegraphed circular to all lines with instructions to stop suspicious telegrams and to report any unusual troop movements. The railwaymen were asked to prevent areas

[1] *Rech'*, 13 Sep. 1917.
[2] P. Miliukov, *Istoriia vtoroi russkoi revoliutsii*, pt i (Sofia, 1921–3), p. 263.

occupied by Kornilov's units from receiving food or other supplies. Vikzhel members personally took over the central telegraph bureau of the Ministry of Ways and Communications and intercepted all telegrams emanating from Mogilev. The Petrograd Soviet and Vikzhel got widespread support from the Russian railways. Telegrams offering support even came from distant Irkutsk, and many messages expressed the sentiments recorded in the following telegram from the railwaymen of Samara on the Volga: ' . . . The traditions of 1905 are still very much alive among the railwaymen, and they will rise as one and stifle any schemes of the counter-revolutionary hydra. . . . Let the Kornilovites not forget that they will die before they can strike a single blow against the revolution.'[1]

The Bolsheviks as usual were the most active in the crisis. The Bolshevik organisation on the Nikolaev railway line got together a group of railway workers who sallied out to Dno station, where the Tsar's train had passed in the February revolution. There they wrecked the tracks and built barricades from sleepers. Between 700 and 800 Petrograd factory workers, most of them from the enormous Putilov metal works, advanced towards Kornilov's forces under the command of three leaders, one of whom, Zaitsev, was a railway worker.[2] Far more effective than threats of force was the propaganda of Bolshevik agitators who infiltrated among the rank-and-file of the advancing troops and pointed out to them that they were helping reactionary political leaders. Prince Bagration, one of Kornilov's military supporters, realised this on 29 August and ordered units to attack Bolshevik agitators on the Nikolaev line, but it was too late.[3]

The defeat of Kornilov gave a tremendous fillip to the left wing and the tide of revolution began to swing in its favour again after the difficult months of July and August. In September some sections among the railwaymen organised themselves for militant action. At their sixth Party Congress held in July the Bolsheviks had encouraged the organisation of armed

---

[1] Telegram no. 7455 in the Archives of the Samara Railway, quoted in Taniaev, op. cit., p. 95.

[2] Z. V. Stepanov, *Rabochie Petrograda v period podgotovki i provedeniia obtiabrskogo vooruzhennogo vosstaniia* (Moscow, 1965) pp. 180–1.

[3] Sidorov, *Revoliutsionnoe dvizhenie v Rossii v avguste 1917 g.*, p. 462.

bands of volunteers who would be prepared to fight for their cause. The relatively small groups of railway workers who joined together to ward off Kornilov's troops remained in some cases as a militia force through September and up to the October coup. For instance, we know from the memoirs of I. P. Golubev, commander of the railway workers' Red Guard in Minsk, that at the time of the Kornilov rebellion two brigades of Red Guards were formed. Eighty men joined from the Minsk railway depot, and 150 from the workshop. Under the supervision of the military revolutionary committee for the western front, which lay near to Minsk, they controlled the railway lines in the area. After the Kornilov affair their numbers grew to 300, and their equipment included 500 rifles and two machine-guns, no doubt illegally obtained from Bolshevik sympathisers in the trenches. They arranged a twenty-four-hour guard on the railways and practised weapon assembly and shooting.[1]

As might be expected, one of the strongest detachments of Red Guards was formed in the engine workshop of the Moscow–Kazan' line in Moscow. Units also sprang up in areas that had no connection with the Kornilov rebellion, like the one in Ekaterinburg in the Urals, which issued the following resolution on 9 September:

> In view of the fact that seven months after the overthrow of the autocracy the revolution is still in danger, and that until the present time neither the land, nor even fields have been handed over, and counter-revolutionary classes are constantly trying by force of arms to destroy the revolutionary organs and are planning to carry out a bloody massacre of the workers, we, the railwaymen, standing guard over the revolution, consider it essential to arm the workers at once.'[2]

Growing militancy on the railways, coupled with continuing reluctance and increasing inability on the part of the Government to satisfy the railwaymen's pay claims, eventually led to Vikzhel's declaration of a rail strike. This was due in particular to a left-wing pressure group within Vikzhel's membership. At first some of the Socialist Revolutionary leaders in Vikzhel

[1] I. P. Golubev, *Krasnogvordeitsy–zheleznodorozhniki*, in *V bor'be za oktiabr' v Belorussi i na zapadnom fronte* (Minsk, 1957).

[2] Sidorov, *Revoliutsionnoe dvizhenie v Rossii v sentiabre 1917 g.*, p. 367.

urged N. S. Chkeidze, the President of the Petrograd Soviet, to
use his influence to get Kerensky to yield to the railwaymen's
demands. Chkeidze failed in the attempt, so Vikzhel formed a
strike committee led by A. Gar, V. Planson and A. Malitsky.
The strike was intended as a temporary demonstration which
would end as soon as the Provisional Government showed signs
of making concessions. On 20 September Vikzhel warned the
Government that unless wage increases were promised immediately, the railwaymen would go on strike at midnight on
23-24 September. Kerensky refused to compromise, and on
21 September Vikzhel sent a telegram circular to all lines
announcing the strike: 'Organise strike committees, establish
contact with the local Soviets of Workers' and Soldiers' Deputies. Allow no separatist speeches. Our strength and the success
of our cause lies in solidarity.'[1]

The plan was as follows. On 24 September all long-distance
passenger trains were to be halted, on the 25th all local passenger trains, and on the 26th all goods trains. On the 27th the
railway administration would close down, and from the 28th
all traffic would stop except for hospital, troop and food-supply
trains. All railway lines near the front and those to the west of
the limit Petrograd–Smolensk–Kremenchug (to the south-east
of Kiev) were excluded from the strike for military reasons. The
response to Vikzhel's appeal was widespread, though not una-
nimous. Shortly before midnight on the 23rd the last long-
distance train for three days left Petrograd.[2] On some lines
round Moscow traffic stopped completely, because the disruption caused by the implementation of the first stages of the
plan was sufficient to bring all traffic to a halt. Altogether,
thirty-nine of the fifty-one main lines in the Empire carried out
Vikzhel's orders. Most of the blacklegs were to be found in the
distant parts of the Empire, like the Far East (the Amurskaia,
Ussuriiskaia and Chinese Eastern Railways). On the other hand
some of the lines in the military areas went on strike against
Vikzhel's wishes, though the main junctions like Pskov and
Minsk behind the northern and western fronts continued to
operate. The number and importance of the local strike committees was greater than in the general railway strike of 1905.
They were also better organised than in 1905. In September

[1] Sidorov, op. cit., p. 322.   [2] *Delo naroda*, 24 Sep. 1917.

one of the local committees on the Nikolaev line intervened in high politics by preventing M. I. Tereshchenko, the Minister of Foreign Affairs, from leaving Petrograd for military head-quarters at Mogilev on 26 September.[1] Vikzhel received nearly 500 telegrams of support from local railway committees on 25 September, and 800 more on the next day.[2] In addition many delegations went to Moscow to confer with Vikzhel.

The reaction of the Provisional Government was sharp and bitter. Before the strike began, Kerensky viewed 'the organisa-tion of the rail strike in wartime as a crime'.[3] A. M. Nikitin, the Minister of Post and Telegraph, sent out a telegram circular to the nation: 'All citizens are summoned to defend the fatherland against a new blow, similar to the Kornilov plot. I order that all the telegrams of clearly criminal content are to be withheld and that I am to be informed of them.'[4] In reply, Kharkov railwaymen protested 'It is not we, citizens Kerensky and Nikitin, who have betrayed the fatherland . . . but the Pro-visional Government with its promises; no words and no threats can stop us now, except the powerful words of our comrades.'[5] As might be expected, however, the solidarity of the railwaymen was not firm. Before the strike began, the Central Committee of the Socialist Revolutionaries passed a resolution calling upon S.R. representatives in Vikzhel to vote against the strike, though in the event five of the eleven S.R.s voted for it, reflecting the precarious state of discipline in this party. Among the rank-and-file of the railway workers there were differences of opinion too. The less militant sectors had not forgotten their promises made after the February revolution to ensure, for example, that 'the normal non-stop work of the railways does not cease for one instant in so far as it is serving the Army and supply needs of the population'.[6]

Sections of the Army that were neither defeatist nor drawn from the officer and N.C.O. classes offered some resistance to the railways. At first representatives of the garrison in Pskov,

[1] *Trud*, 27 Sep. 1917.
[2] *Russkoe slovo*, 26 Sep. and *Delo naroda*, 27 Sep. 1917.
[3] *Novaia zhizn'*, 23 Sep. 1917.
[4] *Delo naroda*, 9 Sep. 1917.
[5] Taniaev, op. cit., p. 119.
[6] Sidorov, *Revoliutsionnoe dvizhenie v Rossii posle sverzheniia samoderzhavia*, p. 546.

the headquarters of the northern front, threatened to take military action against the Nikolaev railwaymen. On another front, the southern Caucasus (facing the Turks), the Executive Committee of the Zakavkazskaia railway agreed to Vikzhel's appeal that it should go on working, as it was situated in a military area; but Bolshevik depot workers on the line protested and formed their own strike committee. As always, the Bolsheviks had their own distinctive views. In Kazan', the terminus of the notoriously left-wing Moscow–Kazan' railway, they formed their own strike committee after quarrelling with the main committee run by railway officials. Having succeeded, they made a plan to stop all railway traffic at once. Further along the same line at Murom, halfway between Kazan' and Moscow, a Bolshevik strike committee organised by a representative from the Moscow Bolshevik railway district endeavoured, with the help of the local Red Guard, to take complete control over this sector of the line.[1] Hundreds of miles on the Trans-Siberian railway were affected when Bolsheviks in Krasnoiarsk repeated a successful 1905 venture by sending out delegates' trains to the east and west of the town, carrying railway agitators to Tomsk, Taiga and other stations. Factory as well as railway workers joined their cause in Tomsk: 'The cause of the railwaymen is our common cause. The sympathy and compassion of revolutionary democracy is on their side, because they are struggling against capital for the sake of the working class.'[2]

The moderate and right-wing press, noting the view of the Bolsheviks that no holds should be barred in the railway strike, accused Lenin of anarchy and of repeating on the left the blind destructive tactics used by the Black Hundred mobs on the far right. In reply the Bolshevik Central Committee declared that 'the responsibility for the strike that has flared up falls entirely on the Provisional Government . . . the way out of the situation consists, not in the criminal breaking up of this strike, but in compelling the Government in the shortest possible time to satisfy the lawful demands of the railwaymen.'[3] Lenin's most

[1] *Rabochii klass i rabochee dvizhenie v Rossii v 1917 g.*, p. 193.
[2] Ibid., pp. 194–6.
[3] *Protokoly tsentral'nogo komiteta RSDRP (b), avgust 1917–fevral' 1918* (Moscow, 1958) p. 69.

bitter political attacks were often directed against the Anar-
chists, but in 1917 *before* the October coup it is possible on
several counts to tar him with the same brush. On the ideological level, it has frequently been remarked that Lenin's
famous work *State and Revolution*, written in August 1917, con-
tains anarchic elements. On the practical level, the Bolsheviks
were well aware between February and October 1917 that a
sure way of pulling political opinion to the left in Russia was to
support the breakdown of all Tsarist institutions. This induced
economic and social chaos, which discredited the Provisional
Government and encouraged left-wing views. On the other
hand the Bolsheviks changed their tune the moment they came
into power, and did all they could to impose order and centralised control over the country. We shall see more of this
attitude when we come to consider the period after October.
At this point it is sufficient to note the tactics used by the
Bolsheviks to gain political control over the railwaymen up to
October. An interesting, though perhaps not altogether reliable,
account of this appears in an unpublished manuscript from the
Hoover Institution on War, Revolution and Peace, at Stanford
University.

In the Central Committee of the Bolshevik Party there
were even then [in April] men who realised that by their
very nature the railways must be administered from one
centre (Stalin, Trotsky, Dzerzhinsky) and that caution should
be exercised here not to unleash social demagogy. Even then
the question was being discussed in the Central Committee
of how best to bring the tempestuous railway complex into
the framework of a single authority. On the other hand, it
was obvious to the Bolsheviks that they could increase their
influence among the railwaymen only by supporting the most
radical and syndicalist sentiments and slogans.

For the purpose of leading the mass of the railwaymen and
for elaborating appropriate directives, the Central Committee
of the Bolsheviks created in July of 1917 a special commission
under the chairmanship of Stalin and three members –
Shliapnikov, L'vov, and Engineer N. . . . Reports on the work
of this commission were made to Lenin by Stalin alone or
together with Shliapnikov. Stalin believed that one-man

management should be introduced among the railwaymen as soon as possible after the seizure of power by the Bolsheviks. He realised the necessity of dominating this most important apparatus. In the opinion of Stalin, the resistance of the railwaymen could be quickly reduced to zero by repressions on the one hand, and by promises of various privileges with respect to food supply, on the other. Shliapnikov maintained a precisely opposite point of view. He insisted on the introduction of democratic principles on the railways in order to put the commission's own adherents in all committees and thus get control over the railway body from within. He emphasised the extreme danger of strict measures, which might repel the railway masses from the Bolsheviks and thus create the danger of either a strike or sabotage. . . . The other two members of the commission took the middle-of-the-road point of view. Without repudiating the need of a one-man authority on the railways, they thought that this was a question for the future, at which time the railways should be won from within. They believed that slogans should be used which the masses could understand and which could aid the Bolsheviks in their struggle with the Provisional Government and Vikzhel. The Central Committee of the Bolsheviks approved the latter tactics and charged the commission with working out a statute of railway administration, based on a wide application of the electoral principle, with the ultimate aim of introducing one-man management as soon as possible without detriment to the work of the railways. The Central Committee adopted this decision at Lenin's suggestion. Lenin believed that as long as the railwaymen were not imbued with Bolshevik propaganda and no sufficiently strong technical apparatus existed to administer the railways from the centre, the most demagogic slogans had to be used until the moment when the authority of the Bolsheviks in the centre was sufficiently strong. . . . At the moment of the October revolution, although they had some ties with the railwaymen (in the Petrograd region and in Moscow), the Bolsheviks nevertheless were quite aware of the fact that winning the railwaymen to their side was no easy matter and that employing totalitarian tactics with the railwaymen might meet with strong resistance. At the suggestion of Stalin's

Commission of the Central Committee of the Party, they decided to continue the game of playing on the democratic strings of the railwaymen. . . .[1]

On the first day of the strike, 24 September, the Provisional Government drew up a decree which granted higher pay for the railwaymen. The increases were not as high as Vikzhel demanded, but at midnight on 26-27 September A. L. Malitsky, the Chairman of Vikzhel, called a halt to the strike and ordered the disbandment of the local strike committees. In his telegram of 27 September, Malitsky informed the railway-men that the Provisional Government now recognised Vikzhel as their legal representative. Railway workers were to have the first claim to food supplies after the military, and the question of working conditions was to be referred to a new government commission. Finally, a Congress representing all the railwaymen was to be convened in December. Malitsky was not over-joyful. His message read, 'We have managed to achieve more or less significant results'. Vikzhel was nervous about antagonising the country any longer: 'The railwaymen undergo the risk of being left in isolation, without the support of the rest of the democratic forces.'[2] The widespread railway strike ended, but, as the S.R. press organ noted in early October, 'Outward calm has descended on the railways, but underneath a storm is still brewing'.[3] In this period local strikes went on in some sectors such as the Petrograd repair shops and the unskilled part of the labour force on the Finnish railways.

When the Bolshevik coup took place on 25 October in Petro-grad, the railwaymen had as little to do with it, as far as preparation was concerned, as any other broad groups of the proletariat. The timing and organisation of the coup was arranged by a very small number of professional Bolsheviks without regard for Bolshevik sympathisers in the railway work-shops, or indeed for any other outsiders. Only when the Military Revolutionary Committee in Petrograd actually moved into the attack did a restricted number of left-wing railway employees give it practical aid, and this was substantial in the

[1] Naglovsky, *Zheleznodorozhniki v russkoi revoliutsii 1917–20 gg.*, pp. 5–7.
[2] Sidorov, *Revoliutsionnoe dvizhenie v Rossii v sentiabre 1917 g.*, p. 337.
[3] *Delo naroda*, 6 Oct. 1917.

cities of Petrograd and Moscow only. In the rest of the country the prevailing attitude, with a few exceptions, was one of apathy or ignorance. The fact that the only active railwaymen were on the Bolshevik side and in the crucial political centres of Russia helped, along with other factors, to weigh the scales of strategy in Lenin's favour.

In the October days it is more appropriate to follow events in Petrograd before turning to Moscow, since the fate of the Bolshevik coup depended initially on its reception in the northern capital, and control over communications to and from Petrograd was essential to them. During the last few days before the Bolshevik coup, the Military Revolutionary Committee under Trotsky was parrying attempts by the staff of the Petrograd military district to keep control over the city's railway stations in the interests of the Provisional Government. On 23 October the Military Revolutionary Committee appointed A. L. Biliakov commissar of the Warsaw station and the railway line in the south-west of Petrograd. On the following day the military district ordered the authorities at the Baltic station, which was next to the Warsaw station, not to admit commissars sent by the M.R.C. It also advised them to 'warn [Bolshevik] troops attempting to seize the Baltic station that echelons are moving up from the front (along the railway line to the station) that are on the side of the Provisional Government'.[1] All this was to no avail. Later on the same day the station authorities reported back that 'a company of the Izmailov regiment has arrived at the Baltic station . . . under the orders of a [Bolshevik] commissar'.[2]

The reference to the imminent arrival of troops from the front who would safeguard the Provisional Government was premature. Kerensky in some ways acted like a doomed man as the coup approached. Not until 2.20 a.m. on the morning of the 25th, when the Bolshevik armed uprising finally took place, did he order military headquarters at Mogilev to send troops by rail, or on foot if the lines were blocked.[3] Mogilev complained that the request had been slow in coming, and would take some time to fulfil, given the atrocious conditions

[1] Sidorov, *Oktiabr'skoe vooruzhennoe vosstanie v Petrograde*, p. 338.
[2] Ibid., p. 342.
[3] S. P. Mel'gunov, *Kak bol'sheviki zakhvatili vlast'* (Paris, 1953) pp. 93–4.

on the railways and possible opposition on the part of some railway workers. Although Kerensky had taken rather half-hearted steps to protect Petrograd's railway stations, he appeared to underestimate the importance of the fact that the capital was virtually cut off from the rest of Russia owing to the state of the railways. Yet he must have known, for instance, that from 15 October, because of rail stoppages, Petrograd had food for only three to four days' rations at a time. The city was near starvation, which could spark off riots even without Bolshevik intervention. Petrograd was also completely cut off from Europe by the war, and even from neutral Sweden by the continuing strikes on the Finnish railways. The first troops to answer Kerensky's appeal were bicycle units from the western front which got to within 70 versts of Petrograd at Peredol'sky station. But there was no one from the capital there to contact them on arrival. When no orders came even as late as 27 October, morale began to break down in the ranks and desertion set in.[1]

The strategy of the Military Revolutionary Committee with regard to the railways could hardly fail to be superior to that of Kerensky. On 26 October the Committee appealed to all railway employees through the All-Russia Union of Railwaymen to stop any troops faithful to the Provisional Government from advancing along the lines to Petrograd.[2] On the 28th the M.R.C. ordered Bolshevik-infiltrated units outside the city to travel into it. At the same time it ordered other units to occupy key junctions, like Dno, which lay between Petrograd and the northern and western fronts.[3] In the capital itself commissars had been appointed to all the mainline stations covering, besides the Warsaw and Baltic stations mentioned above, the Finland station in the Vyborg suburb to the north of the Neva, the Nikolaev station in the south for traffic to Moscow, and the Tsarskoe Selo station in the same area. These commissars took a positive role in the armed uprising as well as merely guarding the stations. For instance the commissar at the Finland station, D. E. Solov'ev, saw to the re-routeing of trains from Helsingfors and Vyborg carrying Bolshevik sailors, troops and ammunition along the city circular line right round the city to the Putilov

---

[1] Ibid., pp. 102–3.   [2] Sidorov, op. cit., p. 663.
[3] Ibid., p. 690.

works railway sidings. There they swelled the ranks of the only really effective factory Red Guard in the October coup.[1] The minutes of an evening meeting of the M.R.C. held on 29 October give us a general picture of the situation, by then almost under Bolshevik control. The commissar in charge of the whole Petrograd railway network is speaking:

> I have been to three stations. 1. Military telegraphists must be sent to the Warsaw station. 2. Help must be given to Biliakov [the commissar of the Warsaw station]. . . . 4. At the Baltic station the points are being destroyed; the Red Guard must protect them. 5. There are provocative rumours about; for example, according to a communication from Kerensky, the station is about to be bombarded.[2]

In Moscow revolutionary action on the railways came under the close supervision of the Bolshevik railway district, as might be expected in view of its active role earlier in the year. The Military Revolutionary Committee appointed T. Gusev as their railway commissar for the city. Gusev imitated Petrograd methods by installing Bolsheviks in all the chief railway stations, and prevented the establishment of a middle-class Committee of Public Safety on the Moscow–Kursk line.[3] The October Revolution in Moscow was longer drawn out than in Petrograd, owing to stubborn resistance from supporters of the Provisional Government who initially dominated the Kremlin and the city centre. The Bolsheviks gained their support from the industrial districts outside the centre of the city and, as the railway stations were also in these areas, the Bolshevik Red Guard and railway sympathisers were able to cut off their opponents from reinforcements sent along the railway lines to succour them. The officer corps in the Kremlin tried unsuccessfully on several occasions to carve a passage through the Bolshevik cordon to the Briansk (now the Kiev) station in the south-west, where supporting troops from the front were expected to arrive.[4] The Bolsheviks were successful in preventing hostile troops from approaching the city. Zimin, one of the three chief Bolshevik

---

[1] Ibid., p. 783.   [2] Ibid., p. 715.
[3] *Zheleznodorozhniki i revoliutsiia*, p. 19.
[4] G. S. Ignat'ev, *Oktiabr' 1917 goda v Moskve* (Moscow, 1964) p. 81; cf. pp. 87, 89–90.

agitators among the railwaymen in Moscow, and a man with whom we are already familiar,[1] went out along the Nikolaev line to deal with an armoured train sent by Kerensky, which was coming in from the direction of Petrograd. Luckily for him, it had already been taken over by Bolshevik sailors when he encountered it, and so the train was allowed to pass through to Moscow.

Gusev used the Moscow railway stations as weapon stores for the Red Guard. Part of the Red Guard was made up of stalwart units of railway workers, like the one formed by the engine workshop on the Moscow–Kazan' line at the time of the Kornilov rebellion. It was probably these same men who made use of the 40,000 rifles that were found in trucks at the Kazan' station during the October revolution. Gusev ordered the trains at his disposal to distribute, as soon as possible after the Moscow coup, Bolshevik broadsheets and newspapers giving their account of what had happened. This was of great propaganda value, both in view of Moscow's commanding position in the railway network, and because Moscow and Petrograd had by no means staged a national revolution, but had to go on to impose the new Bolshevik regime on the rest of the country. Piatnitsky, the Bolshevik chairman of the railway Soviet, sat half a day and through the whole of one night at the railway telegraph of the Nikolaev line, monitoring telegrams that might give him clues as to the movements of troops loyal to Kerensky. He was able to intercept messages concerning the advance of Cossack units on Moscow.[2] Such thorough methods, used by a very small but efficient group of Bolsheviks, go a good way towards explaining why Lenin's party could stage successful coups in the two capitals, given the indifference of the great majority of the population and the bungling of those in the Provisional Government and its supporters among the military.

No sooner had the Bolshevik coup taken place than Lenin was confronted with strong opposition from Vikzhel, with its

---

[1] Cf. pp. 25 ff. above.
[2] The information given in the last three paragraphs is taken from *Zheleznodorozhniki i revoliutsiia*, pp. 19–30. John Reed was exaggerating wildly in *Ten Days That Shook The World* (New York, 1919) p. 329, when he wrote that 'in the general turmoil attending the conquest of the city, the chief railway station had been forgotten by the victors'.

majority of S.R.s and Mensheviks. For the first and last time in
the Soviet period the railwaymen showed how their control
over communications could be used to great political effect.
Their dramatic intervention in high politics at a crucial moment
in Russian history has been recorded already by scholars writing
in English,[1] so that it is necessary to repeat only the salient
points here.

At the second and last session of the Second Congress of
Soviets on 8 November (New Style), the Vikzhel delegate declared his opposition to the seizure of power by one party, and
called for a coalition Government of all the socialist parties.
Vikzhel was also concerned with another fundamental issue
which has been somewhat overlooked, that of whether the new
Government should derive its power from the Second Congress
of Soviets, or whether it should rely on the authority of the
Constituent Assembly which was due to meet in the near future.
If the former came about, the Bolsheviks would be making a
break with the continuity of the regime; if the latter materialised,
the aims of the Petrograd Soviet and the Provisional Government would be fulfilled in a sense, since both organs had looked
to the Constituent Assembly as the arbiter of the future
Government of Russia.

In order to give force to its arguments, Vikzhel assumed
independent control over the railways and threatened to cut
off all supplies from Petrograd if its demands were not met. Two
days later an ultimatum threatening a general railway strike
compelled the Bolsheviks to enter into negotiations with the
other socialist parties for a coalition government. Lenin was in
no position to do otherwise. The railways were vital for preventing troops still loyal to the Provisional Government from
moving on Petrograd, and for supporting the, as yet, unsuccessful rising in Moscow. In the negotiations which followed between the Bolsheviks and the other left-wing parties, two distinct
positions were adopted inside Bolshevik ranks. Lenin and
Trotsky merely played for time in order to gain the upper hand
over Vikzhel; but Kamenev and Zinoviev saw the railwaymen's resistance as a vindication of their personal view that the

[1] See E. H. Carr, *The Bolshevik Revolution, 1917–1923* London, 1952) vol. 2,
pp. 394 ff.; and L. Schapiro, *The Origin of the Communist Autocracy* (London,
1955) pp. 70 ff., 79, 139.

C

time was not yet ripe for a specifically proletarian revolution. A Vikzhel conference worked out a plan for a new government, from which Lenin and Trotsky would be excluded. This prompted Lenin to propose that negotiations for a coalition be broken off at once, but a majority of the Bolshevik Central Committee voted against this. Eventually Kamenev, Zinoviev and three other Committee members resigned. Slowly the general political situation improved in Lenin's favour. The Moscow uprising was successful, Kerensky fled, and the threat of hostile troops descending on Petrograd receded. Lenin appeared to yield somewhat in allowing the admission of a small number of Left S.R.s into the Bolshevik Council of People's Commissars. This was a very astute move. It satisfied the rather simple-minded Vikzhel, and also appeased the Second Congress of Peasant Deputies, which supported the S.R.s for the most part.

The Bolshevik–S.R. coalition did not survive for long, nor did the compromise with Vikzhel. At an All-Russian Congress of Railwaymen held between 18 January and 12 February 1918, Vikzhel persisted in its original political aims by securing a small majority in favour of a resolution supporting the Constituent Assembly. A Bolshevik regulation of January countered this majority by ushering in one of the few measures after the October coup which was tantamount to anarchy of the kind Lenin had encouraged earlier in 1917. The regulation entrusted the running of every railway line to a Soviet elected by the railwaymen of that line. This new organisation built up from below soon destroyed the efficient Vikzhel and replaced the latter by a new Bolshevik-controlled executive body, Vikzhedor, composed from the unsuccessful minority at the Railwaymen's Congress.

This resulted in even more chaos on the railways. The situation took on tragi-comic aspects. ' . . . Trains nowadays often go unlighted without observing any of the regulations with regard to signals, . . . the carriages are never cleaned. . . . At the station of Klin the engine shed has been converted into a club and the locomotives are being repaired in the open air.'[1]

---

[1] From A. G. Shliapnikov's report to the Bolshevik Central Executive Committee, 20 March 1918, in *Protokoly zesedanii Vserossiskogo Tsentral'nogo Ispolnitel'nogo Komiteta 4-go sozyva*, pp. 44–5.

Only on 26 March, after the Brest-Litovsk crisis was over, did the Council of People's Commissars centralise railway control under the Commissar of Communications, who was given dictatorial powers. The era of workers' control was over for the railwaymen.

The bald facts of the Vikzhel episode deserve some comment. The Railwaymen's Union seemed a hard nut to crack, but even it was smashed after a few months of manoeuvring. Vikzhel commanded the Bolshevik's respect at first. Immediately after Lenin's coup the railwaymen had more widespread technical power over Russia at large than any of the political parties. They were in a position to bargain with both sides of the foundering Dual Government, and in fact took advantage of this to send a delegation to Kerensky[1] as well as negotiating with the left-wing parties. Yet in other respects the Vikzhel members turned out to be men of straw. They were imbued with a good dose of simple optimism, and the relative lack of political experience among their ranks showed in their naïve handling of the situation. They were trying to reconcile the irreconcilable – eight months of bitter political in-fighting had seen to that. It was merely a matter of time before inter-party negotiations could be successfully broken off by the Bolsheviks. Lenin feared factionalism within his own party as a result of Vikzhel's proposals far more than the necessity to form a bogus coalition Government.

Vikzhel suffered from another fundamental weakness. It was incapable of enforcing its decisions on the whole body of railway workers. The political differences of opinion between workshop employees, who often supported the Bolsheviks before October, and other railway workers have already been observed. This lack of unity affected Vikzhel's stand against Lenin after the coup. On 13 November Petrograd workshops issued a resolution recommending that 'Vikzhel members should be arrested and handed over to the Military Revolutionary Committee.'[2] The strongest opposition to Vikzhel came from the Moscow workshops, which with Bolshevik encouragement had succeeded as early as June to form a separate Union of Workers and Workshop Men. When Lenin set up Vikzhedor to counter

---

[1] See Oldenbourg, *Le coup d'état bolcheviste* (Paris, 1929) pp. 309–10.

[2] Sidorov, *Oktiabr'skoe vooruzhennoe vosstanie v Petrograde*, p. 757.

Vikzhel, a large number of Vikzhedor's activists came from the Moscow workshops.[1]

Vikzhel was accused of treachery by all parties during its intervention in the realm of high politics. This was only natural in view of the fierce mistrust that each party felt for other groups. The right wing was convinced that 'Vikzhel was on the side of the Bolsheviks, who had their troops in Petrograd and did not need transportation, and that under the guise of neutrality it was preparing to strike . . . at Kerensky'.[2] Fears evinced at the time have been re-echoed by right-wing interpreters since 1917. Thus S. P. Mel'gunov notes that Vikzhel allowed Bolshevik sailors from Helsingfors to get into Petrograd by rail on 9 November.[3] Bolshevik sources still maintain an equally lively suspicion that Vikzhel was in league with groups as far to the right as the Kadets. In reality Vikzhel genuinely tried to keep up a neutral stance, but its members were far too unsophisticated politically to avoid raising suspicions in both camps.

Some conclusions based on the material presented in this essay may be drawn with regard to the way in which the railways and the railwaymen impinged upon the political scene in 1917. Independent political action on the part of the railway workers certainly had a crucial effect at vital turning-points like the fall of the Romanovs and the Kornilov rebellion. The strategic importance of the railways and of the men who operated them was outstanding. Yet these sporadic interventions were not backed up by long-term political thinking. It is true that some sections of the railwaymen gave serious thought over a period of time to the nature of their economic demands and the ways in which they could exert pressure on the Government to attain them. But by 1917 only a very small minority had emerged from the 'Economist' stage, and most of these men were firmly under the thumb of the Bolsheviks, who manipulated them primarily for their own short-term strategic aims. The idea that the railway workers could adopt an authoritative political role of their own accord was much

[1] For more details, see *Zheleznodorozhniki i revoliutsiia.*
[2] S. A. Rappoport, *Posle perevorota 25-go oktiabria 1917 g.*, in *Arkhiv russkoi revoliutsii*, vol. 8 (1923) p. 45.
[3] Mel'gunov, *Kak bol'sheviki zakhvatili vlast'*, p. 192.

more remote. Such an idea was visionary in 1917, given the heterogeneous make-up of the railwaymen, the absence of universal suffrage, the almost complete lack of political education and the high prevalence of illiteracy among the lower ranks.

This helps to explain the Bolsheviks' attitude to the railwaymen. In his theoretical writings Lenin included them with the rest of the Russian proletariat as the eventual leaders of the new state structure that would arise after the revolution. In practice he found himself in an ambiguous position. During 1917 he was probably genuinely interested in the notion of workers' control *per se*; at the same time his ideas helped to attract badly needed recruits among the railwaymen and other sections of the proletariat, many of whom were syndicalist rather than Bolshevik in outlook. Lenin and his colleagues realised that after the Bolshevik coup they might have to impose centralised Soviet government for a time in order to overcome all those local anarchies that had helped to bring about the downfall of the Provisional Government.

Before October, however, the Bolsheviks looked for ways in which the mood of the railwaymen and the state of the railways could be turned to their own immediate aim – the overthrow of Kerensky's Government. During the months after February, there are frequent references to this subject in Lenin's writings and speeches. The strategic importance of the railways must also have become clearer to the Bolsheviks as the year drew on. In February they had almost no influence over the action taken by the railwaymen. At the time of the Kornilov affair they were more involved, whilst in October they directed railway activities in Petrograd and Moscow as part of the strategy of the Military Revolutionary Committees. The technical breakdown of the railway system played into the hands of the Bolsheviks too. Increasing chaos evoked discontent in the nation at large, reducing confidence in the Provisional Government and crippling the war effort which the Bolsheviks opposed. The lack of railway communications also cut Petrograd off from the rest of the country, thus allowing a few political extremists to stage a successful coup in one corner of a vast empire populated by a majority who were indifferent to Bolshevik rule. That is why the Bolsheviks supported the September railway strike, yet did everything in their power after the October coup to prevent further disruption on the railways. After the revolution they stood to suffer in the same way that the Provisional Government had suffered between February and October 1917.

2 Post and Telegraph

> We must combine our three main forces, the fleet,
> the workers and the armed units, so that in the first
> instance (*a*) the telephone network, (*b*) the telegraph,
> (*c*) the railway stations, (*d*) the bridges are occupied
> immediately and held at all costs.
>
> LENIN, *Collected Works*, 4th ed., vol. 26, p. 152

The telegraph was much more important than the post as an
instrument of revolution in 1917. Two other technological
developments of the nineteenth and early twentieth centuries,
the telephone and the radio, also played a minor role in Russia's
upheaval, and will be mentioned here. In order to grasp their
political significance, it is necessary to consider the stage of
technical efficiency they had reached just prior to the revolution. Then a comparison will be drawn between the ways in
which the Provisional Government, the Bolsheviks, other left-
wing parties and the technicians themselves made rival use of
these devices, setting up conflicting communications channels
to the rest of the country beyond the capital. These channels
were manipulated by qualified, skilled men, who, as was the
case with the railwaymen, often acted as a jamming or distort-
ing element on the central policies of all parties when it suited
their independent interests. Finally, the October coup provides
us with a case study of the ultimate clash between the channels
manipulated by the Bolsheviks and the Provisional Government.

POST, TELEGRAPH AND TELEPHONE IN THE LATE TSARIST PERIOD

The postal system is the oldest of the three, yet on the eve of the First World War the Russian Empire contained only 7,618 post offices. Eighty per cent of these were situated in European Russia.[1] The Tsarist Government had permitted the zemstva to organise their own supplementary postal services, but even by 1917 many towns were as far as a hundred kilometres away from the nearest office. In 1913, 58,600 km. of the railway network were used for postal services; sea and river transport added another 39,900 km.[2] The system was really primitive at the grass roots. Most of the mail was carried by carts, and there were only one or two deliveries a week in the rural areas[3] of European Russia. The zemstva employed local shopkeepers and teachers as semi-official distributors.

The telegraph was the first of the more technical forms of communication to appear in Europe. As early as 1794, during the French revolution, an optical telegraph was used over the 225 km. between Lille and Paris in support of the Convention. The method of tapping out a code along a wire was first used commercially in Britain for railway signalling. Even today in Canada the two great railway systems (the C.P.R. and the C.N.) still control the inland telegraph system, reminding us of the links between these two communications systems, which were very close in Russia in 1917.[4]

In Tsarist, as in Soviet Russia, the inland telegraph was run by the post offices, apart from a special section for railway telegraph. The Hughes and Morse systems were used during the late Tsarist period and up to the 1920s. The Hughes machine, invented in 1855, was capable of transmitting between 1,000 and 1,400 words an hour. The telegraph network was fairly well developed in Russia by 1917. The Crimean War had led to a construction boom, so that by 1870 there were 714 telegraph offices and 90,678 km. of line.[5] The First World War had a similar stimulating effect, with the difference that the

---

[1] *Bol'shaia sovetskaia entsiklopediia*, 2nd ed., vol. 34, p. 328. It is interesting to note that neither the poor postal system in Siberia nor the censor prevented Lenin from obtaining books and newspapers through the official post during his Siberian exile.

[2] *Bol'shaia sovetskaia entsiklopediia*, p. 328.

[3] See note 4, p. 100 below, for an explanation of the provincial administrative divisions.

[4] See above, pp. 39, 41, 50.

[5] *Bol'shaia sovetskaia entsiklopediia*, vol. 42, pp. 140, 169-70.

amount of messages passing through the post and telegraph increased heavily, rather than the extent of the systems themselves.[1]

Compared with the telegraph, the more recent invention of the telephone got off to a slower start in Russia. Government regulations of 1881 allowed private entrepreneurs to set up telephone systems for a period of twenty years, after which time they had to revert to state ownership. The first governmental network began in Kiev in 1886. By 1904 the St Petersburg system could accommodate between 40,000 and 80,000 numbers, whilst Moscow could in theory expand to 60,000. The actual total of urban subscribers was much lower.[2] Inter-urban connections were still very weak by 1917. A link was established between Moscow and Kharkov in 1912, but an attempt to link up Kharkov with St Petersburg via Moscow failed. Thus by 1917 European Russia possessed a restricted number of isolated single channels between cities within a certain distance of each other.[3] In general the lines were very little used by modern standards. In 1913 there were two hundred conversations on average every twenty-four hours between the twin capitals. In the same year there were 240,000 telephones in the whole of the Empire, compared with 700,000 for 1912 in diminutive Britain.[4]

The radio, the most recent invention of all, hardly concerns us in 1917. Its full impact did not hit Britain until the 1920s, and in Russia there were very few major broadcasts until 1922.[5] The first time the radio played an eminent role in European

[1] State revenue from the post and telegraph rose from 80 million roubles in 1913 to 154 million roubles in 1916. See A. M. Michelson *et al.*, *Russian Public Finance during the War: Revenue and Expenditure* (New Haven, 1928) p. 191.

[2] *Bol'shaia sovetskaia entsiklopediia*, vol. 42, pp. 169-70.

[3] Ibid., pp. 171-3. Single channels existed between the following cities; St Petersburg–Moscow, St Petersburg–Reval, St Petersburg–Helsingfors, Moscow–Kharkov, Nizhnii Novgorod–Riazan', Baku–Tiflis, etc.

[4] Ibid., p. 172. Chekov's story *U telefona* gives an amusing view of the early inefficiency of the Russian telephone system.

[5] In 1913 A. S. Popov had opened a naval depot in St Petersburg for radio telegraph to ships at sea. Before the 1917 revolution there were no Russian manufacturers of radio apparatus, but there were branches of Siemens and Marconi in the country. See *Bol'shaia sovetskaia entsiklopediia*, vol. 35, p. 557.

politics came some time after the appointment of Goebbels as Hitler's propaganda chief in 1928. In order to sum up this introductory section, the volume of communications may be restated in the way it affected the ordinary Russian on the eve of the First World War. That statistical myth, the 'average Russian', would have posted four letters in the course of the year 1913, received 2·6 newspapers or journals, and sent off 0·26 telegrams.[1] This shows how static a society Tsarist Russia was, despite the fast expansion of facilities.

THE PROVISIONAL GOVERNMENT

Up to the February revolution of 1917, the administration of the post and telegraph came under the Tsarist Ministry of the Interior, that giant among bureaucratic machines, which controlled so many of the tools of repression in the declining Empire. During the war with Germany and Austria, both the Petrograd Telegraph Agency[2] and the mail, especially to and from the fronts,[3] were heavily censored. The old order quickly fell apart in the February revolution. After centuries of almost personal supervision of the reins of government, the Romanovs found themselves at the receiving end of the whip. Trotsky, in his history of the revolution, relates how the Empress 'was sending the Tsar telegram after telegram, appealing to him to return as soon as possible [to Tsarskoe Selo]. But her telegrams came back to her from the office with the inscription in blue pencil: "Whereabouts of the addressee unknown." The telegraph clerks were unable to locate the Russian Tsar.'[4]

When the Provisional Committee of the Duma came into being, one of its very first measures was to set the flow of appropriate political information going out of the capital into all the provinces of Russia. This was done in the fastest possible

[1] Ibid., vol. 34, p. 328.
[2] For details, see T. E. Kruglak, *The Two Faces of TASS* (Minneapolis, 1962), p. 17.
[3] In his famous autobiography, K. Paustovsky relates how he was dismissed from the hospital service in the war for including a harmless joke about the Tsar's visit to the Polish front in a letter he wrote to a friend. See K. Paustovsky, *Slow Approach of Thunder* (London, 1965) p. 176.
[4] L. Trotsky, *The History of the Russian Revolution* (New York, 1932), p. 79.

way, by railway telegraph. In his memoirs, Kerensky describes how A. Bublikov was sent off with soldiers to occupy the central railway telegraph in Petrograd. It was Bublikov who telegraphed the first news of the revolution to the rest of the country.[1] At the same time he took control over the movement of trains.[2] General P. A. Polovtsov, another servant of the new regime in his capacity as member of the Duma Military Commission, received the feedback resulting from Bublikov's efforts. The reactions of local governors, police agents and military staff from all over Russia flowed into his office in the form of telegrams during the days after the February revolution. The political hiatus that existed at this time between Petrograd and most of the rest of Russia can be shown neatly by the fact that Polovtsov was unable to decipher the information, because the local authorities unhesitatingly used the old Tsarist code. After taking the messages to the General Staff for decoding, Polovtsov discovered that the thoughts of these loyal servants of Nicholas's regime were also still tuned onto the old network: for the most part they interpreted the February revolution as a slight temporary disturbance that would neither dethrone the Tsar nor result in any major change of Government.[3]

The Provisional Government established a new Ministry of Posts and Telegraph on 5 May. The first Minister was I. G. Tseretelli, better known as a Menshevik leader in the Petrograd Soviet. In an appeal to postal and telegraph workers, he urged them to stay on in their jobs and maintain discipline. He blamed the Tsarist Government for hanging on to antiquated equipment and methods: they could only survive in sweatshop conditions and would no longer be tolerated. At the same time Tseretelli took good care to forbid the holding of political meetings during working hours and stressed that syndicalism was out of the question.[4] He allowed the *Post and Telegraph Journal*, founded in 1888, to continue printing, and indeed it survived until 1919.[5]

[1] *The Kerensky Memoirs* (London, 1966) p. 201.
[2] See above, p. 21.
[3] P. A. Polovtsov, *Glory and Downfall: Reminiscences of a Russian General Staff Officer* (London, 1935) p. 153.
[4] See *Izvestiia*, 28 June 1917.
[5] *Bol'shaia sovetskaia entsiklopediia*, vol. 34, p. 329.

Tseretelli's time was increasingly taken up with political business in the Petrograd Soviet. In his memoirs he does not often mention his duties as Minister of Posts and Telegraph.[1] On 25 July he was replaced by A. M. Nikitin. Yet the political importance of the telegraph increased as the months went by. The scope of the Petrograd revolution fanned out through most of European Russia and beyond; only the telegraph was capable of linking up the huge areas involved. Geographical space was not the sole factor involved. Only the telegraph could attempt to keep pace with the number of quick political decisions that the Provisional Government had to take and transmit to distant parts of Russia, to the military fronts stretching from the Baltic to the Caucasus, to the fleets in Odessa and Vladivostok, to the scattered settlements of Siberia and Central Asia.

In the end the Provisional Government failed to unite Russia in a liberal mould. The country disintegrated politically, lagging behind the quicksilver mood of Petrograd. But to judge by the sheer volume of orders, information and propaganda put out by the Provisional Government through the telegraph, it did not fail for lack of trying to keep in contact with the nation, but rather because its messages could not be backed up by force if necessary. The most striking evidence in favour of this view is provided by the three volumes of documents on the Provisional Government edited by Kerensky himself, in collaboration with R. Browder.[2] The amount of business transacted in eight months is staggering to contemplate: small wonder therefore that Kerensky's health was failing by October.

Much of the Government's business was transmitted by telegraph. Important decrees were issued to the country by this method.[3] Kerensky also used the telegraph office as a kind of debating chamber on high political issues. When it seemed as though the Ukraine might secede from the Russian Republic in June, he endeavoured to assemble all his ministers at one end of the line in Petrograd, so that they could parley with members of the

[1] I. G. Tseretelli, *Vospominaniia o fevral'skoi revoliutsii* (The Hague, 1963).
[2] R. P. Browder and A. F. Kerensky (eds), *The Russian Provisional Government 1917* (Stanford, 1961).
[3] One of many examples is to be found in Browder, op. cit., vol. II, pp. 892–3.

Ukrainian Rada[1] at the other end in Kiev.[2] The Rada had already realised the political significance of the telegraph in revolutionary conditions; it gave top priority to a demand for independent Ukrainian control over the telegraph network within Ukrainian territory.[3]

Government by telegraph had its dangers as well as its advantages. The attempted coup by General Kornilov in August 1917 provides the best-known illustration of this. Kornilov misunderstood Kerensky's intentions, and vice versa. This was due chiefly to the fumbling of V. N. Lvov, who acted as the intermediary for the other two. However, the confusion was reinforced when Kerensky decided to get in touch with Kornilov on the Hughes telegraph from the War Ministry in Petrograd. Lvov had been asked to attend, but was late, so Kerensky impersonated him in the conversation. Using his own name, Kerensky first asked Kornilov whether he should act 'according to the information given to him by Lvov'. When Kornilov replied in the affirmative, Kerensky assumed the role of Lvov and asked whether it was necessary to carry out the demands which Kornilov had communicated to him through Lvov. Kornilov gave an oblique reply, merely saying that Kerensky should go to see him at Mogilev.[4]

Thus Kerensky neglected to spell out the exact nature of Kornilov's demands that had been put to him in an ambiguous manner by Lvov. Kornilov also avoided the issue. The veiling of fundamental problems and Kerensky's resort to subterfuge in impersonating Lvov would have been ruled out in a face-to-face confrontation between the two leaders. The use of the telegraph eliminated the more subtle aspects of political bargaining. Blind anger was the result on both sides. Kerensky was convinced that Kornilov intended to stage an immediate military coup d'état, and ordered him to resign his post as Commander-in-Chief of the Russian Army. Kornilov in his turn was amazed by Kerensky's action and ordered his troops to march on Petrograd. Although the rebellion failed, it was

---

[1] The Rada had been formed in Kiev on 4 March 1917, by Ukrainian socialists and the Society of Ukrainian Progressives.

[2] *Rech'*, 4 July 1917.

[3] Browder, op. cit., vol. i, p. 398.

[4] See the Archive of the October Revolution, *The Kornilov Affair*, no. 25.

one of the main causes of the subsequent downfall of Kerensky's Government.

THE BOLSHEVIKS

The Provisional Government did not retain the Tsarist monopoly over official telegraph sources. Item 4 in an early resolution passed by the Petrograd Soviet of Soldiers' Deputies stated that 'all censorship on letters and telegrams, except those that are strictly military, is now abolished'.[1] The Bolsheviks went so far as to demand that the Petrograd Telegraph Agency be taken out of the Government's hands, because they claimed that the Agency distorted the news.[2] Neither did the secrecy of military information remain inviolate. Telegrams sent by A. Guchkov, the Minister of War after the February revolution, were sabotaged by a Bolshevik agent,[3] whilst left-wing sailors in Helsingfors, well aware of the terrible military conditions, accused the Petrograd Telegraph Agency of spreading optimistic lies.[4] Attacks on the Provisional Government came from the right as well as the left. The Kadet party complained that falsehoods put out by the Telegraph Agency led to absurd rumours and panic among the population.[5]

In the interval between February and October, the Bolsheviks were in a relatively weak position compared to the Provisional Government with regard to the manipulation of state-run institutions like the post and telegraph. After all, the Provisional Committee of the Duma was in a real sense the revolutionary heir of the Tsarist Government, even if it was only a temporary guardian until a Constituent Assembly could be called that would express the views of the whole Russian nation. It is true that the Petrograd Soviet set itself up as a second arm of the Dual Government, but the Bolsheviks did not gain a majority in the Soviet until September. The Bolsheviks tried hard to gain influence over the rank-and-file of the postal workers.

[1] *Izvestiia*, 15 Mar. 1917.
[2] Sidorov, *Revoliutsionnoe dvizhenie v Rossii posle sverzheniia samoderzhaviia*, p. 80.
[3] This was A. F. Il'in-Genevsky, mentioned in the essay on the press, pp. 127 *et al.* below.
[4] Sidorov, *Iul'skii krizis*, p. 153.
[5] Ibid., *Razgrom kornilovskogo miatezha*, p. 376.

They had much less success in the telegraph offices. If Lenin had been able to win substantial support from the telecommunications workers in Petrograd, the Provisional Government would not have been able to give its orders to the country, since all messages from the centre could have been sabotaged by the technicians who alone were capable of transmitting them.

Actually the situation was roughly the same as in the case of the railwaymen and the printers. Neither the Bolsheviks nor the Provisional Government was sufficiently strong to impose exclusive control over the post and telegraph workers. If anything, Bolshevik policies had rather less appeal for white-collar office-employees like telegraphists and postal clerks, who were more likely to support the Mensheviks or the S.R.s, if they supported any party in 1917. Immediately after the October coup the trade union of postal employees opposed the new one-party Government enforced by the Bolsheviks.[1]

The lowest ranks of the social strata who were employed on the railways were not so numerous in the post and telegraph, where even the humble postman had to be literate.[2] Far more women worked for the Ministry of Posts and Telegraph than on the railways, adding a natural apolitical or even conservative element. When delegates to the Second Congress of Soviets from all over Russia were asked in October 'What contact does your Soviet have with post and telegraph employees – does the Soviet have a strong influence over them?', the most common reply was that relations were better with the local railwaymen, since the post and telegraph workers were apt to be more conservative.[3]

The Bolsheviks attracted a few supporters during 1917, despite these disadvantages. As in so many other spheres, they concentrated with great strategical astuteness on the nerve centres of the communications network, so that they were an equal match for Kerensky's Government in October. It may be useful at this point to look at the methods used by the Bol-

[1] See E. H. Carr, *The Bolshevik Revolution 1917–1923*, vol. II (London, 1952) p. 105, n. 1.
[2] Even in the postal and telegraph services, however, standards were low, as shown in M. Zoshchenko's charming story *Rachis* in which an employee mistakes a telegram from Paris as one from 'Rachis', a fictitious Russian town composed of the Cyrillic letters bearing a close resemblance to the Russian transliteration of Paris.   [3] *Krasnyi arkhiv*, vol. 84.

sheviks in 1917 for infiltrating first into the Petrograd post and telegraph, and then into branches throughout Russia. The chief Bolshevik agent in the Petrograd head post office was K. Ya. Kadlubovsky (1885–1961). Prior to 1917 he had been a member of the Social Democrat party and carried out revolutionary work in Warsaw. He had been arrested three times by the Okhrana,[1] in 1906, 1907 and 1910. In 1915 he began to work as a postman for the head office in Petrograd, and became a member of the Bolshevik party in March 1917. He was responsible for organising the first Bolshevik cell in the post office on 1 June 1917.[2]

Kadlubovsky was helped in his efforts by colleagues like E. M. Salzirn. A Latvian by nationality, she had been a textile worker in Riga, became a member of the Bolshevik party in 1915, and went to Petrograd in April 1917, borne on the flood of refugees from the Baltic provinces as the German army advanced. Like Kadlubovsky, she took a job in the head post office.[3] When the trade union organisation at the post office began to publish a new journal, the *Post and Telegraph Tribune*, in May, Kadlubovsky managed to get the editor's job. Soon the journal was appearing with the headline slogan 'Down with the ten capitalist ministers', which of course was Bolshevik-inspired, although the trade union had a large Menshevik majority. This peculiar situation reminds us of the way in which the railway Soviet of the Moscow Soviet was taken over in May 1917, and run by the two energetic Bolsheviks, Piatnitsky and Aronshtam, even though there was a Bolshevik minority in the railway Soviet.[4] The qualities of energy and dedication in Bolshevik workers counted for more than the mere quantity of Menshevik or Socialist Revolutionary supporters in 1917. The Bolsheviks usually commanded a majority of talent and enthusiasm among the lower echelons as well as in the party leadership.

Bolshevik organisation, though nowhere near as efficient as many Soviet writers have supposed, was probably at least

[1] The Tsarist secret police.
[2] K. Ya. Kadlubovsky, *Sviazisty Petrograda v bor'be za vlast' sovetov*, in *Sviazisty v bor'be za vlast' sovetov* (Moscow, 1964) pp. 17–18.
[3] E. M. Salzirn, *Ot fevralia k oktiabriu*, in *Sviazisty v bor'be za vlast' sovetov*, p. 33.   [4] See above, pp. 25–6.

superior to that of all other parties. Bolshevik workers as a rule were closely knit and reasonably well informed about activities in each other's sectors. In the sphere of communications one sector helped another. When the press of the Bolshevik *Soldatskaia pravda* was burnt down in May, the Petrograd post-office workers collected money to buy another.[1] In June delegates from the second district committee of the Petrograd Bolshevik organisation were instructed to lecture to post and telegraph workers in the city, and even Lenin's wife, Krupskaia, gave them political talks.[2] By the time of the October coup, there were thirty Bolshevik party members in the Petrograd head post office.[3] The membership was certainly not large numerically, but was probably very active.

The spread of Bolshevik organisation beyond Petrograd shows how economically the party harnessed its small force of supporters to the revolutionary task. When Tseretelli withheld a pay increase from the post and telegraph employees at their second All-Russian Congress held on 25 May,[4] a number of Bolshevik cells sprang up in the provinces, no doubt organised partly by angry delegates back from the Congress. Bolshevik groups were formed in Samara, Kazan', Ekaterinoslav, Riga and Tomsk, among other places.[5] Bolshevik workers were scattered very thinly round the country, but they often occupied vital strategic positions. For example, I. I. Chernyshev, a party member since 1907, worked in the railway station post office at Kursk in 1917. He organized a Bolshevik cell there in March. In itself this group would have been unimportant but for the fact that the Kursk post and telegraph office had been set up in 1914 especially to deal with post and messages passing to and from the military fronts. Obviously there was ample scope in 1917 for employees there to gather useful information for their party superiors in Petrograd, and to carry out petty sabotage on their own initiative.[6]

A second illustration of strategic usefulness was M. N. Volin. A Bolshevik supporter, though not a party member in 1917, he

[1] Salzirn, op. cit., pp. 33–4.
[2] Kadlubovsky, op. cit., p. 17.   [3] Ibid., p. 18.
[4] The first Congress had been convened in the revolution of 1905.
[5] *Sviazisty v bor'be* . . ., p. 9.
[6] I. I. Chernyshev, *Pod znamia velikogo oktiabria*, in *Sviazisty* . . ., p. 92.

happened to work in the town of Tver as a postman. Tver was
an important telecommunications centre, through which passed
all messages on tape between Petrograd and Moscow. Moreover
the Tver post and telegraph office was the receiving centre of
the War Ministry which had installed a radio station there.
Volin did what he could in his small way to influence his fellow
workers. He was sent from 100 to 250 copies of Bolshevik leaflets
at a time. Wrapping them up separately in his room, he saw to
it that they were dispatched round the neighbourhood to the
other groups of post and telegraph employees and to the local
committees of their trade union.[1] Yet again one branch of
Bolshevik organisation was helping another – the post office
was planting the seed issued by the central press.

The political activities of the Bolsheviks in the post and telegraph offices did not go unobserved by the Provisional Government, but it was not until the onset of the anti-Bolshevik
reaction, triggered off by the July Days in Petrograd, that any
firm measures were taken. Tseretelli, the minister most closely
concerned, then set up a commission to interrogate all those
post and telegraph employees who were known or thought to
be Bolsheviks. He was aided by top officials who began to collect
signatures for a resolution to the effect that all Bolshevik workers
should be dismissed for the 'crimes' they had committed against
state property.[2]

The venture was a failure like the rest of Kerensky's campaign
against the Bolsheviks after the July Days; it was a half-hearted
affair and had no tangible results. Bolsheviks placed in the post
and telegraph offices of the big cities in European Russia
survived the attack and re-emerged in the political arena after
the failure of Kornilov's attempted coup. In the October coup
they were to aim a crushing blow against the Provisional
Government.

OTHER PARTIES: POST AND TELEGRAPH WORKERS
AS INDEPENDENT AGENTS

A walk round the A. S. Popov Central Museum of Communications in Moscow would be sufficient to convince the visitor

[1] M. N. Volin, *Formirovanie klassovogo soznaniia*, in *Sviazisty* . . ., pp. 86–7.
[2] Salzirn, op. cit., pp. 34–5.

of two things: first, that well before 1917 post and telegraph employees comprised a formidable group of white-collar workers; second, that prior to the 1917 revolution Bolshevik influence over them was small, despite the Soviet historians' attempts to prove the reverse. In an article written for *Iskra* in 1902, Lenin referred to the post and telegraph workers as the 'bureaucratic proletariat'.[1] Many of them stood on the social borderline between skilled labour and the bottom ranks of the lower middle class, thus putting themselves beyond the normal scope of Bolshevik influence. As state employees, they had to promise in the years before the revolution that they would not become affiliated to any political party or trade union. This restriction did not prevent a minority of workers from taking part in clandestine political activity.

The majority were more interested in bettering their working conditions, though the action taken with this aim in mind sometimes led from economic to political demands, as was also the case with the railway workers. Both labour forces were often militant before 1917. In the nationwide strike of post and telegraph employees in the revolution of 1905, it was the workers on the railway telegraph who caused the worst trouble:[2] two of the most powerful labour groups in the country were thus conspiring together. The post and telegraph workers threatened to strike again in 1915, a more audacious move than in 1905, seeing that draconic police measures had been introduced by the Government at the start of the war. They were in sympathy with the Putilov works in Petrograd, which came out on strike in 1915. The Tsarist Government subsequently decided to raise the pay of the more highly skilled elements among the post and telegraph employees, but left the pay of the lower grades as it had been before. The Bolsheviks immediately interpreted this as an attempt to divide and rule.

By 1917 conditions in the post and telegraph offices were atrocious. The length of a working day depended on the amount of mail, telegrams and other incoming business, and there was

---

[1] Lenin, *Sochineniia*, 4th ed., vol. 6 (Moscow, 1941–52) p. 76. Almost without exception, quotations from Lenin are taken either from this edition or from his *Collected Works* in English, 4th ed. (see Bibliography).

[2] For an example of this see J. L. Keep, *The Rise of Social Democracy in Russia* (Oxford, 1963) p. 221.

no extra pay for overtime. The post and telegraph, like the railways, were choked and overloaded through the eight months from February to October. The administrative periphery as well as the centres of government were overburdened. With respect to local agrarian problems alone there was a 'forest of telegrams of protest to headquarters'.[1] The events of 1917 also chivvied the educated part of the population into making its own personal arrangements for dealing with the revolutionary holocaust. The upper classes were writing or sending telegrams to their relations and servants on their country estates, or trying to get in touch with contacts abroad. Businessmen fearful for their interests endeavoured to round off their accounts and correspondence. The whole population, literate and illiterate, was writing or getting letters written to and from the fronts, manned by millions of soldiers. State revenue from post and telegraph went up by an estimated 210 million roubles from 1916 to 1917 as a result.[2]

The cost of running these services also went up correspondingly. In a review of the financial situation of Russia as of mid-August 1917, the Minister of Foreign Affairs stated that 'the increase in maintaining postal and telegraph clerks during this year gave an extra appropriation of 141 million roubles'.[3] When employees began to claim pay rises in the spring of 1917, they were battering against an empty cupboard. Even if it had wanted to, the Ministry of Posts and Telegraph could not have met their demands.

The discontent increased as the summer drew near. The All-Russian Congress of Post and Telegraph Workers in May elected a central committee to negotiate with Tseretelli for a pay rise, which he refused. It was after this Congress that a few of the more militant employees, seeing that constitutional

[1] L. Owen, *The Russian Peasant Movement 1906 to 1917* (London, 1937) p. 165.

[2] Michelson *et al.*, *Russian Public Finance during the War*, p. 191. The figure for 1916 was 154 million roubles, and the figure for 1917 364 million. The final estimate was made in the middle of 1917, and had to be revised, upwards, later. *Izvestiia* alone received 10,000 telegrams in a period of two weeks after the February revolution; see an interesting analysis of some 1,000 messages from all sectors of the population by M. Ferro, 'The Aspirations of Russian Society', in R. Pipes (ed.), *Revolutionary Russia* (Cambridge, Mass., 1968) pp. 143–63.   [3] *Ekonomicheskoe polozhenie*, II, 376–7.

pressure was inadequate, resorted to the political methods of the far left wing, i.e. the Bolsheviks, and called for the expulsion of the Provisional Government. But the majority remained Menshevik or Socialist Revolutionary in outlook, or else, which was more likely, apathetic and ignorant of all the various political platforms. The younger men, being the worst paid and the most impatient, tended to provide the converts to Bolshevism.

The active core of the non-Bolshevik workers was not idle in organising its forces during 1917, though its talents were scattered geographically and shared out between several political parties, so that by October the total effect was less impressive than the monolithic Bolshevik approach. Petrograd was the vital point. The arrival of Lenin in April was welcomed by a small section of the post and telegraph workers, but they still looked to a legally convened Constituent Assembly as the panacea for Russia's political ills.[1] The vision had not faded by the end of September, when two representatives from the post and telegraph sat in the Provisional Council of the Republic, which was supposed to act as the midwife of the new republic to come. The relative weight attached to their political opinion can be judged from the fact that apart from lawyers, teachers and railwaymen (of whom there were five delegates), theirs was the only profession to be represented on a separate basis.[2]

A Soviet of the post and telegraph employees of the Moscow network was formed in September 1917. Unlike the Moscow railway Soviet, it stayed immune from Bolshevik domination. The chief organisers included Miller, the director of the Moscow post office, and Rudnev, a right-wing Socialist Revolutionary.[3] In the post and telegraph offices of provincial towns, workers were in a position to control most of the messages sent out to the rest of Russia. The services in Kharkov were taken over in September by the 'Soviet of the Fifteen'. Among its members were the telegraph office supervisor, the railway post-office clerk and a clerk from the city post office, two technicians, a telegraphist, and a postman from the telephone unit. Between

---

[1] Sidorov, *Aprel'skii krizis*, p. 394.
[2] F. A. Golder (ed.), *Documents of Russian History 1914–1917* (New York, 1927), p. 564.
[3] T. P. Zhmotova, *Proiski eserov i men'shevikov poterpeli proval*, in *Sviazisty*, pp. 49–50.

them they could manage the technical apparatus necessary for their aim, which was to allow no important decisions to pass through their offices without their consent. This was the nucleus of what later became a pro-Bolshevik group. On 2 December, a considerable time after the Petrograd uprising, it began to run the communications system under the direct orders of the Kharkov Bolshevik committee.[1]

The employees resisted Bolshevik infiltration in the remote Siberian town of Omsk between February and October. They gave an enthusiastic reception to the news of the end of Tsarist rule, since among their number were men who had taken an active part in the 1905 revolution. These same men now came to the fore once again.[2] The links between activists in the 1905 and the 1917 revolution were probably far more numerous throughout all walks of life in Russia than is known to us as yet from the sparse evidence that is available. The nature of these links and their changing political character would make an interesting study.

Another interesting thing about Omsk is that these old hands were now joined by technicians who had recently arrived in Siberia as refugees from the occupied Baltic States.[3] There are frequent instances of non-Russians, and especially newly-arrived refugees from the western part of the Empire, taking up the cudgels in the revolutionary cause, more often than not in the camps of the political far left. Support for the Petrograd Soviet was therefore immediate and loud among the Omsk post and telegraph workers. The Tsarist head of the telegraph fled, leaving a Menshevik by the name of Vannikov in charge. He ran the office together with the new censors of the Provisional Government.[4]

Military telegraphists on leave or deserting from the front also helped to run the Omsk station after the February revolution. This soon became a common phenomenon throughout the provinces, but it was more prevalent in European Russia than Siberia, on account of the vast distances involved. If Tsarist officials quit or lost their posts in a small country town,

---

[1] P. N. Telegin, *Sovet piatnadsati revoliutsionnykh sviazistov Kharkova*, in *Sviazisty*, pp. 115–16.

[2] A. A. Tarasov, *U provoda Lenina*, in *Sviazisty*, p. 124.

[3] Ibid.   [4] Ibid., p. 125.

soldiers were often the only ones qualified to take over. They were usually Menshevik, Socialist Revolutionary, and increasingly, as time went on, Bolshevik supporters.

LETTERS

The role of postal workers in 1917 has been mentioned above, but the political content and influence of the mail they carried has not. This should not be neglected. Besides providing information, letters often served as incidental propaganda.

A two-way process operated between the political hub and the provinces. Mail containing propaganda flowed outwards from Petrograd and Moscow through the hands of Bolsheviks like N. N. Baburin, head of a village post office not far from Moscow. Elected by the management of a neighbouring factory to serve in the local Soviet, he was soon organising the post in his own special way. Mail disguised as ordinary letters, but known to insiders to contain copies of *Pravda* from Petrograd and *Sotsial-Democrat* from Moscow, was held back by Baburin and his associates. They opened them, scanned them, and then read them out aloud to groups of Bolshevik sympathisers in the area, often from the local factory. Finally the letters were resealed and sent off again on their way to more distant parts of the country.[1]

Sparks cast in this way into the political darkness of rural Russia sometimes ignited enthusiasm. Then the reverse process occurred. Letters of support and praise of Lenin's aims flooded into Bolshevik headquarters through 1917, providing stimulation and useful political information for the revolutionaries.[2] However scattered and inaccurate such evidence was, it could be used by the leaders in a very general way as a thermometer of public opinion. Here is an example of such letters:

> Dear comrade Lenin,
> I am writing from the town of Krasnoiarsk.
> I am a teacher in the third class of the Krasnoiarsk guberniia girls' grammar school. You are a Bolshevik, and so am

[1] N. N. Baburin, *V. bor'be roslo nashe revoliutsionnoe samoznanie*, in *Sviazisty*, pp. 55–6.
[2] See the interesting selection of letters of this kind in *Pis'ma trudiashchikhsia k Leninu* (Moscow, 1960).

I. Please send instructions to our school to stop compulsory scripture lessons; ours is a bourgeois school and has always made scripture compulsory. And I beseech you to send me a personal reply, however short. . . . I await your letter.

Zhenia Zamoshchina[1]

Amazingly, Lenin found the time to answer this and many other letters from private individuals. He was a stickler for detail and thoroughness. On many of the letters he received, Lenin wrote hastily and laconically 'V arkhiv', 'For the archives'; he was already thinking of posterity.

Letters on other channels beyond the crucial two-way one discussed above may have been more effective in spreading Bolshevik ideas, since they were not preaching to the converted. The tides of private correspondence that passed to and from the military fronts were in a sense better propaganda than many deliberately organised campaigns. Peasants inside Russia learnt to be unconscious defeatists through reading letters from demoralised relatives fighting at the front.[2] The letters the peasants sent back to the Army were full of disturbing and exciting news about the dismissal of Tsarist officials, the flight of the gentry, and above all the hope of land redistribution. It was news of this kind that made the soldiers desert, thus promoting the Bolshevik cause in their turn.

Letters to the front were often more than private messages between two people. Soldiers read out their contents to their fellows, and letters of special interest were reproduced on a hectograph; soldiers' revolutionary committees also used information culled from letters for composing satirical verses of a political nature.[3] Bolshevik support whipped up by these means prompted other letters from private soldiers to Lenin, of which the following extract is an example:

In Petrograd I picked up newspapers and pamphlets which I distributed all the way [back to the front], and in Kotel'nich I gave out about 120 copies of various kinds. According to

[1] Ibid., pp. 29–30.
[2] Soldiers were able to send letters home post-free. Non-commissioned officers and Sisters of Mercy acted as scribes for illiterates. See R. S. Liddell, *On the Russian Front* (London, 1916) p. 234.
[3] *Letopis' velikogo oktiabria, aprel'–oktiabr' 1917* (Moscow, 1958) pp. 62 ff.

the villagers and the people in the town, they have received nothing but bourgeois papers so far. . . . I humbly ask you, comrade Lenin, to take very decisive action for the town of Kotel'nich. . . . Comrades, excuse my bad grammar.[1]

THE TELEPHONE

The telephone played a minor role in the political upheavals of 1917, because of the comparative lack of inter-urban lines in Russia. For the most part it was only inside the separate towns of European Russia that the telephone was used. Like the telegraph, but on a much smaller geographical scale, it came into its own at moments of sudden crisis. During the February revolution politicians, intellectuals and public-minded individuals in general picked up the telephone to find out what others were thinking and to get a clearer view of the confused situation inside Petrograd.[2]

No one expected the February revolution to occur exactly when it did, but the abortive uprising in July was quite different. The Bolsheviks, the Petrograd Soviet and the Provisional Government were aware before the event that trouble was in the air. On this occasion the telephone was used for specific political aims. On the night of 5 July, the Provisional Government took two strategic measures to reduce the risk of a successful uprising. The bridges leading across the Neva from the working-class quarters to the city centre were cut off, and the central telephone exchange was ordered to boycott calls requested by Bolsheviks.[3] At the same time Sukhanov relates how the Petrograd Soviet used the telephone as a means of ensuring that factories in the suburbs remained loyal to it and did not collaborate with the Bolshevik sailors coming into the city from the island fortress of Kronstadt.[4] In the October coup the telephone was put to even better and more calculated use.

[1] *Pis'ma trudiashchikhsia k Leninu*, p. 27.

[2] See, among many others, the memoirs of V. Shulgin, *Dni* (Leningrad, 1925) and D. Francis, *Russia from the American Embassy* (New York, 1921).

[3] See O. N. Znamensky, *Iul'skii krizis 1917 goda* (Moscow, 1964) p. 106, and Il'in-Genevsky, op. cit., p. 66.

[4] N. N. Sukhanov, *The Russian Revolution, 1917: A Personal Record* (London, 1955) p. 422.

THE OCTOBER COUP

Both the Bolsheviks and the Provisional Government recognised the supreme importance of telecommunications in the October coup. The lengths to which Lenin went to take over the telegraph, the post office and the telephone network in Petrograd and Moscow, and the care Karensky took to protect them, are clear evidence of this. Since the details of the seizure of these installations in Petrograd have been related by previous scholars, they are dealt with briefly here, and attention is also given to the rest of the country.

Control over the railways, supplies and the press was important throughout 1917, and during the months between February and October the political problems concerning them were probably of more weight than any to do with telecommunications and the postal service, But at a time of swift action in October, when the fate of the Government was in the balance, it was vital for both sides to have access to a correspondingly swift means of communication. Even if Petrograd fell to the Bolsheviks, the rest of the country needed to be persuaded to follow suit. The telegraph and telephone were essential for information and propaganda purposes. In Lenin's words, 'We must . . . occupy the telegraph and the telephone exchange at once; move *our* insurrection headquarters to the central telephone exchange and connect it by telephone with all the factories, all the regiments, all the points of armed fighting'.[1]

In the popular mind revolutions are labelled indiscriminately with the epithet 'bloody'. On the whole the Russian revolution of 1917 was accompanied by little bloodshed. Certainly the October coup in Petrograd caused very small loss of life. The protracted civil war which followed was a different matter. The only physical struggles in Petrograd during the fatal October days occurred around the Winter Palace, where Kerensky's Government was entombed, the railway stations, bridges, and the telegraph, telephone and post offices. Even these restricted tussles were amazingly subdued. Part of the reason for this was that the Bolsheviks had pre-planned the coup, so that all vital positions had been taken before Kerensky could summon troops to the captial. Kerensky's reactions were slow in any case. The

[1] Lenin, *Sochineniia*, 4th ed., vol. 26 p. 27 (13–14 Sep. 1917).

result was not a straight walkover for the Bolsheviks, however, since their actual execution of the coup was not nearly so efficient as has sometimes been thought.[1]

Although armed volunteers from the Bolshevik Red Guard had been meeting in the post and telegraph workers' club from 21 October onwards,[2] the central telegraph office was eventually taken on 24 October by a Bolshevik commissary, A. M. Liubovich, and a handful of soldiers from the Keksgol'msky regiment.[3] According to a very detailed non-Bolshevik source, they were unarmed.[4] On 25 October, a Junker regiment tried to retake the central telegraph for the Provisional Government. It was too late. However, most of the telegraphists refused to work for the Bolshevik intruders, so it was left to a group of sailors from Kronstadt to struggle with the apparatus in an attempt to inform the country about Lenin's first decrees on peace and land. They soon found that they could not cope with the task: some of the apparatus and the supply of current had been sabotaged.

The Bolsheviks put up a large placard outside the telegraph office, pointing out what had happened and asking for assistance. Eventually, after angry Bolshevik sympathisers from the factories had arrived and intimidated the telegraphists, some of them returned to their posts.[5] The sailors saw to it that a strict censorship was imposed on outgoing news.[6] Trotsky was so eager to use the office that he sent out a telegram to the military fronts at 2.35 a.m. on 25 October, to the effect that the Winter Palace has fallen to the Bolsheviks.[7] In reality the Provisional Government did not capitulate until the evening of that day.

The head post office fell more smoothly into Bolshevik hands, thanks to the earlier work of men like Kadlubovsky. A revolutionary committee had been founded just prior to the coup, and no doubt it was composed of some of the thirty Bolshevik

---

[1] For a recent reassessment of Bolshevik efficiency in the coup, see R. V. Daniels, *Red October: The Bolshevik Revolution of 1917* (London, 1968).
[2] Salzirn, p. 38.   [3] Kadlubovsky, op. cit., pp. 18–19.
[4] S. P. Mel'gunov, *Kak bol'sheviki zakhvatili vlast'* (Paris, 1953) p. 108.
[5] Kadlubovsky, op. cit., pp. 18-20.
[6] A. L. Sidorov, *Oktiabr'skoe vooruzhennoe vosstanie v Petrograde*, p. 344.
[7] Mel'gunov, op. cit., p. 125.

party members already in the office.[1] The committee called for an armed guard from the local district Soviet and carried on routine postal work during the coup. The triumphant Bolshevik employees were proud of this feat, for, as they declared, 'the success of the revolution depends on the proper working of the post and the telegraph'.[2]

The telephone exchange suffered rather rougher treatment than the post office. The Junkers got there before the Bolsheviks and managed to cut off Smolny, Lenin's revolutionary headquarters on the bank of the Neva. Soldiers from the Keksgol'-msky regiment subsequently managed to oust the Junkers, but this was not the end of the Bolsheviks' trouble. As in the case of the telegraph, the telephonists refused to co-operate. They were in a special trade union closely directed by the municipal authorities, who were far from being favourably inclined to the Bolsheviks. The Bolshevik Military Revolutionary Committee sent Kadlubovsky to command the telephone exchange. He succeeded in repulsing a delegation from the municipal authorities headed by Bas, a Socialist Revolutionary. Kadlubovsky was backed up by the district Soviet, which sent him factory telephonists to replace those who had deserted the central exchange. Later on the Moscow Bolshevik committee sent another twenty girl telephonists to help with the large volume of work that needed to be done during and after the coup.[3] By these means the Bolsheviks soon gained a hold over the telegraph, post and telephone systems.

In the Winter Palace, the headquarters of the Provisional Government, Kerensky was unable to use the central telegraph after it had been seized by insurgents, but at first one of his ministers, S. L. Maslov, was able to ring through to the city Duma on an unregistered telephone. The Duma sent out a delegation to support the Provisional Government.[4] The Winter Palace, already virtually cut off from the rest of Russia, now had its ordinary telephone system disconnected, so that it be-

[1] Cf. p. 67 above.
[2] Kadlubovsky, op. cit., pp. 20–2.
[3] Ibid., pp. 22–7. See also Sidorov, op. cit., pp. 888, 897, 900, for documents concerning this episode.
[4] Mel'gunov, op. cit., p. 125. The Duma members were stopped on their way through the streets of Petrograd and did not manage to reach the Winter Palace.

came isolated from Petrograd as well.[1] The Bolsheviks were not quite so efficient as all that, however, nor was Kerensky so negligent. He had arranged for a system of runners in case the city telephones ceased to work.[2] There was also a single direct wire connecting the Provisional Government with Army head-quarters at Mogilev. The Bolsheviks had made a detailed plan for seizing strategic points in Petrograd as early as July, but they still forgot to capture the telephone in the War Ministry in October.[3] Thus the Provisional Government was able to send out appeals until late in the evening of 25 October, like this one sent to Mogilev: 'Let the country and the people reply to the mad effort of the Bolsheviks to raise an uprising in the rear of the fighting Army.'[4]

The October coup in Moscow led to more disorders than was the case in Petrograd. The Moscow Bolsheviks were not so skilful and stubborn as Lenin and Trotsky, and the Junkers offered more resistance. The latter held the centre of Moscow, whilst the Bolsheviks were scattered round the suburbs. As a result, fighting went on for a week. Bolshevik troops of the 56th regiment took over the guard of the central telegraph office in Moscow on 25 October, but during the night of the 27th and 28th the Junkers retook it, together with the central telephone station and the post office. This victory upset Bolshevik efforts to co-ordinate communications between the two capitals.[5]

[1] Sidorov, op. cit., p. 353. Sukhanov, op. cit., p. 621, observes that the Bolsheviks cleverly seized communications in the city before they stormed the Winter Palace. Before being cut off from Petrograd, the Provisional Government had tried to cut off the Bolsheviks' telephones in Smolny.

[2] Ibid., p. 406. The Bolsheviks used long-distance couriers to avoid uncertain postal services: seventy-five couriers reported to the Central Committee after its historic meeting of 10 October. A few of them came from Transcaucasia. See John Keep, 'October in the Provinces', in Pipes (ed.), *Revolutionary Russia*, p. 188, n. 30.

[3] Mel'gunov, op. cit., pp. 108, 123.

[4] Quoted in W. H. Chamberlin, *The Russian Revolution*, vol. 1 (New York, 1965) p. 317. The full text of the main telegraphic exchange between the Winter Palace and Mogilev is contained in the *Arkhiv russkoi revoliutsii*.

[5] On 24 October a meeting of the Bolshevik Party Central Committee in Petrograd had carefully assigned functions to its members during the uprisings. The key roles were given to (1) Bubnov, who was to establish connection with the railwaymen, (2) Dzerzhinsky, liaising with the post and telegraph workers, and (3) Lomov, who was sent to Moscow in person to co-ordinate activities. See Chamberlin, op. cit., pp. 310–11.

The central telegraph was reoccupied temporarily by the Soviet of post and telegraph employees under the leadership of the Socialist Revolutionaries.[1] All telegrams passing through Moscow on the way to Petrograd from the provinces were intercepted. Those coming from local Bolshevik military revolutionary committees were not allowed to pass. Outgoing news telegraphed from Moscow on the development of the uprising was distorted in the Junkers' favour.[2] The Junker forces which took the telephone station saw to it that all Bolshevik and Soviet organs in the city had their lines cut off. Listening devices were used for other calls. The building was nine storeys high and so provided a good defence point in addition. It was the last to fall to the Bolsheviks after the post office and the central telegraph.[3]

The physical struggle was soon over in the twin capitals, but the central committee of the trade union of post and telegraph workers continued to resist the Bolsheviks. Telegrams from Bolshevik military revolutionary committees in the provinces were often delayed or not delivered at all. Local telegraph offices where Bolshevik telegraphists had been installed as commissars found themselves mysteriously cut off from the capitals.[4] In Kharkov, messages intended for Bolshevik organs were sent to the wrong address.[5] On 18 November (Old Style) a meeting of delegates from the post and telegraph workers' trade union met in Nizhnii Novgorod (it was not safe to meet in either of the capitals) in an unsuccessful attempt to whip up a general strike among their co-workers.[6] Back in Petrograd there was political trouble with the civil servants in the Ministry of Posts and Telegraph, who were in league with the higher officials of the trade union. Within a few days after the October coup, only eighty-eight employees remained in the Ministry: the rest had left their jobs. Only on 12 November was Lenin able to establish a new People's Commissar (Minister) of Posts and Telegraph, N. P. Avilov. Two of Avilov's close advisers now

---

[1] See p. 71 above.

[2] Zhmotova, op. cit., pp. 49–50.

[3] A. G. Anisimova-Slesareva, *Bor'ba za moskovskuiu telefonnuiu stantsiiu*, in *Sviazisty*, pp. 62-5.

[4] M. V. Khodeev, *Po puti, ukazannomu Leninym*, in *Sviazisty*, p. 73.

[5] N. S. Zubavnikov, *V. bor'be za vlast' sovetov*, in *Sviazisty*, p. 101.

[6] *Sviazisty*, p. 11.

appointed were Kadlubovsky and Liubovich, as a reward for their revolutionary work mentioned earlier in this essay.[1]

The new Bolshevik regime soon began to assert a tighter hold over telecommunications beyond Petrograd. The Military Revolutionary Committee organised a special journal for recording news of political changes coming in over the telephone from nearby centres in European Russia.[2] From the provinces local pro-Bolshevik Soviets were asking for new direct telephone lines with Petrograd to keep them informed of the latest government moves.[3] In areas closer to Petrograd and Moscow, Bolshevik Red Guards were sent out from the cities to protect local communications centres. A group of seven arrived in the night of 26–27 October at the post office near Moscow where N. N. Baburin worked, to help him in ensuring Bolshevik supremacy there.[4] (Baburin was the postman referred to above, p. 73.)

In most of European Russia and in every part beyond, the telegraph was the Petrograd Bolsheviks' only means of fast information. Bolshevik telegraphists in distant Omsk at once passed on the news of the October coup to the local factories, where public meetings were called. Omsk was on a newly constructed direct line to Petrograd using the Murray apparatus. Unfortunately for the local Bolsheviks, many of the Omsk telegraph workers could not be trusted politically. The Bolsheviks got round the difficulty by passing their information to the capital on the old Morse apparatus still operating in the town. This link was often sabotaged at intermediate stations by anti-Bolshevik workers who cut off discussions or drowned the reception.[5]

While petty tussles of this kind were going on in the telecommunications network throughout the length and breadth of Russia, the rival leaders were drawing near to the end of their struggle at the political hub of the country. After the initial Bolshevik coup d'état in Petrograd, many decisions of supreme importance were carried out by telephone and telegraph. Thus when Kerensky tried to join forces with General Dukhonin, the

[1] Kadlubovsky, op. cit., in *Sviazisty*, pp. 24–5.
[2] V. D. Bonch-Bruevich, *Vospominaniia Lenina* (Moscow, 1965) p. 247.
[3] Sidorov, op. cit., p. 571.
[4] Baburin, op. cit., pp. 59–60.
[5] Tarasov, op. cit., pp. 127–30.

military chief of staff, in order to march on Petrograd, telephone contact between the two men was prevented by General Cheremisov, the commander-in-chief of the northern front, who according to Kerensky was 'flirting' with the Bolsheviks.[1] Again, on 7 November, after Kerensky had left the country, the Soviet Council of Peoples' Commissars sent Dukhonin a message ordering him immediately to propose an armistice to all the belligerent countries. No reply came, and when Lenin, Stalin and Krylenko, the Commissar for War, communicated with Dukhonin over the direct line on 9 November, the latter refused to obey. He was instantly dismissed from his post by an order sent on the direct line.[2] This was revolution by telegraph indeed.

[1] *The Kerensky Memoirs*, pp. 439 ff.
[2] Lenin, *Collected Works*, 4th ed., vol. 26, pp. 308–12.

3 Supplies

> Bread for twelve hours!
> Note scribbled on a piece of paper by Kerensky
> and found on his desk after his flight from the Winter
> Palace in October

The Russian Minister of Foreign Affairs noted shortly before
the October coup with respect to the state of the railways and
the supply question:

> ... Notwithstanding all the difficulties we are experiencing,
> our position, objectively, still includes enormous resources
> both with respect to manpower reserves and food supplies. ...
> The difficulties, however, arise from the shortage and the
> poor functioning of transport. That is why much of what is
> happening in our country is completely incomprehensible to
> foreigners, be they our enemies or our allies.[1]

The railway situation in Russia may serve as an introduction
to the politics of the supply problem. The collapse of the railway
system, enhanced in the revolutionary months by the actions
of the railwaymen, was the main cause of the breakdown in
supplies.

Before investigating supplies for the civil and military population, a word on water and road transport would not be out
of place at this point. Although it is true that the railways were
of overriding importance in the transport system of Russia,
rivers like the Volga carried large volumes of grain, oil and
timber along their great lengths. Unlike the railways, river
traffic was run on a completely private basis. Only as late as

---

[1] *Kommissiia po inostrannym delam, Byloe*, VI, no. 12 (1917) pp. 9-23.

January 1916 did the state begin to control the passage of fuel and other military supplies.[1] By this time it was far too late to remedy the crippled state of water communications, which was almost as bad as that of the railways. Many shipping companies were losing money from 1913 on. River-boat workers were quitting their jobs in large numbers because the pay and conditions were so low, indeed far worse than on the railways. Some vessels would reach their journey's end with only two of the crew left on board. Fewer new boats were built after 1910, and the old ones were over-used and under-repaired. By the winter of 1916–17 there were 2,246 craft on the Volga, or 7 per cent less than there had been in 1912.[2]

In the revolutionary months class hatred incapacitated river traffic even further. The shipowners of the Volga basin formed themselves into one group, their employees and the sailors into a second, and the Union of Stevedores into a third. The latter succeeded in holding the owners to ransom by demanding and getting as much as a hundred roubles a day. The tale went round that red caviar, not kasha, was now their staple diet. In April the Provisional Government stepped in, allowing supply committees to requisition the services of the local population for loading the river boats.

The backward state of Russian roads has already been alluded to. They can be ruled out as a major form of transport. Even as an ancillary service they were of little use by 1917, partly because over two million horses had been taken over by the military authorities. A British officer on the Russian front commented on the position in a dispatch of 10 August 1917:

The delivery to railhead is a problem in itself. Horse requisition has been overdone. There is no mechanical transport. There are practically no metalled roads in the grain-bearing districts, and the roads are often impassable in spring and autumn. Just now such means of transport as the peasant possesses are engaged in the actual harvesting and no grain is being delivered to railhead. Horse-drawn transport is so limited that grain cannot be conveyed from long distances. In fact, it amounts to this, that the army and the town

[1] I. A. Shubin, *Volga i volzhskoe sudokhodstvo* (Moscow, 1927) pp. 846–7.
[2] Ibid., pp. 729–34.

population of Russia have to depend for their existence on a narrow strip some fifteen miles wide on either side of the railways.[1]

SUPPLY AND DEMAND

The supply crisis of 1917 would have been more acute had the export of food, raw materials and manufactured goods continued on a pre-war scale. Before 1914, Russian foreign trade showed a large excess of exports over imports, but in the first year of the war, August 1914 to July 1915, exports declined to 13·3 per cent of the pre-war figure, although this sudden drop was reversed slightly in 1916 and 1917.[2] Trade with Germany, Russia's traditional partner, stopped altogether, and ties with the rest of the world were virtually severed owing to Russia's isolated position and the general lack of goods. The vast ranks of Russia's armies swallowed up what she could not export, and more than that in so far as food, clothing and armaments were concerned. The millions of peasants in uniform were at first often better fed and clothed than they had been in their own villages before the war.

The new and urgent demands of the military were not counterbalanced by a slackening of demand on the part of the civilian urban and rural population. During the period 1908-16 the working-class population of Petrograd and the surrounding area had increased two and a half times. Roughly 40 per cent of the Petrograd proletariat was mobilised in 1914, but the gap was soon made up by a new influx from the countryside. The total urban population of Russia before the war was about 22 million. By 1916 the figure had risen by another 6 million. A large labour force was needed to man the new war industries. Peasant military recruits were moved from the country into city barracks which later had to accommodate the sick and the wounded as well. Last but not least, hundreds of thousands of refugees flooded into Russia's western cities, particularly Petrograd, as the Germay Army advanced eastwards. When most of

[1] Dispatch sent to England by Brigadier-General Sir Alfred Knox, quoted in N. Golovine, *The Russian Army in the World War* (New Haven, 1931) pp. 173-4.
[2] Baron B. E. Nolde, *Russia in the Economic War* (New Haven, 1928) pp. 124-6.

Riga's factories were evacuated in July 1915, only 3 per cent of the city's metalworkers stayed on, and the total population declined from half a million to two hundred thousand.[1]

In the countryside material prosperity grew in the early stages of the war. There were fewer mouths to feed owing to the exodus of the male population to the front or to the cities. At the same time the large government contracts for foodstuffs provided the peasantry with more ready cash than it had ever controlled before. As a result the demand for a more varied diet and more manufactured goods increased.

The Russian economy was unable by 1917 to meet all these demands, either with regard to food or to other goods.

FOOD

The condition of a nation's stomach would seem to be a vital factor in political revolutions. The French revolution was touched off by the acute rise in the price of bread in Paris, and the February revolution of 1917 by unruly queues outside the bakeries in Petrograd. An eyewitness at this time noted that in order to 'obtain the miserable dole of bread from one of these shops it was necessary to stand in a long queue and wait your turn. Some of these queues were often over a mile in length with people waiting four deep. This does not sound so terrible a hardship until one learns that the temperature would sometimes be 70° to 80° F. below freezing point with a cutting wind blowing.' The same eyewitness had been called on business to the Urals a few weeks before the February revolution, where 'food was very plentiful and could be obtained at almost pre-war prices, transport being the only difficulty to be overcome. ... In one instance many tons of the best cream butter, which was retailing in Petrograd at between seven and eight shillings the pound, were sent to a soap works to be made into soap. For this transport trucks were available, and yet such trucks were not permitted to take butter to Petrograd.'[2] These are the revealing but isolated impressions of one individual. Taking a

[1] See Ia. Kaimin', *Latyshkie strel'by v bor'be za pobedu oktiabr'skoi revoliutsii* (Riga, 1961).

[2] Stinton Jones, *Russia in Revolution, being the Experiences of an Englishman in Petrograd during the Upheaval* (London, 1917) pp. 68, 70–1.

wider view, it was calculated after 1917, though no doubt with
some exaggeration, that at the time of the February revolution
for the country as a whole there was sufficient grain available
to supply only 50 per cent of military demands and 41 per
cent of civilian requirements.[1]

Bad food distribution to the cities, especially to Petrograd,
which was penalised by its swollen population and an isolated
geographical site, soon led to a rapid increase in food prices. In
the short period between the start of the war and the end of
1914, the cost of butter in the capital rose by 30 per cent, and
the price of salt by 57 per cent.[2] Increases of this kind continued
right up to the October coup. Although Soviet figures are
probably too sanguine, a recent estimate which puts the number of workers' strikes in Petrograd, from 19 July 1914 to
31 July 1915, at 147[3] does not appear to be wildly overstated
in view of the food situation which so often helped to instigate
them.

What caused such acute shortages and inflated prices in
Petrograd? We already know of the greatly increased demand
for food in the war. On the whole the peasants preferred to give
up their crops to the Army rather than to the town. They had
been compelled to send their sons to the front, so they reckoned
that their grain should follow them. We know too of the state
of transport in Russia, and that the northern half of the country,
including Petrograd and Moscow, were non-producing areas
which relied heavily on the south and west for food. New
factors assumed great importance in the food crisis by 1917.
Even before the February revolution Russia had ceased to be
a unified market. The countryside was refusing, even if it was
wholly competent, which it was not, to supply the towns with
food. Economic disintegration preceded the political localism
of 1917. In an atmosphere of *sauve qui peut*, the peasants in the
producing regions held back available supplies for themselves.
By May 1917 the price of rye bread, traditionally the staple

[1] Z. Lozinsky, *Ekonomicheskoe polozhenie vremennogo pravitel'stva* (Leningrad,
1929) p. 124.
[2] A. P. Pogrebinsky, *Sels'koe khoziaistvo i prodovol'stvennyi vopros v Rossii v
gody pervoi mirovoi voiny*, in *Istoricheskie zapiski* (Moscow, 1950) vol. 31, p. 45.
[3] I. P. Leiberov, *Statechnaia bor'ba petrogradskogo proletariata v period pervoi
mirovoi voiny*, in *Istoriia rabochego klassa Leningrada* (Leningrad, 1963, p. 166.

peasant food, was as high as twenty kopecks a *funt* (nine-tenths of a pound). As a result the towns went short, the Army suffered, and fellow peasants in the non-producing provinces went hungry as well.

When the effect of the February revolution spread like a slow fuse from the big industrial cities to the countryside in European Russia, food supplies were disrupted even further. Because of the political backwardness and apathy of the peasants and the enormous distances separating the Russian provinces, the agrarian movement in 1917 got off to a later start than the trouble in the cities and the trenches. In the late spring threats and petty trespass were the main ways in which the peasants showed their hostility to the local gentry. Then in spite of the hay-cutting season, June saw no abatement in the harassing of the landowners. By the autumn the peasants were burning crops, destroying houses and killing their occupants.

In a questionnaire handed out at the second Congress of Soviets held in the capital during the October coup, delegates were asked if there were food shortages in their districts. The great majority admitted that there were, though the blame for them was often laid erroneously on the Jewish merchants or the Black Hundreds.[1] Even at this late stage in the revolution, few Russians could grasp the basic reasons for the food crisis, but the whole nation suffered from its effects:

> The question which agitated the minds of both village and town (and more urgently the town) was the food question, which overshadowed the land question. Indeed, . . . an examination of the abundance of documentation upon the whole peasant question in 1917 [shows] that it was largely the food question which brought the year to its catastrophic close. If there was an 'elemental' movement in September and October, it was 'elemental' because it was based upon the satisfaction of 'elementary' needs of life – food supply in particular. The lofty schemes of constitutionalists, politicians and even economists are liable to collapse over such a homely, yet vital problem.[2]

[1] *Krasnyi arkhiv*, vol. 84, question no. 12. The Black Hundreds were an extremist monarchist organisation with a terrorist character, founded in 1905.

[2] L. Owen, *The Russian Peasant Movement 1906–17* (London, 1937) p. 173.

OTHER GOODS

The lack of manufactured products by 1917 was such that on
24 April the Provisional Government found it necessary to
establish a commission to examine the question of supplying
the population with consumer goods. Articles in very short
supply included many basic necessities like kerosene, soap,
textiles, paper, leather and metal products. By October the
cumulative effect of these shortages was taking its toll of human
patience in the same way as the food crisis. As a result bare-
footed railwaymen came out on strike, and in the Ufa guberniia there was even a riot caused by the shortage of galoshes –
a good example of Russian 'laughter through tears' that would
have appealed to Gogol.[1] To some extent the reasons for the
lack of manufactured goods were the same as those for the food
shortage, including bad transport and increased demand. The
Army swallowed up a tremendous amount. 'When it developed
that the greater portion of production must be diverted to the
needs of the Army – upward of 60 per cent of cotton goods and
up to 100 per cent for woollens – the population was faced with
a veritable famine in regard to the most necessary articles of
daily living.'[2]

In the case of manufactured goods, the lack of fuel for the
factories was an extra cause of falling output. The example of
coal mining in the Donets region is interesting, since it shows
how a vicious circle was operating. During the first half of
August 1917, this area managed to send off only 32 per cent
of the coal required for shipment. Yet the disruption of railway
transport played no part in the reduction. Other complex
factors were at work. There was a shortage of metal and coal
carts, not enough timber for the reinforcement of coal pits, nor
sufficient funds for exploitation work. Thus it cost nearly twice
as much to extract the same amount of coal compared with the
pre-war period. Finally the shortage of food and political fric-
tion between the owners and the workers had led to a lowering
of labour efficiency.[3] One factor reinforced another, pulling the
whole industry downhill. Nor could any substitute for coal be

[1] *Krasnyi arkhiv*, vol. 84, question no. 12.
[2] *Russkiia vedomosti*, 3 June 1917.
[3] Information taken from ibid., 8 Sep. 1917.

found. The oil industry of Baku was practically at a standstill. In May the Petrograd Soviet put out an appeal to the peasantry to meet the entire coal deficiency by collecting firewood. The peasants remained uncooperative.

THE 'SCISSORS' PROBLEM

The shortage of manufactured goods led to huge price rises. This was not only disconcerting in itself, but also exacerbated the food problem. In March 1917 the Provisional Government established a fixed price for grain; the Tsarist regime had already made compulsory grain levies. The effect in the cities was disastrous, as the press soon pointed out:

> During the past months a decrease has become evident in the flow of food and fodder supplies to the market. This decrease, by the way, can be explained by the fact that the peasants found it disadvantageous to sell grain at fixed prices while prices on all manufactured goods were rising continuously, reaching incredible levels. And even with these fantastic prices, which, not infrequently, were five to six times as high as pre-war prices, one was often unable to purchase the most vital necessities. In this connection, the question was raised more than once of establishing statutory prices on all the most important manufactured goods, vital to the peasant farm, concurrently with a statutory price on grain. But the matter did not go beyond the stage of general discussion. The Tsarist Government did not even attempt to undertake any steps in this direction. The Provisional Government now considers it essential to give priority to this matter.[1]

In the event, the Provisional Government fared little better than its Tsarist predecessor. Most manufactured articles went unregulated throughout 1917. Ineffective controls were placed on the production of wool, cotton and leather goods. On 19 July a belated attempt was made to impose fixed prices on metal goods.[2] The worried officials of the Provisional Government found it 'essential to give priority' to virtually every crisis that confronted them in the spring and summer of 1917; and there was no sphere of government without its particular crisis in the

[1] Ibid., 30 Apr. 1917.
[2] *Sobranie uzakonenii i rasporiazhenii pravitel'stva*, I, 2, no. 1078.

revolutionary months. The task of the state was overwhelming, and neither the Provisional Government nor the Soviets could take steps fast enough to cope with the speed at which different problems were hurled at them. Like the Red Queen in *Alice through the Looking Glass*, they were running as fast as they could in order to stay in the same place.

The basic forces that caused the Russian peasant to produce more food than he or his family could eat were taxes, rents and mortgage payments. Over and above this he needed several commodities and coveted a few petty luxuries. In 1917 even basic necessities were beyond the means of the rural population, so what was the point of keeping the towns alive with grain that was kept at an artificially low price? As for rents, mortgages and even taxes, the land-hungry peasantry under the influence of Bolshevik propaganda came to believe that these would vanish overnight, since the wide fields of Russia were soon to belong to them outright.

This divergence of agricultural and industrial prices was to be a running sore through the new Soviet economy. After the revolution Trotsky, with his genius for graphic, abstract generalisation, noted that the diverging trends resembled the widening of a pair of opening scissors, and labelled the phenomenon the 'scissors' crisis.

Once again the economic problem had disastrous political effects. Internecine hatred sprang up between the town and village dwellers. This affected those peasants who had very recently been drafted into the ranks of industry. Their loyalties were divided, but as the revolution dragged the country deeper into chaos, they often voted with their feet and returned to their village homes, where, if they were lucky enough to come from a producing area, they could at least get sufficient food, even if there was no kerosene for the lamp in the evening nor any soap for an occasional wash. Meanwhile in the towns, at the front, and in the non-producing rural areas hunger threatened the very basis of civilised society, as the Provisional Government admitted in the closing phrase of this appeal of 29 August 1917:

The food situation in the Army and the country is extremely grave. The government supplies are constantly decreasing.

D 2

Cities, entire guberniias, and even the front suffer an acute shortage of grain, although there is plenty of it in the country. The turnover of the government authorities established by law is very poor. Many have not handed in even those supplies which they had left over from the previous harvest. There are also those who forbid and prevent others from fulfilling their duty to the motherland. The danger which threatens the country is increased further because of the fact that in a number of guberniias grain in sufficient quantities could be delivered only by water routes. And if delivery is not made within the next few weeks, these regions will be doomed to starvation in the winter. Famine brings anarchy and loss of the freedom gained by the revolution.[1]

THE COLLAPSE OF THE WAR EFFORT

Just at the time when the supply problem was taking on frightening dimensions, the size and therefore the demands of the Army increased. Prior to September 1915, the ranks of the military comprised between 3 and 4 millions. By January 1916 this figure rose to over 6 millions, and on the eve of the February revolution stood at approximately 7 millions.[2] Shortly afterwards, on 18 March 1917, the Director of Military Operations issued reports from representatives of the main Army branches. The food situation headed the list: 'Not only do we find it impossible to build up food reserves at the front, but we will not receive enough for daily needs. It is necessary for the Army either to cut down the number of men and horses or to reduce rations. The latter is dangerous, therefore the number of men should be reduced.'[3]

This suggestion was not taken up by the authorities. Their ranks were indeed reduced, but it was by death and desertion, and this did not ease a situation that was already critical after

[1] Quoted in *Ekonomicheskoe polozhenie Rossii nakanune velikoi oktiabr'skoi sotsialisticheskoi revoliutsii*, Akademiia nauk SSSR (Moscow, 1957) vol. II, p. 343.
[2] These figures, which cannot be estimated with greater precision, are taken from Golovine, op. cit., chap. 9.
[3] M. N. Pokrovsky and Ya. A. Yakovlev (eds), *Razlozhenie armii v 1917 godu* (Moscow, 1925) p. 10.

the February revolution. The political implications did not fail to attract the notice of General Alekseev, the Supreme Commander, who wrote on 12 March: 'The question of food acquires a special significance in days of moral unrest. A soldier who is well fed feels that he is being taken care of by his superiors and is more inclined to obey the voice of reason, which calls him to order, to obedience, to maintaining the moral strength of his company and of his regiment. At the moment we are in a constant state of food crisis and live from day to day.'[1] Eleven days before this was written, the Petrograd Soviet issued Order No. 1, which speeded up the election of committees of soldiers in all Army units and paved the way for insubordination in the ranks. The Order appealed to a wide audience at the front. This is not surprising in view of the appalling conditions there.

The Army had top priority in the struggle to obtain food, but on 20 March Alekseev was compelled to order a reduction in rations issued to the rear units. In the province of Nizhnii Novgorod twenty thousand military equipment workers found themselves without bread by May. The only way to obtain it was to buy at prohibitive rates in neighbouring areas, but there were local regulations against the transfer of bread. Riots broke out among the workers, and the Army went short of more equipment.[2] This example was but one among many. The food shortage affected the whole country in 1917, except for some producing areas. The military and civil sectors were both caught up in the crisis and affected each other.

Civil transport difficulties in the rear affected the Army, especially units on the northern and western fronts, which were far away from the crop areas. It is perhaps significant that these fronts provided most of the Bolsheviks' supporters among the military. In a dispatch sent through the British Embassy in August, Brigadier-General Knox reported that as the railway lines were blocked, 'food [for the front] must be carried by the waterways. The idea, however, of carrying grain to the Volga by railway, transferring to lighters for conveyance to the north, and transferring later to railway trucks is largely checkmated by the exorbitant wages demanded by dock labourers, wages

[1] Ibid., p. 30.
[2] *Krasnyi arkhiv*, vol. xv, p. 52.

which make it possible for them to work, not eight hours a day, but far less.'[1]

By October, on the eve of the Bolshevik coup, all pretences at co-operation between the civil and military populations had been abandoned. Both were competing openly in order to survive. On 19 October the commander-in-chief of the western front reported to Kerensky that

> following threats by the starving population of the city and the surrounding area to pillage and burn down the commissary storehouses, the commander of the Viazemsk garrison ordered seven cartloads of flour to be released from the commissary to the population. Requests supported by references to possible excesses and pogroms are arriving from the food-supply committees in the cities near the front to release food for the population. Thus the front, already in an extremely grave situation, is facing a great new danger from the starving population. This portends a complete breakdown in supply.

In desperation, the commander-in-chief finally requested that 'extra measures be taken to provide both the front and the population with foodstuffs; otherwise the most dreadful consequences are inevitable'.[2]

The position with regard to equipment for the Army was not much better than the food problem. Approximate figures given by the Russian Central Statistical Department claimed that in the course of the war the following quantities were supplied to the Army: 65 million pairs of leather boots, 21 million heavy undershirts, 217 million horseshoes, etc.[3] The fact that these figures were on the ministries' order books does not mean that articles all reached the front, nor that they were used properly if they did. Many railway trucks originally intended to carry military equipment had to be converted into hospital trains, baths, laundries and mobile shops. Brand-new boots were often sold for profit by the soldiers, whilst Army tents were used for making skirts for peasant women. After the

[1] Dispatch D.3., 10 Aug. 1917, from the British Embassy, Petrograd. Quoted in Golovine, op. cit., pp. 173–4.
[2] *Ekonomicheskoe polozhenie Rossii*, vol. II, p. 290.
[3] Figures quoted in Golovine, op. cit., p. 181.

February revolution and Order No. 1, pilfering from government stores increased. The rank-and-file believed that the Treasury purse was inexhaustible, and that state property was theirs to do as they liked with. The military authorities were often very wasteful too. Their cavalier misuse of rolling stock on the railways was also extended to supplies. 'While there was no leather on the market, hundreds of thousands of hides, taken from slaughtered cattle, were rotting at the front.'[1] Checks by the civil authorities on the quality of equipment were also very lax, so that replacements were continually needed. 'And the Army depots! Huge vaults crammed with hats that came to pieces in your hands, greatcoats made of cloth as thin as canvas, caps with broken peaks and badges, boots with rotten soles. . . .'[2]

Short of food, short of clothes, the Russian soldier with any guts left to fight in 1917 often found himself without any weapon to fight with either. One-third of the number of rifles required at the front were lacking in 1917. Those who had no weapons waited for their fellows to die, desert or get wounded in order to obtain a rifle. As for heavy guns, even the Romanian Army had more howitzers at its disposal than the Russians.[3] The factories of Petrograd were responsible for supplying 70 per cent of all arms to the front in 1916, and the massive Putilov plant manufactured a large proportion of this amount. In the course of the revolution elements from this same factory played a leading role on the far left wing in support of the Bolsheviks. The heart of the armaments industry was thus disrupted beyond repair. Moreover, after the February revolution Workers' committees partly took over the running of many Petrograd arms factories which were state-controlled. Tsarist state managers with no financial stake in production soon quit their jobs to escape the wrath of the workers.[4]

In their efforts to maintain supplies of food, equipment and arms for the military it must be admitted that the Tsarist and

[1] A. Lukomsky, *Memoirs of the Russian Revolution* (London, 1922) p. 36.

[2] K. Paustovsky, *Slow Approach of Thunder* (London, 1965) p. 173.

[3] Golovine, op. cit., pp. 133, 141.

[4] V. I. Selitsky, *Nekotorye voprosy bor'by petrogradskikh rabochikh za kontrol' nad proizvodstvom v period mirnogo razvitiia revoliutsii (mart-iun' 1917 g.)*, in *Istoriia rabochego klassa Leningrada* (Leningrad, 1963) pp. 188, 190–1.

later the Provisional Government were dealing with an operation of unprecedented size in Russian history, although the
Crimean War had presented enormous problems which had
also been tackled lamentably in their time. The task in the
World War was rendered twice as difficult in that the military,
unlike the civil population apart from refugees, was frequently
shifted from place to place. Strategic advances, retreats and
concentrations repeatedly altered the supply problems along
the fronts from the Baltic to the Black Sea. Not long after the
start of the war large-scale evacuations added new problems.
After the failure of the Russian counter-attack in Galicia in
1915, it was particularly difficult to retreat on account of the
local narrow-gauge railways which did not link up with the
Russian wide-gauge tracks. Later in the war all the hospitals
and most of the factories and offices had to be evacuated eastwards out of a large city like Warsaw, causing congestion when
they came up against the westward flow of traffic to the fronts.
In 1917 deserters mixed with the movement away from the
fronts, adding to the traffic burden. In the rush to leave the
war-weary battlefields, soldiers had no thought for those left
behind. Thus, for instance, demobilised troops in Georgia com-
mandeered a grain ship on the Black Sea to take them home,
and in this way deprived their comrades on the Turkish front
of vital food supplies.[1]

The political effects of the military supply situation in 1917
were of crucial importance. This was because the war issue
formed one of the basic elements of Lenin's political position as
laid down in his April Theses. He was determined that Russia
should withdraw entirely and as soon as possible from an
imperialist war which, he claimed, was sponsored by capitalist
forces. This 'defeatist' attitude was opposed by the 'defensists',
who were equally determined to continue the war. By 3 May
1917, however, P. N. Miliukov, the first Foreign Minister of
the Provisional Government, resigned on account of the intense
opposition to his efforts to maintain Russia's pre-revolutionary
annexationist policies. His fall heralded the demise of the
right-wing defensists.

As the revolutionary year advanced and the war effort
weakened day by day, the ranks of the 'defeatists' broadened

[1] D. M. Lang, *A Modern History of Soviet Georgia* (London, 1962) p. 198.

in the Petrograd Soviet, and their policy, after being suitably vulgarised into popular propaganda, had an immediate appeal for the suffering soldiers at the fronts. Long before October the common soldier was taking the law into his own hands by deserting or helping to form defeatist military committees. There is no doubt that the state of supplies was chiefly responsible for the decline of morale in the Army. Indeed, it may be argued that even if the Tsarist regime had survived 1917, the Russian military machine would still have broken down.[1] Certainly it would have taken an administrative genius of the first order to set the country right in this respect.

As it was, the fact that the Provisional Government could not control the armed forces between February and October 1917 created the sort of climate in which social and economic chaos thrived, and with it the political forces of the extreme left. There was no coercive weapon at hand with which to attack the growing anarchy through 1917. The breakdown of the war effort had another important political result. The backbone of the Russian Army consisted of peasants in uniform. Fleeing from the front in their thousands, they were the chief supporters in the countryside of Lenin's second basic idea, that the land should be handed over to the peasants outright. It was the deserters and other returning soldiers who gradually infected the dormant provinces of Russia with the extremist fever that was already sweeping the city proletariat.

INEFFECTIVE REMEDIES

The Provisional Government did what it could to improve the flow of supplies through Russia, but eventually it became clear that not only were the measures ineffective, but also that they stirred up political hornets' nests of a new kind. The Provisional Government attempted to deal with the problem in three ways – by establishing a grain monopoly, by imposing ration cards and by relying on local supply committees to get the crops delivered.

[1] Prior to the February revolution the supply problem had already led to acute political tensions between the Voluntary Organisations and the Tsarist Government that reached into the realm of high politics. See G. Katkov, *Russia in 1917* (London, 1967) pts i and ii.

98 THE SPREAD OF THE RUSSIAN REVOLUTION

The reasons for introducing the state grain monopoly on 25 March 1917 may be summed up in the words of A. V. Peshekhonov, the Minister of Food: 'During the war we were forced to come to the conclusion that even the slightest participation of dealers led to a sharp and rapid increase in prices. The people began to be very reluctant to give up the grain, saying: Why should we give our grain today when the price on it will be still higher tomorrow? Speculation began to run high; it was followed by bribery, graft on the railways, and the appearance of speculators.'[1] A fixed price was set on grain, a price that was higher on average by 60 per cent than those prevailing in September 1916. The Provisional Government also contracted through its agents to protect all crops and to reimburse peasant owners whose crops were destroyed as the result of agrarian disturbances.[2]

The new laws antagonised both the peasants and the grain merchants, the two groups most directly affected. From their point of view, the merchants argued that 'in various regions of the Empire [sic] there are great quantities of grain which could be drawn out only by commercial circles:'; however, 'the grain monopoly, setting aside a whole army of experienced workers, substitutes for them new organs that are totally unfit for the task. In the opinion of this group, the grain monopoly and fixed prices will inflict innumerable calamities on the business of supplying the country with food products.'[3]

The peasants for their part looked upon the monopoly as a kind of legalised robbery. Keenly aware of the 'scissors' position, they complained that while they were being bled of their resources, the rich in the towns escaped restrictions on their way of life. Thus fierce class hatred often came to the villages before Bolshevik city agitators carried it there. Instead of turning over grain, the peasants used it for themselves, hoarded it, sold it to private speculators, or else put it in illicit distilleries to make liquor, a profitable pastime in an age of prohibition.

[1] *Izvestiia*, 7 June 1917. The Russian for 'speculator' in this quotation is *tolkach*, or 'pusher', a term and practice that has recurred in the overcentralised Soviet economy.
[2] *Sobranie uzakonenii i rasporiazhenii pravitel'stva*, 1, 1, no. 498.
[3] *Den'*, 17 May 1917.

Faced by the lack of any co-operation, the Provisional Government in vain cajoled the farmers to hand over their crops and stored grain. Finally, on 27 August, the Ministry of Food decided to double the fixed prices on grain[1] despite the fact that earlier in the month it had guaranteed not to raise the prices.[2] This move came too late to cure earlier ills, and the way in which the Government ate its own words did much harm to its public image.

The collapse of the monopoly scheme was not due to the peasants and merchants alone. The central administrators in the Government had neither the time nor the power to enforce the monopoly. The course of the revolution went at such a speed, and remedies were delayed through bureaucratic procrastination. The grain monopoly became law on 25 March, but the Government's instructions to local supply committees did not go out until 3 May, although it expected them to make a thorough survey by 31 May. In the early summer the Moscow Soviet discovered that no census of grain crops and stores had been taken still in thirty-two out of the thirty-eight provinces it investigated. Until a proper census was taken, it was impossible to determine how much grain each farm would be allowed to keep back for its own consumption.

The question of the Government's physical authority was important. Local commissars were given special powers, but were unable to enforce them. The feebleness of the Provisional Government was transparent by August. On 20 August it called for the use of armed force in the struggle to provide grain, yet seven days later it had to appeal to the peasants' economic instinct instead, by doubling the fixed prices. For the most part, the peasant-soldier refused to fight the peasant-farmer in order to get food to the towns.

The only thoroughgoing change effected by the grain monopoly was that some millers were employed on a full-time basis by the Government to grind grain, whilst the rest were excluded. Once again the result was that another section of the population was antagonised. Millers who were left out of the government scheme turned to work for illegal speculators.[3]

[1] *Sobranie uzakonenii*, i, 1, no. 1393.
[2] *Vestnik vremennogo pravitel'stva*, no. 123, 5 Aug. 1917.
[3] *Krasnyi arkhiv*, vol. XXI, p. 129.

The rationing of bread, a necessary corollary of the grain policy, was introduced slowly after the February revolution. In Petrograd it went into effect as early as 24 March, the day before the announcement of the grain monopoly. It led directly to ill feeling between the civilian population and the military garrison. The soldiers did not receive their ration cards on the first day and so demanded bread from the city bakeries. Consequently some civilians went without. In Moscow many bakeries were short of flour in March and had to cut their production by half; at the same time the surrounding population crowded into Moscow in search of bread. On 29 April rationing for grain products was extended over the whole territory 'of the Russian State, with the exception of Transcaucasia and the oblasts [regions] of the Turkestan governor-generalship'.[1] By the time of the October coup, ration cards were apparently in wide use in European Russia,[2] but what was the good of a card system when food supplies were in a chaotic state? As with so many other administrative measures of the Provisional Government, the system looked well on paper, but was never carried into effect.

The same could be said of the food-supply committees, which were called into existence by the Provisional Government in order to regulate food rationing and the grain monopoly. On 19 March 1917 a central State Committee on Food Supply was established under the chairmanship of the Ministry of Agriculture.[3] This Committee was intended to co-ordinate the work of the local supply organs that were created at the guberniia, uezd and volost levels.[4] A perusal of sources describing the activities of the local supply committees seems to indicate that they were not wholly incompetent. Often they put a stop to the machinations of swindling grain merchants, and managed to counteract the trend towards autarchy, when grain-producing

[1] *Sobranie uzakonenii*, I, I, no. 581. An *oblast'* was a large administrative division in the Caucasus, Central Asia and the Far Eastern Territory.

[2] *Krasnyi arkhiv*, vol. 84, answers to question 15 in the questionnaire handed out to delegates to the Second Congress of Soviets.

[3] *Sobranie uzakonenii*, I, I, no. 358. The Petrograd Soviet elected a food supply commission on the night of 27–28 February.

[4] The *guberniia* was the major administrative division of the Empire. Each *guberniia* was subdivided into *uezds*. The *volost* was a peasant administrative division of the *uezd*.

areas threatened to refuse to export their crops.[1] The committees saved much valuable food and property by taking over the
administration of estates abandoned by the local gentry, and
were frequently strong enough to exert social pressure on
individual hoarders.[2]

On the other hand the ways in which the committees were
run sometimes provoked more social and political unrest than
their technical help was worth. Their composition often en-
gendered class hatred. In localities where peasants of middling
substance got themselves elected to the committees, the scale
of wanton requisitioning from the landlords' estates led to
economic chaos rather than to order.[3] As a rule, though, it was
the rich and the powerful who appeared on the committees,
and the tables were turned. Local class squabbles could have
wider repercussions, as the following appeal from members of
an Army committee at the front to their place of origin shows:
'We beg you, comrades, on receipt of this letter, to ensure that
the merchants, landowners and rich peasants in all the volost
committees do not suppress the people. We, the people, have
the right to arrange our own lives, and this time we will allow
no one to prevent us from arranging our affairs. We will not
cede land and liberty to anyone.'[4] This climate of opinion soon
led to desertion, as anxious soldiers returned home to protect
their own interests.

When, in an attempt at fair representation, a supply committee drew on both the political left and right for its members,
the practical result was even worse. In the words of the chairman of a provincial Soviet, 'The conduct of affairs in the
committee is so bad that the committee cannot even elect a

---

[1] For examples of these illegal activities, see Sidorov, *Revoliutsionnoe
dvizhenie v Rossii v aprele 1917 g.*, pp. 218, 367.

[2] See, for example, Sidorov, *Revoliutsionnoe dvizhenie v Rossii v mae-iune
1917 g.*, pp. 417, 432: 'The peasants . . . requested the local supply com-
mitte to requisition 200 puds of wheat held by the priest Ivanchenko. The
committee therefore compelled the priest to sign a promise that he would
not sell the wheat to outside buyers without prior instructions from the local
volost committee.'

[3] Sidorov, *Revoliutsionnoe dvizhenie v Rossii v iule 1917 g.*, pp. 466, 473–5.

[4] Excerpt from a letter sent by the committee of the pioneer detachment
of the 21st Muromsky infantry regiment to the Aleksandrovsk *uezd* committee, 9 July 1917, in Sidorov, op. cit., pp. 454–5.

chairman. This is because the committee members chosen by
the Soviet do not attend the meetings of the supply committee;
only three out of eight members attend regularly. A personal
struggle took place in the Committee . . . with the result that
the whole administration of supplies may get delayed.'[1] As
social disruption spread through the countryside, and peasant
anarchy reared its head, so 'the management of supplies suffered greatly in the villages from the lack of enlightened or even
literate people, as the more enlightened peasants and even the
representatives of the co-operative societies are frequently
boycotted.'[2]

The root of the problem was that the Government was incapable of enforcing its orders. The local Tsarist police had
been replaced by a militia with officials chosen by popular
election, but this new organisation was powerless. Sir John
Maynard, a shrewd observer of the Russian peasantry, concluded that 'the lack of an adequate police must be placed high
among the causes of the overthrow of the Provisional Government: for rural disturbances involved a virtual severance of the
economic tie between town and village, and cut off supplies of
food and fuel from the capital and from the Army at the front'.[3]

The local supply committees have been singled out for study,
but they formed only one of several systems that tried to deal
with the food problem. In the revolutionary months of 1917
numerous organisations were involved. The zemstvo system,
established in the reign of Alexander II, did what it could to
keep the country on its feet, but after the February revolution
the leading positions in the reformed zemstvo assemblies were
occupied by persons who had hardly any experience of public
work and who very often had absolutely nothing in common
with the life of a particular area. The local Soviets that sprang
up in 1917 also intervened in the administration of food; like
the reformed zemstvos, they were chiefly made up of untried
men; they were less effective than the zemstvos in that they allowed political considerations to prejudice their decisions more.

[1] Sidorov, *Revoliutsionnoe dvizhenie v Rossii v avguste 1917 g.*, p. 142.
[2] Excerpt from the data of the Provincial Section of the Provisional
Government, quoted in C. E. Vulliamy (ed.), *The Red Archives* (London,
1929) p. 256.
[3] Sir John Maynard, *The Russian Peasant* (New York, 1962 ed.) p. 89.

What Russia needed after the February revolution was a centralised supply system that would have precedence over all other systems and could use force. Neither condition existed in fact. This was clearly seen by the Minister of Finance in the Provisional Government, A. I. Shingarev. Addressing the Food Congress in May, he admitted: 'Citizens, the danger that faces the country is all the more grave because the country does not have the most elementary organisational control, and, regardless of how deep was the confidence expressed by the masses, regardless of the endless number of welcoming telegrams they sent to the Provisional Government, these are nothing but words.'[1]

His views were echoed later in the year by the press, which laid the blame on the selfishness of the different factions:

At no time has there been so much talk in our country about the need for total unity and solidarity in the face of the catastrophe threatening our country, about forgetting mutual grudges and personal, narrow class interests and the need to take a national point of view. And at no time, it would seem, have the various public groups reacted so differently to these appeals for unity and reconciliation. At no time has there been so little evidence of actual sacrifice, willingness to give up one's own narrow interests for the good of all.[2]

The way in which the supply of raw materials and manufactured goods was tackled in 1917 is further proof of this disintegration. The Provisional Government and the Petrograd Soviet were both very slow to remedy the situation,[3] and the field was left open to heavily prejudiced class interests, represented on one side by the manufacturers and owners of capital, and by the trade unions and the revolutionary factory committees on the other. The trade union leaders accused the

[1] *Vestnik vremennogo pravitel'stva*, 24 May 1917, p. 3.
[2] *Russkiia vedomosti*, 5 Aug. 1917.
[3] The proposal for the establishment of a high government organ to deal with general planning problems was only acted on with the creation of the Economic Council and the Central Economic Committee on 21 June 1917. The first body never achieved anything of positive value, and was abolished on 11 Oct. 1917, shortly before the Bolshevik coup d'état.

factory committees of anarchist tendencies in the matter of workers' control over supplies. Trends in this direction were indeed apparent in some cases, as Lenin was to discover to his cost after seizing power. Prior to October, many cases of irresponsibility did occur, but they were often triggered off by economic hardship or class hatred, and were not protests against all forms of government.

Sometimes the factory committees were far better organised than other supply authorities. In many of the larger Petrograd enterprises the committees worked out carefully how their productive capacity could be geared to the restricted supplies of coal, and reported their findings to the Central Council of Factory Committees so that it could co-ordinate fuel rationing in the city and prevent the closure of some plants.[1] Individual committees took the initiative squarely on their own shoulders by sending off delegations to Kharkov to negotiate with coal merchants there. A group from a gun factory in Petrograd shipped back twenty-eight train trucks of coal by rail in this way.[2] Admittedly the notions of uneducated workers thrown into temporary prominence after the February revolution were often naïve rather than helpful, as in the case of some local committees that wanted to make immediate use of local waterfalls for the production of 'white coal'.[3]

It may seem strange that the rank-and-file of the city proletariat should be so interested in keeping capitalist industry ticking over, yet their motives were not exactly altruistic. Changes in economic production due to the war effort had created pockets of unemployment, and after February 1917 factory after factory was compelled to close down in the towns of the north and west for lack of fuel and raw materials, throwing thousands out of work. It has been estimated, for instance, that at the Putilov works in Petrograd over ten thousand workers were idle by the second half of October 1917.[4] Small wonder that this section of the population became the most active supporters of the Bolsheviks.

[1] A. A. Sviridov, *Proletariat Petrograda v bor'be za rabochii kontrol' v period organizatsii shturma*, in *Uchenye zapiski LGPI im. A. I. Gertsena*, vol. 102 (Leningrad, 1955) p. 16.   [2] *Rabochii put'*, 15 Oct. 1917.
[3] *Krasnyi arkhiv*, vol. 103, pp. 111-12.
[4] M. Mitel'man, *1917 god na putilovskom zavode* (Leningrad, 1939) p. 142.

Naturally the factory committees became entangled in arguments with works owners over the supply question. This element in the class struggle had been foreseen early in the war by the president of the Moscow Association of Merchants and Manufacturers, who warned the Tsarist police that any major shortage of raw materials would lead to social unrest in industry.[1] In 1917 an owner who wished to wind up his business, in order to get his capital into liquid form that could be exported for greater security, was often opposed by his employees, who saw through his excuse that he was only quitting because of lack of raw materials or fuel. Orders from the management were frequently ignored, and it was not unusual by October for a factory committee to run a plant on its own, paying scant attention to the advice it received from a barely tolerated employer. In the struggle to keep workers employed, the Bolsheviks encouraged some factories to go over to peacetime production and turn swords into ploughshares, in line with the Bolsheviks' defeatist policy.[2] Yet the same party did not hesitate to make profitable use of rifles and bullets supplied by committees at arms factories to detachments of the Red Guard in the October revolution.[3] Through its increasing control over production and supply, the proletariat was able on occasions to threaten the owning classes at the point of a gun.

FISCAL MEASURES

The amount of money entering the coffers of the Russian Treasury is another aspect of the supply problem that cannot be neglected. Colossal expenditure on the war and the virtual termination of all exports led to an ever-increasing deficit after 1914. In his history of the Russian economy, P. I. Liashchenko gives the following table:[4]

[1] A. T. Vassiliev, *The Okhrana* (London, 1930) pp. 126–7.

[2] Thus the Sestroretsky Armaments Works in Petrograd was urged to turn to the production of agricultural machinery: see *Rabochii put'*, 4 Oct. 1917.

[3] Z. V. Stepanov, *Rabochie Petrograda v period podgotovki i provedeniia oktiabr' skogo vooruzhennogo vosstaniia* (Moscow, 1965) p. 121.

[4] P. I. Liashchenko, *History of the National Economy of Russia* (New York, 1949) p. 769. Any precise assessments for 1917 must be taken with a large pinch of salt.

Years	Military expenditure	Budget deficit
	(in millions of roubles)	
1914	1,234	1,898
1915	8,620	8,561
1916	14,573	14,573
1917	22,561	22,568

The measures taken by the Provisional Government to cover the expenditure inherited from its Tsarist predecessor were clearly doomed to failure in view of the fact that the Government was given only eight months in which to operate. Unfortunately the few futile attempts it did make only served to exacerbate political and class rivalries and to alienate confidence in the Government's ability.

As of February 1917 there was a large quantity of idle cash in Russian banks which the new Government tried to attract into the new Liberty Loan of 27 March.[1] The general reaction of both the sophisticated and the non-moneyed classes may be summed up in a remark from one group of peasants, who said 'we would have subscribed but all kinds of people explained that the papers would soon have no value whatsoever'.[2] More general plans for financial reform were held up until the summer, and were never acted upon subsequently. An increase in the war profits tax was levied in June,[3] but it brought in little additional revenue and antagonised industrialists, who started up a kind of blackmail by warning the Government that they would be unable to maintain armaments production for the forces.[4] The Treasury was caught between Scylla and Charybdis on the question of the war effort, since Russia's allies asserted that they would continue to lend funds to the Provisional Government only so long as Russian troops went on fighting.

Open pressure of this kind certainly lent force to Lenin's arguments about the pernicious influence of capital on the conduct of the war. It may have created more sympathy for the financial policy of the Bolsheviks before the October coup. This policy included three main points: the annulment of the financial obligations of previous Russian governments, especi-

[1] *Sobranie uzakonenii*, I, 1, no. 408.
[2] *Den'*, 4 Aug. 1917.
[3] For details of this and other tax reforms, see A. M. Michelson *et al.*, *Russian Public Finance during the War* (New Haven, 1928) pp. 195 ff.
[4] *Ekonomicheskoe polozhenie*, I, pp. 228–9.

ally to foreign powers; the nationalisation of the banks; and the cessation of any further issues of paper money.[1]

On the question of paper currency, the prestige of the Provisional Government suffered yet another blow. The budget deficit was reflected in a progressive currency inflation, and the rouble had been forced off its gold basis. Between February and October nine milliards of roubles were added to the note issue. The paper currency began to depreciate in value very rapidly, while the price of goods rose, aggravating the catastrophic economic condition of the country still further. All social groups lost confidence in the rouble. The upper classes, 'more moved by the approaching panic than by patriotism, are striving by fair means or foul to liquidate their holdings in Russia and transfer the proceeds into foreign security or values. Money has been sent out of the country by every conceivable means. . . .'[2] The temporary Treasury notes issued in 1917 came to be called 'kerenki' after Kerensky, the head of the Provisional Government. Like their namesake, they soon became unpopular, and the lower classes began to hoard Romanov notes which they erroneously believed would be more stable. Inflation, combined with the scarcity of notes in circulation, finally drove the Treasury into proposing that notes already issued should be cut in half, but the October coup put a stop to this rather ludicrous project.[3]

ECOMONIC AND SOCIAL COLLAPSE

The supply problem in 1917 would have proved too much even for a strong Government. It crippled Kerensky's regime. Failure to adopt adequate remedies led to further disorders. Since neither the Provisional Government nor the Soviets were able to speed up supplies, speculators came into their own as the chaos increased through 1917. The townsmen believed that the peasants were profiteers, and vice versa. In fact both sides were guilty, as is clear from the accounts of Soviets from all over the country. Repeated but ineffective fines were imposed on both

[1] For the fate of these policies after the October revolution, see E. H. Carr, *The Bolshevik Revolution 1917–1923*, vol. II (London, 1952) pp. 131 ff.
[2] *Sobranie uzakonenii*, I, I, no. 734.
[3] On the currency question see Michelson, op. cit., pp. 385–8.

peasant and merchant speculators. Occasionally government agents carried out, or attempted to carry out, arrests.[1] The widespread appearance of speculation was blamed on the authorities in the capital, as Ilia Ehrenburg records: 'Once I saw two officers take a bag of granulated sugar from a woman. She howled :"Bandits!" As she walked away, one of the officers shouted after her that she would soon be shot: Kerensky was on the side of the black marketeers, but Kerensky wouldn't last much longer.'[2]

Sabotage was another phenomenon that grew in importance towards October, and afterwards. Lenin put the blame for this on the owning classes: 'The capitalists are deliberately and unremittingly sabotaging (damaging, stopping, disrupting, hampering) production, hoping that an unparalleled catastrophe will mean the collapse of the republic and democracy, and of the Soviets and proletarian and peasant associations generally, thus facilitating the return to a monarchy and the restoration of the unlimited power of the bourgeoisie and the landowners.'[3] It was by no means only the working classes and the peasants who became obstructive: there was some truth in Lenin's accusations.[4] But it was also true, as has been seen with regard to the railways, that the proletariat often resorted to what amounted to sabotage.

The situation in the northern cities, which were the worst hit by the lack of supplies, deteriorated rapidly towards the end of the year. From August onwards the Provisional Government seriously contemplated evacuating Petrograd and moving the capital to Moscow, but this was opposed by the left wing in the Petrograd Soviet. In any case there was no means of transport at hand for such a huge operation.[5] Instead, large elements of the population of Petrograd began to leave the city. The gentry fled to salvage what they could from their estates, the middle

[1] *Krasnyi arkhiv*, vol. 84, question no. 13.
[2] Ilia Ehrenburg, *First Years of Revolution* (London, 1962) p. 10.
[3] V. I. Lenin, *Collected Works*, June–Sept. 1917, p. 323.
[4] 'Every day brings news of the closing of a number of factories and plants. And if, in certain cases, this closing is caused by shortages of raw materials and fuel, then in many other cases it is done by the businessmen on purpose in order to frighten both the workers and the Provisional Government.' *Den'*, 17 June 1917.
[5] See below, pp. 187–8, for more details of the plan to evacuate Petrograd.

class departed with their liquid assets, and the peasant-worker returned to his locality to protect his family, to ensure his claim to the land, and often just to get more food than he could in the city. The depleted population that remained behind still ate faster than it could be supplied with agricultural produce.

The Russian peasant-worker had somewhere to go to on leaving the city, but this was not the case for the great influx of Poles, Balts and Ukrainians who had been driven eastwards by the war. It was frequently the latter groups who made up the unstable rabble of the Petrograd streets, and names from these nationalities also cropped up in the lists of newly-recruited Bolshevik sympathisers among the city proletariat. At a Petrograd Bolshevik city committee meeting held on 10 October, a spokesman commented that only in eight of the nineteen districts of Petrograd were the workers in a fighting mood; three of these were non-geographical 'districts', comprising the Latvian, Estonian and Finnish minority groups in the city.[1]

As October drew near, social unrest inspired by the lack of the common necessities of life grew in intensity and bitterness. Beyond those cities in European Russia which registered the most feverish political temperature, the peasantry resorted increasingly to violence. Local food offices were destroyed, and the Bolshevik slogan of 'Down with the Food Committees' became more popular. At the front soldiers were writing vicious letters to their homes and to the left-wing newspapers:

Shame on the socialists who lag behind the people and hold up the powerful impetus of the revolution by taking grain away from the hungry population. We know very well that there's lots of grain in the country, but they are sending it off to England and America in order to get shells in return. May the bourgeosie be crushed by these shells. We have realised that the only way out of the oppressive situation the country is in is to hand over the power to the Soviets of workers', soldiers' and peasants' deputies.[2]

Sentiments like these found a solacing echo in some of Lenin's

[1] S. P. Mel'gunov, *Kak bol'sheviki zakhvatili vlast'*, p. 24.
[2] Letter sent to the newspaper *Proletarskaia mysl'*, quoted in *Bol'shevistkie organizatsii Ukrainy v period ustanovleniia i ukrepleniia sovetskoi vlasti; sbornik dokumentov i materialov* (Kiev, 1962) pp. 527–8.

more fiery affirmations, no less utopian and stinging in their content: 'We shall take away all the bread and boots from the capitalists. We shall leave them only crusts and dress them in bast shoes. We shall send all the bread and footwear to the front.'[1] This is Lenin the revolutionary agitator, talking to the suppressed in their own language. At a more sophisticated level, he did what he could to use the economic disorganisation of Russia as a political lever for future state supervision of the country's resources. Initially he looked to workers' control over industry as the solution; but already in May 1917 he foresaw that 'the aim of a state organisation should be to organise on a broad, regional and subsequently country-wide scale the exchange of agricultural for manufactured goods'.[2] *Izvestiia*, the organ of the Petrograd Soviet, stated the issue more openly: 'In short, the solution to the problem of supplying the population with goods is unavoidably that of supervising and controlling the very process of manufacture in addition to supervising distribution.'[3] These statements look forward to the future of Soviet Russia, but before state control could be imposed the country had to tread a long road of recovery in order to escape from the combined political and economic effects of 1917.

[1] Lenin, op. cit., vol. 26, p. 25.
[2] Ibid., vol. 24, p. 514. See also vol. 25, pp. 426–7 (*The State and Revolution*) where Lenin proposed the reorganisation of the whole economy 'on the lines of the postal service'. By this he meant that even before the October coup the postal system was a state monopoly, albeit a 'state-capitalist' one. All that was needed was a change in its 'social management' to put it to a worthy use in the new Bolshevik regime.
[3] *Izvestiia*, 30 Apr. 1917.

4 The Press

'A newspaper is not only a collective propagandist and collective agitator; it is also a collective organiser.'

LENIN

THE PRESS UP TO 1917

The Russian revolution took place in a country that had not yet entered the age of mass media. Powerful forces like the radio, films and television, which can play a large part in the formation of opinion nowadays, had no political influence in 1917. The Russian public relied heavily for news on the written word. For this reason the role of the press in the pre-revolutionary period was very significant; but there were other factors which tended to diminish this role.

In the first place, the press was not run in the same way in Russia as it was in Britain by 1917. From the 1830s onwards the British public had been used to popular journalism of a type that hardly existed in Tsarist Russia, where the press confined itself to serving the sophisticated literary and political interests of a small sector of the population. Neither were there any commercial empires in the Russian press world that were comparable to the chains of newspapers and magazines ushered in by the 'Northcliffe revolution' of the 1890s. Circulation figures in Russia were minute by the side of those built up as a result of Northcliffe's economic reorganisation of his newspapers.

Another factor which seriously limited the scope of the Russian press was the size of its audience. According to the census of 1897, only one-third of all males and 13 per cent of all females in European Russia were literate; 54 per cent of all townsmen were literate, and in St Petersburg three-quarters of the working male population were, although some of these could read but not write. In the countryside only 27 per cent of the men and 10 per cent of the women were literate.[1] Not enough was done between the 1890s and the 1917 revolution to improve the situation of the 'dark people'. Serious thinking on the need to reform Russian spelling began in 1901, but it took a political revolution to achieve anything concrete. When the orthographic reform went through in 1917, a liberal newspaper claimed that 'it was no secret to anyone that reactionary Ministers of Education – and other ministers, too – would not support this reform, as they did not support anything that tended to benefit the common people'.[2]

The low level of literacy in Russia acted as an informal censor that was far more efficient than the official Tsarist censorship. Even many of the so-called literates suffered from this barrier against the spread of knowledge. For instance, General Knox observed at the outbreak of the World War that, although 50 per cent of the Russian reservists were classed as literates, many of them had had one or two years at school at the age of eight to ten, but had never seen a book or newspaper since; so that when they wanted to communicate with their families, their letters were usually written for them by non-commissioned and junior officers. It was widely known that letters went through a double censorship, first by the regimental officer, and then by the official censor.[3]

The Tsarist censor was aimed against the small reading public. This public formed a restricted circle, but a brilliant one, to judge by the achievements of the Russian intelligentsia of the nineteenth and early twentieth centuries. In the reign of Nicholas II the censorship was not a downright authoritarian system, as it was to become in the Stalinist period, but rather an authoritarian system with a conscience, better styled as paternalism. Censorship was widely used in the period prior to 1917, but it was defended on the grounds that some elements of the populace needed protection against certain social and

[1] T. H. von Laue, 'Russian Peasants in the Factory 1892-1904', *Journal of Economic History* (1961) pp. 68–9.

[2] *Russkiia vedomosti*, 2 June 1917.

[3] Sir A. Knox, *With the Russian Army, 1914–1917* (London, 1921) p. 389.

political ideas that would be harmful to them. Before the Soviet period the press was not viewed as part of the total machine through which a small minority coerced a society.

The Tsarist censor had originally been imposed in order to shield Russia from the harmful effects of the French revolution.[1] It was never a very efficient method. The most famous example of laxity was the permit given for the publication of Marx's *Das Kapital* in Russia, on the grounds that the book was so obscure that no one would read it. In general, weighty and expensive volumes were considered to be less dangerous than cheap, short pamphlets. After the 1905 revolution, preliminary censorship of newspapers, periodicals, books and pamphlets was abolished in all the cities of the Empire. Newspaper material only went to a committee of inspection after publication, so that if the committee disliked the tone of the contents, not more than 10 to 20 per cent of the circulation could be confiscated, because it was too late to retrieve the rest. In the period between the 1905 and 1917 revolutions many journalists were arrested, but there was a wide amnesty in 1913, and often the so-called 'editor' of a newspaper was a mere dummy or paid hireling who was prepared to be removed to jail.

Before the reforms of 1905 and 1906 a newspaper could be started only with the permission of the Minister of the Interior, but after that time an editor could get a licence to publish by sending certain information to the local governor, who was normally obliged to issue the licence within a fortnight.[2] Under the new regulations it was possible for a Communist paper like *Pravda* to operate almost continuously from 1912 until it was closed by the new military censorship in 1914. This was because, although it was shut down eight times, it could at once reopen under a different name, using the same plant and publicising the same policies.

Heavy and arbitrarily imposed money fines were more

[1] In May 1792 Prince Prozorovsky wrote to ask the Empress Catherine 'to take measures to prevent the delivery of books, especially from disturbed France, which serve to lead astray and pervert people who have no foundation in the principles of honour'. See N. Engelhardt, *Sketch of the History of the Russian Censorship in Connection with the Development of the Press, 1703–1903* (St Petersburg, 1904).

[2] V. F. Deriuzhinsky, *Politseiskoe pravo*, 2nd ed. (St Petersburg, 1908) pp. 229–30.

crippling than legal action for left-wing Russian newspapers after 1905. Occasionally the autocracy poured out money in aid of the right-wing press, as in May 1916 when the Minister of Finance induced the Tsar to allow him to bribe the editor of the paper *Novoe Vremia* to the tune of 880,000 roubles, so that there should be at least one major organ which supported government policy.[1] Sustained opposition to government control of the press came from the ranks of those revolutionary parties that were to emerge into the open in 1917, but which were trying to make themselves heard through the medium of the press for a long time before then. Sporadic yet powerful opposition in the 1905 revolution came from those employed in the printing trade itself. The very first Soviet in Russia, formed in the textile town of Ivanovo-Voznesensk on 15 May 1905, consisted mainly of textile workers, but engravers and compositors dominated the presidium.[2] By September 1905 the Moscow printers' Soviet was the leading trade organ in the city; it stood at the centre of the general Moscow strike.[3] During the St Petersburg strike, only the government press and that of the General Staff continued to function. The St Petersburg Soviet was able to end the censorship, since the printers' show of strength in 1905 was remarkable.[4] It is true that they represented some of the best-educated elements of the proletariat, yet their ties with their apolitical peasant background were still very close.[5]

By 1917 the Social Democrats had almost twenty years of

[1] *Krasnyi arkhiv*, vol. 21, pp. 223 ff. Half of this sum was paid out before the February revolution. Subsequently the Provisional Government demanded the return of the money.

[2] O. Anweiler, *Die Rätebewegung in Russland 1905–1921* (Leiden, 1958) p. 50.

[3] V. Nevsky, *Sovety i vooruzhennoe vosstanie v 1905 godu* (Moscow, 1931) pp. 29–34. The printers' Soviet included 264 delegates from 110 printing houses.

[4] S. S. Harcave, *First Blood: The Russian Revolution of 1905* (London, 1965) pp. 178, 212, 214.

[5] It was found in investigations shortly before the World War that there was still a strong tie between the printers and the countryside. Among workers in the Moscow printing trade, 46 per cent were still conducting farming operations, while another 16·7 per cent were no longer personally engaged in farming but still had households in the village. See V. P. Miliutin, *Selsko-khoziaistvennye rabochie i voina* (Petrograd, 1917) p. 12.

experience behind them with regard to propaganda among the masses. The bulk of it found expression in illegal underground activity, in spreading political programmes among the industrial workers and the liberal intelligentsia. The revolutionary press played the leading part in this, and the Bolsheviks proved to be the best journalists of all the left-wing factions. Their chief inspiration was Lenin himself, who devoted a considerable portion of his energies and time to the organisation of the Bolshevik press. His career in exile as editor of *Iskra* had given him a long training, and it was not for nothing that he gave his profession as that of a journalist for use in official documents.

Besides being engaged in practical work, Lenin, as in all things, also contrived a clear theory of the role of the press as a revolutionary weapon. He gave lectures on journalism in Paris in 1911,[1] and evolved guiding principles in the subject long before 1917. The key to any understanding of the Soviet press is contained in Lenin's remarks on its function. For him a paper was much more than a published newsheet. It had to be a collective propagandist, agitator and organiser as well. He compared the press to a scaffolding, surrounding a building under construction (the workers' state), which marked the outlines of the structure, facilitated communication among the builders, enhanced the effective assignment of tasks, and made possible a clear view of the achievements of the builders.[2]

The roots of the Bolshevik press go back to 1900, in which year the original issue of *Iskra* appeared. *Pravda* first came out on 5 May 1912, and continued to be published under various names until the printing plant was destroyed by the Tsarist police on 8 July 1914, the eve of the war. The regular daily Social Democratic press was crippled, but reviews, pamphlets and weeklies were able to come out during this time; and in 1917 dailies appeared sporadically. After the start of the war the Social Democrats produced illegal leaflets on underground presses. By 1915-16 the Petrograd Bolshevik organisation was able to turn out more than a hundred different leaflets on nineteen presses.[3] Activities spread to Moscow, Reval, Khar-

[1] N. K. Kruspkaia, *Memories of Lenin* (London, 1930) p. 167.
[2] Lenin, *Collected Works*, vol. 4 (1) (London, 1927) p. 114.
[3] I. G. Levitas, M. A. Moskalev, E. M. Fingerit, *Revoliutsionnye podpol'nye tipografii v Rossii, 1860–1917 gg.* (Moscow, 1962) p. 337.

E

kov, Kiev, Ekaterinburg, the Caucasus and the military fronts. It is interesting to note that one of the earliest and most important of the Moscow presses was run by Latvian refugees from the Baltic seaboard.[1] The conditions under which the revolutionaries worked were appalling. They fondly called their underground presses 'revolutionary Hades'. The machinery was hidden in badly lit and ventilated rooms which the printers did not dare to leave for twenty-four hours at a time.[2] Fear of immediate arrest was constant, and during the war there was no hope of reprieve.

When *Pravda* reappeared legally on 5 March 1917, after the February revolution, the leading article reminded readers of the long history of the Bolshevik press. At the very start of the revolutionary year, Lenin's favourite weapon was sharp and poised for action, with many battles already lost and won. For this reason alone it is worth recalling the years before 1917.[3]

PRAVDA IN 1917

The freedom of the press granted by the Provisional Government and endorsed by the Petrograd Soviet after the fall of the monarchy unleashed a flood of revolutionary literature. Without a doubt, *Pravda*, the organ of the Central Committee of the Bolshevik Party, soon outshone rivals like *Delo Naroda* (for the Socialist Revolutionaries) and *Rabochaia Gazeta* (for the Mensheviks). *Pravda* was better organised, better written and more efficiently distributed. In part it lived up to Lenin's ideal of a newspaper that was more than a mere medium of information. During the eight months between the two revolutions, when no faction had sufficient physical force at hand with which to control the course of political events, the Bolshevik press was a powerful instrument of persuasion. It deserves detailed attention.

After February the editorial office of *Pravda* was situated awkwardly in a two-room flat on the Moika Canal, an aristo-

---

[1] Ibid., p. 338.   [2] Ibid., p. 369.
[3] An interesting article on the revival of *Pravda* in 1917 enhances this view, since it shows that the Bolsheviks were well prepared for the reopening of their organ. See Peter Frank and B. C. Kirkham, 'The Revival of *Pravda* in 1917', *Soviet Studies* (Jan. 1969).

cratic area of Petrograd and very near the right-wing General Staff building. It was cut off from the working-class district of Vyborg, which lay across the other side of the wide Neva. In the same building the Bolsheviks seized the press of the *Sel'skii Vestnik* on 4 March, and it was used for printing *Pravda* until 5 July. The arrangement proved to be unsatisfactory, because anti-Bolshevik workers employed on this press sometimes sabotaged editions of *Pravda* by dislocating the rotary machine[1] In mid-April Lenin negotiated for the press of the newspaper *Trud* as well, so that the Central Committee was now able to bring out more publications than previously. But the new press suffered from technical faults and had to be used to turn out *Soldatskaia Pravda* besides *Pravda* from May onwards; so that when Lenin urged supporters to write for *Pravda*, he demanded that they write 'extra-short' articles – 'there's very little space'.[2]

Lenin's thoughts on his return to Russia on 3 April were directed at once to *Pravda*. The moment he met Kamenev on Russian soil, Lenin's first remark was 'What's this stuff that's being written in your *Pravda*? We saw some numbers and heartily cursed you.'[3] With Lenin's arrival in Petrograd the political line of *Pravda* changed to suit his own ideas expressed in his April Theses. Lenin's interest in the paper may be gauged by the amount of material he wrote for it between March and October 1917 – 180 pieces in all.[4] Much of his time from April to July was spent in the flat on the Moika Canal, writing, editing and talking to sympathisers who treated the *Pravda* office as one of their natural party headquarters, together with the town house of Ksheshinskaia, the famous ballet-dancer and favourite of Nicholas II, which the Bolsheviks acquired. The Moika site was guarded by armed volunteers, whose vigilance saved Lenin on several occasions. Lenin's sister, M. I. Ulianova, who worked in the office, remembers one such instance: 'One

[1] B. Zaslavsky, I. Sazonov, Kh. Astrakhan, *Pravda 1917 goda* (Moscow, 1962) p. 66.

[2] Lenin, *Sochineniia*, 4th ed., vol. 36, p. 405.

[3] *Proletarskaia revoliutsiia*, no. 1 (1923) p. 221. *Pravda* maintained a defensist policy on the war until Lenin returned to Russia and put forward the defeatist line in his April Theses. His *Letters from Afar* also attacked the conciliatory line of Kamenev and Stalin.

[4] V. P. Budnikov, *Bolshevistskaia partiinaia pechat' v 1917 godu* (Kharkov, 1959) p. 53.

evening, when Il'ich was in the editorial office, one of the comrades ran up and persuaded him to leave – there was a hostile demonstration just outside. Accompanied by a soldier with a rifle, Vladimir Il'ich left the office in a cab and went to an acquaintance's flat. . . .'[1]

How was *Pravda* distributed and financed? In a doctoral thesis on the Bolshevik press in 1917, a Soviet historian claims that on 5 March, the day of the first issue, 200,000 copies were distributed gratis.[2] Even if the figure is reduced when partisan exaggeration is taken into account, it is still very impressive; for there was bitter truth in Lenin's outcry that the so-called 'free press' allowed by the Provisional Government was not so in fact, since a real stranglehold was still maintained over the press through the 'sacred proprietary right of the exploiters to the printing houses and paper stores seized by them'.[3] Yet *Pravda* was able to achieve a phenomenal success on the first day of publication.

Much of the paper, machinery and other equipment used for publishing Bolshevik materials was stolen or taken by force in the lawless conditions prevailing during the revolutionary months, and so was never paid for at all. Soviet sources naturally play down this aspect, whilst making all they can of the fact that voluntary contributions were given by Bolshevik supporters.

Financial help of this kind was certainly substantial, especially when it is related to the low pay of the city workers who were the chief contributors. On 13 April 1917 the Petrograd Bolsheviks published an appeal in *Pravda* for 75,000 roubles, to be collected within five days.[4] The money was to be used for the purchase of printing plant. The response from the factories, the sailors and the city garrisons was apparently more than satisfactory. On 14 April, the first day of the appeal, *Pravda* received 3,472 roubles and 33 kopecks, on the second day 9,794 roubles and 74 kopecks, and 28,691 roubles 81 kopecks on the following two days.[5] Admittedly several large sums came from

[1] *Lenin v oktiabre-vospominaniia* (Moscow, 1957) p. 197.
[2] Budnikov, op. cit., p. 13. Many sources put the figure at 100,000.
[3] Lenin, *Sochineniia*, vol. 25, p. 351.
[4] Sidorov, *Aprel'skii krizis*, p. 52.
[5] *Pravda*, 16, 18, 20 Apr. 1917.

rich individuals like Maxim Gorky, who gave 3,000 roubles,[1] but there is no denying the enthusiasm and sacrifice of many workers in these early days of revolutionary euphoria. This was the response of Moscow trade unionists to a similar appeal broadcast in Moscow on 12 April:

> ... In our working-class struggle for freedom, bread and peace, our main weapon is the workers' socialist press, created with our kopecks, borne on our shoulders, and carrying the legacy of the international proletariat's revolutionary struggle. We protest against the unfair distribution of paper, which goes exclusively to the presses of bourgeois newspapers. ... We appeal strongly to worker comrades to subscribe one day's pay on 22 April, Workers' Press Day, to the fund of the workers' press – the liberation of the working class is the task of the workers themselves.[2]

The administration of voluntary funds was time-consuming. Every evening at eight o'clock, workers from Petrograd factories arrived at the *Pravda* offices laden with heavy packets containing mainly five-kopeck pieces. A group of medical students were the self-appointed cashiers; they counted the money and delivered it to the bank.[3] The larger factories in Petrograd later resorted to more ambitious methods of helping *Pravda*. In May workers at the Novyi Lessner plant collected over 30,000 roubles for sending revolutionary literature to the military forces.[4] The famous Putilov factory went so far as to send thirty-three workers with two railway wagonloads of newspapers and presents to the western front.[5] This kind of collaboration not only improved the Bolsheviks' newspaper circulation; it also promoted common ties between the city proletariat and the peasant soldiers at the fronts, a union which Lenin desired for strategic and ideological purposes. Here is just one example of the military's recognition of the workers' help: 'You are aware of the Army's great significance at the present time, and of the part played by the printed word in the education of the masses. But there is little use in merely being aware of the facts, words have still to be translated into deeds. You have really known

[1] Budnikov, op. cit., p. 14.   [2] *Sotsial-demokrat*, 14 Apr. 1917.
[3] Zaslavsky, op. cit., p. 65.   [4] *Soldatskaia pravda*, 19 May 1917.
[5] Budnikov, op. cit., p. 106.

how to do this and have come to the help of us poor soldiers. . . .
In unity lies strength!'[1]

Whereas Soviet historians tend to exaggerate the financial
support of factory workers for the Bolshevik press, some non-
Communist writers attach too much importance to the role
played by German money which found its way by devious
means into Bolshevik pockets. Certainly there is no denying the
authenticity of the following telegram sent on 3 December 1917
by the German Minister of Foreign Affairs to Kaiser Wilhelm II:
'It was not until the Bolsheviks had received from us a steady
flow of funds through various channels and under varying
labels that they were in a position to be able to build up their
main organ, Pravda, to conduct energetic propaganda and
appreciably to extend the originally narrow base of their
party.'[2] However, the national donors of aid of any kind are
always apt to overestimate its influence. Also the 40,580,997
German marks (about two marks to the rouble) allocated for
Russia from the Special Fund for Propaganda and Special
Expeditions up to 30 January 1918 represented only about 10
per cent of the Fund's total expenditure. The total sum from
all German sources received by the Bolsheviks has been estimated by one scholar to be 80 million gold marks, but this
covers a much longer period than the revolutionary months
between February and October 1917.[3] Several scholars have
laid stress in recent years on the newly-revealed sources concerning German financial aid to the Bolsheviks, but in doing
so have tended to exaggerate its role. In the future this will no
doubt be allotted its substantial, though not disproportionate,
place in the history of the Bolshevik revolution.

What was the circulation of Pravda in 1917? How efficiently
was it distributed? The answers to these two questions must
remain tentative, and may never be very accurate, even if the
archives are fully opened. It is doubtful whether the Bolsheviks
kept a completely accurate tally of circulation figures through
1917. The number fluctuated considerably from one week to
another, and there is little external evidence left to support or

---

[1] Sidorov, op. cit., p. 149.
[2] See International Affairs, London (Apr. 1956) p. 189.
[3] Fritz Fischer, Griff nach der Weltmacht: Die Kriegszielpolitik des Kaiserlichen Deutschland, 1914–1918 (Düsseldorf, 1961) p. 176, n. 127.

disprove the figures now given in Bolshevik secondary sources. It is even more difficult to discover how many printed copies of *Pravda* reached their intended goals: high circulation figures were not a certain indication of a high level of receptivity, especially at a time when transport was in such a chaotic condition.

Nevertheless in some respects Soviet accounts appear to be remarkably frank on these matters. Of the supposed total circulation of about 200,000 in the weeks immediately after 5 March, between 85,000 and 100,000 copies did not get beyond the confines of Petrograd.[1] Admittedly there was a large audience inside the capital, but this piece of information lends weight to the view that Petrograd occupied a position of overriding importance in Bolshevik strategy. When the Bolshevik Petrograd City Committee in May clamoured for a separate press organ besides *Pravda* that would represent local city interests, Lenin replied: 'My own view is that there is no fundamental need for a special organ of the Petrograd committee. In view of the *capital's* leading role and country-wide influence, only *one* organ of the Party is needed there, namely, the Central Organ.'[2]

Lenin also believed in the monolithic unity of the Bolshevik press, and his second reason for turning down the proposal was a foretaste of the way in which the future Soviet press would be run: 'I believe that the decision of the Petrograd Committee's Executive to establish a special newspaper in Petrograd is utterly wrong and undesirable, because it splits up our forces and introduces into our Party the elements of conflict.'[3] That was the first thought to come into his head. Apparently it did not occur to him that a new party press organ might reinforce the Bolshevik cause in the capital.

The total circulation of *Pravda* dropped suddenly with the fortunes of the Bolshevik party after the abortive July uprising in Petrograd. At the beginning of September only approximately 50,000 copies of *Rabochii put'* (*Pravda* under another

[1] *Protokoly VI s"ezda RSDRP* (*b*) (Moscow, 1919) p. 39.
[2] Lenin, *Collected Works*, vol. 24, p. 553.
[3] Ibid., p. 554. There were practical reasons too. Petrograd took a large proportion of *Pravda*'s circulation in any case; and *Pravda*'s unpaid labour force might have been syphoned off drastically to start up the new organ.

name) were being issued daily. By October the figure rose again to 100,000.[1] Many of the *Pravda* copies for the capital were distributed to the Bolshevik factory committees on a regular basis, and special transport was organised to take the paper to the sailors on the island of Kronstadt. On 25 May an article in *Pravda* recommended the establishment of city district offices to improve distribution methods. A bookshop was opened in the working-class suburb of Narvskaia. It was open from five o'clock in the morning until late at night, so that the workers from nearby factories could find time to collect Bolshevik literature there.[2] Sympathisers who had neither the time nor the money to buy a copy of *Pravda* could often listen to extracts read out aloud by fellow workers. This custom was widely prevalent in a society still submerged in mass illiteracy.

Copies of *Pravda* which were sent outside Petrograd were aimed chiefly at the Army fronts and the other large industrial centres of European Russia. We have already noted the efforts of Petrograd workers to get the newspaper to the fronts. Moscow Bolshevik organisations claimed to have sent to the fronts 7,972 copies of *Pravda* and 30,375 copies of their own newspaper, *Sotsial-Demokrat*, in the short period between 24 March and 1 May 1917.[3] It was a valiant effort, but it was a tiny drop in the ocean of propaganda spread among the millions of soldiers by non-Bolshevik sources during the same period. According to a Soviet estimate, the Kadet, Socialist Revolutionary and Menshevik parties between them were issuing 150 papers and pamphlets of various kinds, all of them intended solely for the armed forces.[4] At the beginning of September 1917 the Bolshevik Central Committee wrote to 515 local Bolshevik organisations, urging them to increase the distribution of *Rabochii Put'* (*Pravda*) in their areas. As a result, 600 copies a day were sold in Minsk, 300 in Arkhangel and 200 in Odessa. The circulation in the Vitebsk area west of Moscow rose dramatically from 50 to 300 a day between August and the end of September.[5]

[1] Zaslavsky, op. cit., pp. 178-9.

[2] *Narvskaia zastava v 1917 godu v vospominaniiakh i dokumentakh* (Leningrad, 1960) pp. 83-4.   [3] Zaslavsky, op. cit., p. 98.   [4] Ibid.

[5] *Perepiska Sekretariata Tsk RSDRP (b) s mestnymi partiinymi organizatsiiami* (Moscow, 1957) vol. I, pp. 287, 295.

Pravda hardly penetrated beyond the frontiers of Russia in the first three months of the revolution. On 14 April Lenin lamented: 'Abroad, where no paper more left than *Rech'* [the organ of the Kadet party] ever penetrates, and where the English and French bourgeois papers speak of an all-powerful Provisional Government and the "chaos" represented by the Soviet of Workers' and Soldiers' Deputies, nobody has any clear idea of this dual power.'[1] The situation improved slightly in June when a *Pravda* bulletin began to appear in German and French in neutral Stockholm.[2]

A regular subscriber to *Pravda* throughout 1917 would have noticed how its layout changed somewhat. The original number, issued on 5 March, presented a very sober first page to the world. There were no large headlines, no subheadings, and an almost complete absence of exclamation marks. The Russian press, we must remember, was in a pre-Northcliffe state. But by the autumn the image was rather different. The issue of *Rabochii put'* announcing the success of the October revolution (issued on 26 October) was full of heavy type and dramatic punctuation.

Bernard Pares received a poor impression of the style used in Russian journals: 'We were flooded with all sorts of new papers, which printed little news and plenty of theories and programmes. The Russian journalese was never good, and now the language was almost debauched with sheer blather.'[3] If the style of *Pravda* was undistinguished, at least it was clearer and simpler than that of most 'bourgeois' newspapers. Lenin, better than any other writer in 1917, adapted his style to the thought-processes of the common worker and soldier. Contact between the Bolshevik Central Committee and receptive elements among the general population was the quicker for this.

The great political weight attached to views put forward in the main party organs, however badly expressed, was undeniable in the revolutionary months. Many of the party leaders wrote constantly for their organs, and directed them personally from day to day. Since no single group possessed enough power to maintain a majority in a national Government, a great deal

---

[1] Lenin, *Collected Works*, vol. 24, p. 142.
[2] *Perepiska . . .*, op. cit., vol. II, p. 73 n.
[3] Sir Bernard Pares, *My Russian Memoirs* (London, 1931) p. 445.

E 2

of effort was devoted to trying to persuade the population of the correctness of a particular party programme and of the stupidity of all the others. Two isolated events in 1917 may serve to illustrate the vital position of the party press. Immediately after the February revolution, the best and perhaps the only way to gain an understanding of the viewpoints of the various political groups which emerged was to read the literature they put out. This was particularly true with regard to the Bolshevik party, which had not been well known to the general public prior to 1917, and which even after February was badly represented in Petrograd, since its leading figures were still in exile. After an initial tussle with the temporary editorial board of *Pravda*, Stalin, Kamenev and Muranov superseded it, and on 15 March adopted a conciliatory attitude towards the Provisional Government in a leading article. The policy of *Pravda*'s editorial board thus ran quite contrary to Lenin's ideas, but he was stranded abroad and had no secure means of getting his view across to the Russian public. When the first of Lenin's *Letters from Afar* appeared in *Pravda* on 21–22 March, it came as a complete break with the previous party line. As a result the reading public was confused and the situation was only clarified after Lenin's return to Russia on 3 April. The Bolsheviks' first essay in mass communication was nearly a fatal one. It is all the more to their credit that *Pravda* subsequently gained such an eminent place among the revolutionary journals. Lenin's rather dictatorial attitude to the Petrograd City Committee on the question of a separate press organ may have been motivated partly by this earlier experience.

Another illustration of the key role of the political press may be taken from the *Kerensky Memoirs*. The first intimation Prime Minister Kerensky received that Miliukov, the head of the Kadet Party, was supporting General Kornilov's 'counter-revolution' in August, came when one of Kerensky's aides rushed into his office and showed him the large blank in the Kadet newspaper *Rech'*, where the leading article should have been. Miliukov, like Lenin, was the chief editor of his party organ. According to the compositor of *Rech'*, Miliukov's censored article had welcomed General Kornilov's action and had demanded that the Provisional Government come to terms with him at once. On the basis of this information alone, Kerensky

took instant measures to make Miliukov relinquish his leadership of the Kadets. Three Kadet spokesmen were called in and
persuaded to tell Miliukov that he would have to resign.
Kerensky adds: 'My visitors carried out this rather delicate
mission very tactfully, and Miliukov left for the Crimea almost
immediately after they had spoken to him.'[1]

OTHER BOLSHEVIK NEWSPAPERS

With his usual clarity of vision, Lenin concentrated the
efforts of the Bolshevik press outside Petrograd as far as he
could on the two elements in the population that seemed likely
to provide the most converts to his cause – the proletariat in
Russia's larger towns, and the military, including the sailors
as well as the land forces. The peasantry came as an afterthought,
corresponding to Lenin's late inclusion of this class as a potential revolutionary weapon in the struggle for a Bolshevik
victory.

Moscow's *Sotsial-Demokrat* was the most powerful Bolshevik
voice after *Pravda*. The first issue was put out on 7 March. Ties
with Petrograd were close, because at the end of March the
editorial board was headed by M. Ol'minsky, who had just
returned from the capital after helping to organise the press
there. The circulation of *Sotsial-Demokrat* began at 60,000 but
was reduced to 47,000 by the autumn, mainly owing to the
Provisional Government's ban on its delivery to the fronts. Of
the 47,000 copies, 20,000 were distributed in Moscow, 5,000 in
the surrounding countryside, 2,000 in the neighbouring guberniia, and the remaining 20,000 in other Russian cities.[2]

Local Bolshevik newspapers in towns not far from Petrograd
and Moscow soon followed on the heels of *Pravda* and *Sotsial-
Demokrat*. In the first weeks after the February revolution news-
papers appeared in Kronstadt, Helsingfors, Riga, Reval and
Vyborg. On 10 March Kharkov witnessed the first issue of
Proletarii. A week later an article in *Pravda* congratulated
Proletarii for its simple, intelligible style, which 'every worker
. . . will understand – from the first word to the last'.[3] Not all

[1] *The Kerensky Memoirs*, pp. 406–7.
[2] Budnikov, op. cit., p. 92.
[3] *Pravda*, 17 Mar. 1917.

the large towns of the new Republic were supplied with Bolshevik journals, but they did crop up in some very remote localities. A flourishing little newspaper started in Yakutsk, in the depths of Siberia, between March and May. It was run by a group of Bolsheviks who had been there in forced exile, and who were unable to leave Siberia until the summer of 1917.[1]

Distant Vladivostok had to wait until June for the organisation of a Bolshevik journal. The Mensheviks, backed by local businessmen in the port, had forestalled their rivals.[2]

The press network of the Bolsheviks in Russian towns and cities was impressive, though rather haphazardly arranged. The activities of the different centres were poorly co-ordinated. Some local organs continued to put out Stalin's 'defensist' line on the war after Lenin took over the management of *Pravda* in April. A questionnaire on the state of the party press, given out at the Sixth Bolshevik Congress at the end of July, contained inaccurate information. Non-Bolshevik organs were classified as Bolshevik, and a whole series of newspapers were incorrectly titled. Thus *Golos pravdy* was referred to as *Kronshtadtskaia pravda*, and *Privolzhskaia pravda* as *Pravda povolzh'ia*.[3] Liaison between the Bolshevik Central Committee and local press organisations cannot have been good. The disruption caused by attacks on the Bolsheviks after the July Days may have accounted for some of the deficiencies; but it is clear from the questionnaire that even local delegates made incorrect statements about their own press arrangements.[4] High enthusiasm often helped to repair poor contacts. In September we find the proud editors of a new journal in a provincial town in Samara guberniia sending their first number to the Bolshevik Central Committee, and asking for a copy of *Pravda* in return. In this way they took the initiative and made themselves known to the party centre.[5]

The ban on the delivery of Bolshevik newspapers to the front did not prevent the establishment of a new organ, *Soldatskaia pravda*, which was first issued on 15 April under the auspices of

[1] Budnikov, op. cit., p. 18.
[2] D. I. Boiko-Pavlov and E. P. Sidorchuk, *Tak bylo na dal'nem vostoke* (Moscow, 1964) p. 45.
[3] *Protokoly VI s'ezda RSDRP (b)*, p. 73.
[4] Ibid. Kamensky, a delegate from the Donbas, referred to a local newspaper, correctly named the *Donetskii proletarii*, as the *Donetskaia pravda*.
[5] Sidorov, *Revoliutsionnoe dvizhenie v Rossii v sentiabre 1917 g.*, p. 82.

the military commission of the Petrograd Bolshevik committee. Resources for the paper were collected by soldiers of the Petrograd garrison and workers from the main Petrograd factories, including the Putilov works. Circulation started at 50,000 copies. Of this figure, 24,000 were sent off to the fronts daily.[1] Most of them successfully avoided the postal checks and military censor offices of the Provisional Government.

The editorial board of *Soldatskaia pravda* consisted of N. I. Podvoisky (a member of the Bolshevik Central Committee), V. I. Nevsky and A. F. Il'in-Genevsky. Il'in-Genevsky was an officer in the Petrograd reserve, who was acting at the same time as private secretary to A. I. Guchkov, the Minister of War in the Provisional Government. This incongruous combination of duties, involving dual loyalties to two incompatible policies, could not last long. Il'in-Genevsky soon began to sabotage Guchkov's activities. 'Thus, in reply to a telegram demanding a fight to a victorious finish, I wired the slogan of peace without annexations or reparations. In answering a telegram calling for the annihilation of the accursed Germans, I spoke of international solidarity, etc. The two colonels [in Guchkov's office] began to consider me with suspicion. Once or twice I noticed that the text of my telegrams had been surreptitiously altered.'[2] When Guchkov's Cabinet fell and Kerensky became War Minister, Il'in-Genevsky lost his job.

In his memoirs Il'in-Genevsky makes some revealing observations on the style of Bolshevik press reports in 1917:

The purposes of our paper [*Soldatskaia pravda*] determined its character and contents. First of all, the paper had to be made appropriate for an ill-prepared and little-educated reading public. Therefore our articles and paragraphs were written in a very colloquial style, and always started with the ABC of any question that was brought up. Highfalutin words were absolutely taboo. In order to give the articles a form best suited to soldiers, we almost always changed the articles which we had written, to be simplified if need be. Another feature of the paper was its avowed purpose to throw light

[1] *Partarkhiv Leningradskogo OK KPSS*, f. 1, op. 1, d. 9.

[2] A. F. Il'in-Genevsky, *From the February Revolution to the October Revolution 1917* (London, 1931) p. 50.

on the peasant question. We took into account the fact that the overwhelming majority of the Army consisted of peasants in soldiers' uniforms.[1]

After the July Days both *Pravda* and *Soldatskaia pravda* were suppressed in the capital. Il'in-Genevsky boasts in his book that he and his fellow editors succeeded in reviving *Soldatskaia pravda* before *Pravda* appeared again under another name. They approached various printing plants, referring to their paper as a Social-Democratic rather than as a Bolshevik organ.

Eventually they won over a plant owner to their revolutionary purposes, though their methods were heavily traditional: 'In order to get in still more with the owner, a special supper party was arranged with plenty of liquor on the table, something very rare at that time.'[2] When the paper was reissued, the real editors used a worker by the name of V. I. Narchuk as a fictitious 'responsible' editor, who would be the one to go to prison if the necessity arose.[3]

Soldatskaia pravda was aimed in the first place at the Petrograd military garrison, a vital factor in Bolshevik strategy. The front-line soldiers' thirst for news on the state of the towns and particularly the countryside soon led to the appearance of the multitude of papers issued near the fronts by the soldiers themselves. The leading Bolshevik organ was *Okopnaia pravda* (*Trench Pravda*), first issued in Riga on 30 April. The initiative for this venture came from private soldiers stationed on the northern front in the ranks of the 436th regiment of the Twelfth Army. According to one of the soldier-editors, he and his comrades had already been producing Bolshevik leaflets on a hectograph prior to the February revolution.[4] Would-be Bolshevik editors were in keen competition with Socialist Revolutionary and Menshevik rivals who also wished to set up their own military press organs. At first there was a squabble between the Socialist Revolutionaries and the Bolsheviks over the control of the plant which turned out *Okopnaia pravda*. The Bolsheviks prevailed

[1] Ibid., p. 51.
[2] Ibid., p. 78.
[3] This system was of course a direct continuation of Bolshevik tactics under the Tsarist regime. Cf. p. 113 above.
[4] D. Grazkin, *Soldatskaia gazeta*, in *Letopis' velikogo oktiabria, aprel'–oktiabr' 1917* (Moscow, 1958) p. 64.

through persistence and some bullying. Their journal increased in stature during 1917. Starting from its lowly origin as the propaganda organ of a single regiment, it was eventually taken over on 5 July by the military organisation for the whole of the Twelfth Army,[1] The road of expansion was not a smooth one. Printing equipment and experience were lacking, and the soldiers could only work on the paper at night. The second number of *Okopnaia pravda* did not appear until four days after the first.[2] Thereafter it came out three to four times a week. Circulation figures varied between 5,000 and 10,000 copies. Small-scale distribution in the early days was carried out by regimental signalmen. Next a system of couriers was established. In the effort to broaden the net, copies of the papers were soon being sent to more distant parts. They were disguised as private letters, wrapped up in envelopes bearing semi-literate addresses to conceal their origin. The Provisional Government censor could not possibly interfere with more than a minimal fraction of these 'letters'.[3]

The foundation in Helsingfors of *Volna* (*The Wave*), the most influential of the Bolshevik journals addressed to the Navy, was engineered from Petrograd. In March a group of Bolsheviks from the capital and from Kronstadt, the naval base in the Gulf of Finland, decided to go to Helsingfors and form a Bolshevik organisation there. The group was led by Il'in-Genevsky. He promised the party Central Committee that he would set up a Bolshevik newspaper within three days of his arrival in Helsingfors.[4] This seemed a rash promise. True, the future capital of independent Finland was at that time the headquarters of Russia's Baltic Fleet. It had more than the usual complement of Bolshevik sympathisers in its ranks – in both the 1905 and 1917 revolutions the Navy provided the party with backbone support which was in some respects more important than that of the famed 'proletariat' – but the trouble was that the Mensheviks had a majority in the town Soviet.

Il'in-Genevsky entered into a contract for a printing plant in Helsingfors without a kopeck in his pocket to pay for it.

[1] Budnikov, op. cit., p. 95.
[2] Grazkin, op. cit., p. 70.
[3] Ibid.
[4] Il'in-Genevsky, op. cit., pp. 26–8.

Luckily the crew of the *Emperor Paul I* (renamed the *Respublika*) decided on their own account to contribute a thousand roubles from their mess fund to pay for the plant.[1] Il'in-Genevsky took advantage of this warm tribute to call a town conference in order to elect a party committee. The organisers of the Bolshevik press in 1917 were never mere editors. They were journalists, proof-readers, orators, money-raisers and party organisers all rolled into one. The first issue of *Volna* appeared on 30 March; Il'in-Genevsky had kept his promise. The articles in the paper had been written by him and his colleagues during the train journey from Petrograd. In the next few days the pressure of work was great, and a continuous flow of excited visitors made it hard to work in the newspaper office. So Il'in-Genevsky 'found a fairly light, but perfectly quiet and secluded place for my work. This was – the toilet. I locked myself in here and though I had few comforts, at least there was peace and quiet to write my articles.'[2]

Within a very short period *Volna* was being produced on a more proficient press; this was none other than the printing press of the Finnish Senate, the supreme governing body of the Grand Duchy of Finland. Finnish nationalism was sufficiently extremist by March 1917 to ensure that a majority of the Senators were sympathetic towards the Social Democrats, including the Bolsheviks on their left wing.[3] Soon the new press organ was running smoothly. Sailors collected 100 copies each a day and sold them on the streets and the ships at three kopecks a time. Before long *Volna* was reaching Petrograd and other important Baltic ports like Riga and Reval. It even sold fifty copies a day in Orlia, a town 250 miles south of Riga.[4]

THE NON-BOLSHEVIK PRESS

At the time of the October coup the Bolsheviks were publishing approximately seventy newspapers and journals.[5] This was a massive achievement, when one considers that before 1917 their views could scarcely find expression in a single Russian

[1] *Proletarskaia revoliutsiia*, no. 5 (1923) p. 121.
[2] Il'in-Genevsky, op. cit., p. 36.   [3] Ibid., pp. 34–5.
[4] *Arkhiv IML pri Tsk KPSS*, f. 17, op. 1, d. 278, l. 12, quoted in Budnikov, op. cit., p. 91.   [5] Budnikov, op. cit., p. 91.

newspaper. The successes and tribulations of the other party presses are of paler interest by comparison. The volume of their output was higher than that of the Bolsheviks, but it had started from a more substantial base, built up before 1917. This was especially the case with regard to the liberal political groups. In September 1917 Lenin estimated that the 'Socialist Revolutionaries, Mensheviks, and Bolsheviks ... command from three-quarters to four-fifths of the votes [in Petrograd and Moscow], while the circulation of the newspapers they publish is certainly less than a quarter, or even less than one-fifth, that of the whole bourgeois press'.[1]

It is virtually impossible to calculate the exact number of political newspapers that came out during 1917. For one thing, there is no clear way of differentiating between a full-scale newspaper and an ephemeral leaflet. Again, many publications were fly-by-night affairs, which petered out almost as soon as they began. Lack of precise information on this point is not so frustrating as it might seem, since the mere production of literature was not the most vital factor in the fight for men's minds. It is more important to consider how well the literature was distributed and how it was received by those whom it reached.

The political groups represented in the Provisional Government certainly had some advantages over the Bolsheviks with regard to the operation of the press. The Kadets and the Octobrists had longer experience, but being better known and established, their organs and printing plants presented a more obvious target for attack in 1917. They possessed a clear advantage in their financial hold over the Russian press. Only the rich had the means to run a newspaper and maintain the machinery and labour which this required. Paper and ink in large quantities were expensive. Lenin never ceased to point these facts out. He also noted something else: 'Look at *Russkoe slovo, Novoe vremiia, Birzhevka, Rech'* etc. [papers supporting the Provisional Government] – you will see a multitude of private advertisements, which yield a tremendous income, in fact the principal income, to their capitalist publishers. This is how bourgeois papers hold sway, how they get rich, and *how they deal in poison for the people* all over the world.'[2] Lenin proposed

[1] Lenin, *Collected Works*, vol. 25, p. 376.   [2] Ibid., pp. 376–7.

'banning advertisements anywhere *outside* the newspapers published by the Soviets in the provincial towns and cities and by the *Central Soviet* in Petrograd for the whole of Russia'. By this means he hoped that the countryside 'would be able to have *Soviet* papers, with supplements for the peasants, at a very low price or even free of charge'.[1]

The 'bourgeois' newspapers also had the whip hand over journalists and other writers, who naturally preferred them for the higher fees they offered. A good deal of political conviction or independent means were necessary to keep contributors faithful to the left-wing press. Gorky had both and refused to write for the liberal organs in 1917. He published a paper of his own, *Novaia zhizn'*. The official local press distribution was firmly in the hands of the Provisional Government as well, inherited from the previous regime. There was less need to construct a network almost from scratch, as the Bolsheviks had to do in 1917. Thus the Russian resident in the distant Emirate of Bokhara automatically saw to it after February that the press organs of the new Provisional Government were published there without restriction.[2] This sense of continuity had its drawbacks though, since the new regime was sometimes associated too closely with the old, with unfortunate political consequences.

The main newspapers of the influential parties to the right of the Bolsheviks were *Rabochaia gazeta* (Menshevik), *Delo naroda* (S.R.) and *Rech'* (Kadet). *Izvestiia* was the organ of the Petrograd Soviet, which included all these parties except for the Kadets.

A suitable printing plant for *Izvestiia* was found as early as 27 February, but according to Sukhanov it possessed 'neither funds, essential for wages, nor supplies, nor safety'.[3] He set off on a prolonged search for food for the printers, conscious of the difficulties involved arising from 'the atmosphere of the crowd, the muddle, and the general nervous strain from the mass of grandiose feelings and niggling details'.[4] The first number of *Izvestiia* was more like a leaflet than a newspaper. In Petrograd

[1] Ibid.
[2] *Krasnyi arkhiv*, vol. 20, p. 81.
[3] Sukhanov, op. cit., p. 89.
[4] Ibid. and see pp. 89–92.

it was distributed mainly by being scattered from cars moving through the streets. Curious passers-by who picked up copies were informed that there was as yet no time to publish real newspapers because events crowded in so rapidly.[1] Although *Izvestiia* turned into a fully-fledged newspaper, with a circulation estimated at 100,000 by the start of April.[2] it remained little more than a personal letter issued by a single editor, Yu. M. Steklov. 'The general tone of the articles, the selection of editorials, the decision of what should or should not be published, and even the misprints – everything revealed the hand of the editor and his assistants, who advocated views of their own and not at all those of the committee [the Executive Committee of the Petrograd Soviet]. *Izvestiia* was regarded by an overwhelming majority of the members of the Committee as something foreign and outrageous.'[3] The situation was remedied when a new three-man editorial committee was appointed, consisting of Sukhanov, Stankevich and Dan.

INTER-PARTY RIVALRY

Competition between the Provisional Government and the Bolsheviks was not restricted to strident propaganda fanfares alone. In the turbulent conditions of 1917 other less peaceful means were frequently used. Neither side had the upper hand at any time. The Provisional Government controlled more presses, but the Bolsheviks were by no means penniless, since they were helped by German money and their own supporters' kopecks.

For the most part the Soviet had a closer influence over the 'typographical workers', as Miliukov admitted to a public meeting in the Tauride Palace on 2 March.[4] When Miliukov,

[1] Stinton Jones, *Russia in Revolution* (London, 1917) pp. 139–40. The Bolsheviks, succeeded in printing a supplement to the first number of *Izvestiia* without asking the permission of the editorial board. See Katkov, op. cit., p. 369.

[2] M. N. Pokrovsky and Ya. A. Yakovlev (eds), *1917 god v dokumentakh i materialakh*. vol. 1: *Petrogradskii sovet rabochikh i soldatskikh deputatov; protokoly zasedanii ispolnitel'nogo komiteta i biuro I.K.* (Moscow, 1925) p. 82.

[3] V. B. Stankevich, *Vospominaniia, 1914–1919* (Berlin, 1920) pp. 88–90.

[4] *Izvestiia revoliutsionnoi nedeli*, no. 6. 2 Mar. 1917, p. 1.

acting for the Provisional Government, was asked on the previous day by Sukhanov, acting for the Soviet, where he would get the new constitution printed, Miliukov was forced to reply, 'I don't know. The printing presses are more under your control.'[1] Yet all the printers in Petrograd were not in agreement with the politics of the far left either. As a rule their representatives, drawn from the skilled labour force, were S.R. or Menshevik adherents rather than Bolsheviks. The editors of *Pravda* had to deal with extensive sabotage to their press in the weeks after the February revolution.

No less underhand means were employed throughout 1917 to obstruct the distribution of newspapers, if and when they survived suppression in the workshops themselves. The Provisional Government ordained that 'the press and trade in the publications of the press are free. They are not subject to administrative penalties',[2] but from the start it was reluctant to allow the defeatist literature of the far left wing to reach the front. Innumerable witnesses recorded the ways in which Bolshevik publications were hindered. The Executive Committee of the Tiflis Soviet was accused of confiscating 40,000 copies of *Pravda* which Georgian workers were preparing to dispatch to the Caucasian front.[3] Post offices in Riazan' guberniia let all except Bolshevik literature through to the front;[4] and we find simple soldiers complaining bitterly that they paid subscriptions for *Pravda*, but could only get *Rech'* and *Den'*. They demanded that the offending post-office workers be thrown out of their jobs.[5]

In theory the soldiers' rights were already supposed to be protected by Order No. 8, issued by Kerensky as one of his first acts as the new Minister of War in May. Item 6 stated that 'all printed matter without exception (periodical or non-periodical) must be delivered to the addressee without any interference'.[6] In actual fact, the situation deteriorated during 1917. Another

---

[1] Sukhanov, op. cit., p. 157.

[2] *Sobranie uzakonenii i rasporiazhenii pravitel'stva*, I, I, no. 597.

[3] *Protokoly VI s'ezda RSDRP (b)* (Moscow, 1919) p. 85.

[4] *Arkhiv IML, fond Tsk RSDRP (b), 1917 g.*, quoted in Budnikov, op. cit., p. 93.

[5] Sidorov, *Revoliutsionnoe dvizhenie v Rossii v mae-iune 1917 g. — iun'skaia demonstratsiia*, p. 358.

[6] *Vestnik vremennogo pravitel'stva*, no. 54, 14 May 1917, p. 1.

impeding factor were the Army officers, as the editors of
Soldatskaia pravda well knew from angry letters reaching them
from privates, who wrote that 'the officer gentlemen hold back
the . . . paper for their own purposes, realising that owing to
it the soldiers may cause them harm'.[1]

In the middle of July the Provisional Government reimposed
military censorship of the press, acting in accordance with the
wishes of the General Staff. The main reason given for this
move was not that it seemed a good way of attacking the
Bolshevik press (in the event it turned out to be ineffective
anyhow), but that 'beginning with the month of March, the
Austrians and the Germans had no need for an intelligence
service. It was enough to get all the Russian papers. From them
it was possible to re-create a complete picture both of the location and the *condition* of all Russian Army corps.'[2]

The Provisional Government and its supporters failed to
check substantially the flow of undesirable literature to the
front. Soon they adopted new tactics by trying to cut off the
fountainheads. The main assault on Bolshevik presses was
timed to coincide with the party's momentary decline after the
abortive uprising in Petrograd during the July Days. As early
as 13 May, however,

two officers and one civilian made their way into our editorial rooms [*Soldatskaia pravda*] in Ksheshinskaia's Palace.
They poured gasoline on bundles of papers laying about on
the floor, which had been prepared for dispatch to the front,
and set fire to them. Having done their vile work, they
jumped into a waiting automobile and disappeared. Luckily
our comrades were awakened and the fire was quickly
extinguished. About forty thousand copies of the paper were
thus destroyed and the walls and ceiling slightly blackened
with soot, but no one was injured.[3]

On 5 July the plants of both *Pravda* and *Soldatskaia pravda*
were wrecked on government orders. The damage was estimated at 150,000 roubles. Six days later the Provisional
Government ordered the discontinuance of the publication of

[1] Quoted in Il'in-Genevsky, op. cit., p. 53.
[2] *Russkiia vedomosti*, 19 July 1917.
[3] Il'in-Genevsky, op. cit., pp. 56-7.

Pravda, Okopnaia pravda and other Bolshevik organs. From this time onwards *Pravda* played a hide-and-seek game with the Government, appearing and disappearing in succession under the names *Listokpravdy, Rabochii i soldat, Proletarii, Rabochii* and *Rabochii put'*. When one press was seized, another took over the torch. The Bolsheviks gained breathing-space owing to the surprising leniency of the Provisional Government. When the commander of the Petrograd military district asked the Minister of the Interior to allow him to arrest the editors of *Rabochii*, as *Pravda* was called in mid-September, the Minister prevaricated for six days, and then stated that the problem would have to be referred to the Ministry of Justice for a decision.[1]

The Provisional Government did go so far as to order all postal, railway and military authorities to stop deliveries for subscribers to Bolshevik newspapers, but this barrier was soon overcome. As we know from a previous essay, the Government could by no means rely on the lower echelons of the railway workers to obey its orders. Also the central illegal Bolshevik presses began to send copies out in bulk direct to local party committees, which saw to their distribution among individual subscribers. Special couriers were organised in Petrograd to pick up papers in the middle of the night or at dawn, and to deliver them to Finland, the northern front and nearby towns. By the last week in July the circulation of *Rabochii i soldat* stood at about 20,000 copies, but soon it swelled to between sixty and seventy thousand.[2]

As for local Bolshevik presses, perhaps the best survey is to be found in information given by delegates to the Second Congress of Soviets, convened in Petrograd at the time of the October coup. 343 delegates were asked, 'Were there any attempts to restrict freedom of political agitation and the press in your locality?' Of the 135 who gave replies, 81 said no, 20 admitted to unsuccessful interventions by the censor, and 34 affirmed that their organisations had been disrupted.[3] It is indicative of the Provisional Government's ineffectiveness at the local level to find such a high proportion of unchecked areas, particularly when one considers that the delegates hailed

---

[1] *Krasnyi arkhiv*, vol. 58, pp. 131–2.
[2] Budnikov, op. cit., p. 140.
[3] *Krasnyi arkhiv*, vol. 84, reply to question no. 7.

mainly from the most active and best-known regions of Bolshevik activity in the country.

Lenin's party took its revenge during the October coup for the persecution it had suffered through the eight previous months. The techniques the Bolsheviks used for capturing the presses of the Provisional Government on 25 October were copied in some detail from the methods employed against them earlier in the year. But instead of closing down the plant, they set to work immediately on turning out their own literature on the machinery. Thus as soon as the press of *Russkaia volia* was seized on 25 October, the editor was ordered to produce 100,000 copies of *Rabochii put'* for instant free distribution to the front.[1] On 28 October the Petrograd Military Revolutionary Committee commanded the stationmaster of the Nikolaev railway line to ensure the unobstructed passage of Bolshevik newspapers.[2] On the same day the Committee also requisitioned lorries in the capital for distributing leaflets and papers.[3] Instructions were given to the main Petrograd post office on how to expedite the handling of *Derevenskaia bednota*, the Bolshevik peasant newspaper.[4] Within a week channels that had been assiduously blocked by Kerensky were opened and cleared.

The triumphant insurgents did not stop at that. After clamouring since July for complete freedom of the press, they now proceeded to throttle all rivals, in order, they claimed, to 'save the Revolution'. Their initial reprisals naturally fell on Kerensky; the plant used for printing his decrees was put under guard, and the state press was searched.[5] At this point we may close with a resolution of the Petrograd Printers' Union which protested in vain against this type of action: 'Having discussed the situation created in connection with the political upheaval that has occurred, the administration (1) demands that an immediate stop be put to the fratricidal slaughter, (2) demands that the Military Revolutionary Committee restore freedom of the press at once. . . .'[6]

[1] *Rech'*, 26 Oct. 1917.
[2] *Dokumenty velikoi proletarskoi revoliutsii* (Moscow, 1938) vol. i, pp. 70–1.
[3] Sidorov, *Oktiabr'skoe vooruzhennoe vosstanie v Petrograde*, p. 883.
[4] Ibid., p. 897.
[5] Ibid., p. 703.
[6] P. Garvi, *Profsoiuzy Rossii v pervye gody revoliutsii*, MS. in the Hoover Institution on War, Revolution and Peace, p. 19.

Perhaps Lenin's single greatest achievement in 1917 was his magnificent use of propaganda, and the Bolshevik press was his main instrument. But even the genius of Lenin must not blind us to the essential point that however brilliant the press campaign was in 1917, the unemancipated mind of the Russian nation provided a very weak receptacle. The military were one of Lenin's foremost targets, yet apart from an attentive minority, their understanding of revolutionary politics often cannot have been far above the level observed by General Polovtsov, the commander of the Petrograd military district:

> While I was visiting Gatchina an amusing incident occurred. Some kind of Bolshevik demonstration had taken place the day before, and huge red posters were lying about in different corners of the barracks. Noticing one with 'Long live the International' written on it, I inquired of one of the soldiers whether he had marched under this motto. He replied 'Yes', so I asked him what the word 'International' meant. He was very much embarrassed, and had to admit that he did not know, but assured me that his deputy in the soldiers' committee knew, so I at once turned to this fellow, a stalwart N.C.O., and put the question to him. Without a moment's hesitation he replied: 'International means the interests of the nation.'
>
> This showed that the Bolsheviks had not yet had time to explain the aims of their Third International to the soldiers, or perhaps they did not care to do it. It was not by explanations and reasonings that they influenced the crowds, but by short slogans. As for the word 'International', in the minds of the soldiers it apparently stood for the name of a new and mysterious deity; for instance, on the railways they invaded the cars, irrespective of class, broke the windows, tore the cloth from the seats, and so on, but they always treated with the greatest respect the car bearing the inscription 'International Sleeping Car Co.'[1]

Even at the political centre there was a shortage of educated talent. S. V. Malyshev, the secretary of *Pravda* in 1914 before he was arrested, stressed how difficult it was then and in 1917

[1] General P. A. Polovtsov, *Glory and Downfall: Reminiscences of a Russian General Staff Officer* (London, 1935) p. 206.

to 'know how to organise and manage a working-class newspaper. We had never been able to go to school. We were all semi-literate Bolsheviks – we all put off studying until we were imprisoned, as we nearly always were. There, day after day, we wrote out declensions, verbs, subordinate clauses and participles. When we were released from prison, we sat down at a secretary's or editor's desk on party orders.'[1]

The Bolsheviks worked to the limit of their capacity in 1917 to impress their views on the wide public through the press. Nevertheless the result of national elections of the Constituent Assembly in November gave the Bolsheviks only 175 out of 707 representatives. Viewed in these terms, their campaign had been a failure. But after the October coup, voting figures do not tell the whole story. The eight revolutionary months of freedom were past. During that time persuasion had been the supreme political art. From October on the realities of power favoured Lenin. The Bolsheviks' strength lay in the political hubs of Petrograd and Moscow, where they commanded a majority, and in the ranks of the Army. In the civil war that followed, the sword was mightier than the pen.

[1] S. V. Malyshev, *Na proletarskikh stupeniakh*, '*Molodaia gvardiia*', no. 2–3 (1925).

5 Propaganda and Political Rumours

> The 'Jingoes' who . . . sang 'We've got the ships, we've got the men, we've got the money too' accurately diagnosed the three essential elements of political power: armaments, man-power, and economic power. But man-power is not reckoned by mere counting of heads. The art of persuasion has always been a necessary part of the equipment of the political leader.
>
> E. H. CARR, *Propaganda in International Politics*

The 'art of persuasion', as E. H. Carr calls it, was one of the main ingredients of political authority in the Russian revolution. This was because the officers who held the trigger of Russia's 'armaments' were in neither one political camp nor the other in 1917 in a sufficiently large majority to provide substantial support to either side. 'Economic power', or what there was left of it after three years of a terrible war followed by violent revolution, was also disputed between the Provisional Government and the Soviets. In this context one has only to remember the way the railways, the supply system and the press would not function exclusively according to the demands of either partner in the Dual Government. Some of the more tangible channels of political propaganda like the telegraph have already been examined in previous essays. The medium of the press was especially important in 1917. The newspaper offices organised oral agitation, political circles, posters and slogans on a grand scale which went far beyond the limited bounds of the printed word. The railways also played a crucial part in the spread of propaganda. They were the main, and often the sole, carrier of the newspapers, the leaflets and the party agitators sent out to all regions of Russia.

It may be useful at this point to summarise what is meant by propaganda in general and to set it against the particular background of the Russian revolution. The word originates from the Latin *propagare*, which refers to the gardening technique of inserting the fresh shoots of a plant into the earth in order to reproduce new plants which will later take on a life of their own. The term 'propaganda' was first used officially in human affairs when Pope Urban VII established the Congregatio de Propaganda Fide in 1633. This body attempted to diffuse certain opinions and suppress other opinions contrary to them. The same technique is also fundamental to all modern propaganda: 'Inasmuch as he is *for* the creation of certain attitudes, the propagandist is necessarily *against* others; and the extirpation of what he regards as false beliefs and doctrines is as much his concern as the propagation of the 'right' ones. This suggests the important rule that one can only speak of propaganda when alternative views exist, and it is therefore not propaganda to teach a belief which is universal at the particular time or place'.[1] Russia in 1917 abounded with widely varying programmes for her future political development, and her leading spokesmen did indeed appear to devote just as much energy to attacking their opponents' propaganda as to promoting their own views.

In mid-twentieth-century terms, propaganda has been defined as 'an attempt to influence opinion and conduct – in such a manner that the persons who adopt the opinions and behaviour indicated do so without themselves making any definite search for reasons'.[2] It is obvious from this definition that propaganda techniques were peculiarly well fitted to Russian society in 1917. If only the great masses of the peasantry and the soldiers could be jolted out of their apathy into accepting political opinions handed out to them from above – a task which was by no means an easy one – they were unlikely to ponder long on their reasons for holding these views.

[1] J. A. C. Brown, *Techniques of Persuasion* (London, 1963) p. 13.
[2] F. C. Bartlett, 'The Aims of Political Propaganda', in *Public Opinion and Propaganda*, ed. D. Katz *et al.* (New York, 1954) p. 464.

The difference between education and propaganda in the best of worlds should be that the former teaches people how to think for themselves, whereas the latter tells them what to think. But in the early stages of development of political societies as well as of individuals, education must perforce take on some of the characteristics of propaganda. This is why Lenin in 1917 and the Soviet Government afterwards have regarded propaganda and education as virtually identical processes. Until the proletariat became 'conscious' in Marxist terms of its historical role, the Communist Party had to maintain the 'dictatorship of the proletariat', in education as in all other spheres of life. Although this theory was misused for the purpose of holding on to political power in Soviet Russia, it did relate quite closely to the true situation in 1917, when the political knowledge of most of the population was childlike in its naïvety.

The propagandist was better adapted to the events of 1917 than the educator in another sense. Education can only yield dividends very slowly, but propaganda aims at producing quick results; and quick results were vitally necessary for any political party in 1917, given the enormous speed at which the revolution progressed. When Gorky suggested to Lenin that a history of literature should be published for the workers' self-education, Lenin replied curtly, 'there is no time for writing thick books; a thick book would be read only by the intelligentsia . . . newspapers and brochures are what we need.'[1] Educational methods rely on rational and dispassionate arguments to drive home their points; but in 1917 emotion and irrational bias swayed most Russians, and this is exactly the stuff that propaganda is made of. The Russian revolution was one of the first political phenomena in which modern technology was used on a wide scale for propaganda purposes. The Bolsheviks can claim the doubtful privilege of being pioneers in this field, as in so many others. The first initiative in using propaganda as a normal instrument of international relations also lay with the Soviet Government.

The qualities which make for successful propaganda are clarity, simplicity of interpretation, repeated application and firm direction from above with the aim of appealing to as many

[1] Maxim Gorky, *V. I. Lenin* (Moscow, 1931).

basic desires as possible. Lenin's propaganda campaign in 1917 possessed all these qualities to a high degree. Only the Bolshevik party after Lenin's return to Russia had a clear policy, which was so original that even some of Lenin's supporters could not swallow his April Theses at first. Lenin had worked out the broad lines of his programme before he arrived at the Finland Station. The detailed propaganda campaign fitted logically into place afterwards.

The details all derived from a few simple home truths about the Russian situation which formed the core of Bolshevik propaganda. Lenin told the soldiers to leave the war and the peasants to take the land, giving a handful of simply stated reasons why they were entitled to do so. People like to feel that issues are simple, even if they are not, particularly when the solutions offered confirm their own prejudices. This was the case in 1917. During the revolutionary months Lenin discarded sophisticated Marxist arguments of the type he had used previously against Plekhanov or the Mensheviks. Instead he applied a greatly watered-down version of Marxism to the practical problems which were worrying the largest social groups in the nation. He tried to use terms which they could understand. To a great extent he succeeded, as even Lenin's opponents admitted. At the height of the February revolution Sukhanov overheard a Petrograd worker summarising the needs of his class; ' "What do they want? They want bread, peace with the Germans, and equality for the Yids." 'Right in the bull's eye, I thought, delighted with this brilliant formulation of the programme of the great revolution.'[1]

Propaganda must be repeated endlessly in order to take full effect. Goebbels stated this as one of his three general principles with regard to propaganda techniques, but Lenin had acted on the same notion a generation earlier. No one knew better than he how vital it was to drum facts incessantly into the heads of ignorant workers and soldiers. Goebbels' two other principles were that propaganda must begin at the optimum moment, and reach the audience ahead of competing propaganda.[2] Lenin was wise to this too. His slogan 'All Power to the Soviets' was turned on and off abruptly according to whether the

[1] Sukhanov, op. cit., p. 17.
[2] *The Goebbels Diaries* (New York, 1945).

Petrograd Soviet happened to be useful to him or not at the time.[1] The care with which the fastest carriers of propaganda like the telegraph and the railways were handled indicates Lenin's acknowledgement of the second principle.

Lenin also knew instinctively that political propaganda should flow strongly from a single source: many variations on a theme lead to a swamp of inertia. With this in mind he attacked savagely all minor divergences from the stereotyped programme which he himself promoted. That is why he would not tolerate the establishment of a separate Petrograd party newspaper. Bolshevik propaganda was highly restrictive at its source, but was intended to be all-embracing at its destination, the working masses of Russia. Communists make a peculiar semantic distinction between the words 'propaganda' and 'agitation'. According to Plekhanov, a propagandist explains sophisticated, intellectual concepts to the initiated few; an agitator presents vulgarised versions of these ideas to society at large. According to this definition, Lenin addressed the Russians as an agitator in 1917.[2] No theoretical study of propaganda in the broader sense of the word can be completely satisfactory, since propaganda bends like a reed before the facts of the given political situation. Universal truths do not exist on this subject, so that almost everything worth saying on it may have to be said in an individual context. The Russian revolution makes an interesting case study.

Prior to 1917, Tsarist propaganda was poorly organised, and in many areas almost non-existent. Writing on the press and propaganda of the old regime, General Denikin, one of its supporters, observed with regard to military affairs: 'It must be admitted that when we occupied Galicia [in 1915] we did

[1] 'This slogan was valid during a period of our revolution – say between 27 February and 4 July – which is now over once and for all. This slogan has obviously ceased to be valid at present. . . . Every single slogan must be deduced from the sum total of the specific features of a given political situation': from Lenin's directive *On Slogans*, written in the middle of July 1917 and issued as a leaflet by the Kronstadt Committee of the Russian Social Democratic Workers' Party. This pronouncement did not deter Lenin from supporting 'All Power to the Soviets' again before October.

[2] As early as 1902, in *What is To be Done?*, Lenin summed up his future method as 'the work of political agitation, unified throughout all of Russia, explaining all aspects of life and directed to the broadest masses'.

not take the trouble to establish the basis for national uni-
fication; we did not manage to win over public opinion in
Rumania, occupied by our troops; we made no effort to stop
the Bulgarians from betraying the interests of the Slavs; finally,
although a large number of prisoners of war were on Russian
territory, we did not take advantage of this to give them a fair
view of our country.'[1]

The Bolsheviks were more efficient than the Tsarist Government, despite the fact that they were working in underground
conditions most of the time. Yet even Lenin's propaganda did
not often lead directly to the workers' strikes and acts of
political hostility to the regime. This was particularly the case
in the early years of Lenin's close contact with the St Petersburg
proletariat, in the 1890s. At that time there was a definite
hiatus between Lenin's literary polemics and the more mun-
dane wage demands of the rising labour movement. Strikes
occurred independently, and only afterwards were their effects
harnessed to Marxist propaganda.[2] The gap was not closed
completely throughout 1917 despite considerable vulgarisation.
It was very noticeable during the February revolution, for
instance, as the Social Democrats themselves remarked: 'the
tempo of the revolutionary events was such that our slogans
were already lagging behind it. By the time the leaflets had
penetrated into the thick of the troops, the latter had already
come over.'[3]

After February the Bolsheviks managed their propaganda
better than any other party. They alone kept nearly abreast of
the quicksilver political mood of the country, and they did it
with a marvellous economy of means and expression. After the
battle of Gettysburg the Hon. Edward Everett spoke for three
hours. Lincoln spoke for five minutes. The Provisional Government reminds one of the Honourable Edward Everett. Lincoln
once said, 'he who moulds public sentiment goes deeper than
he who enacts statutes or pronounces decisions'. In 1917 the
Bolsheviks concentrated on moulding public opinion – they

[1] General A. I. Denikin, *La Décomposition de l'Armée et du Pouvoir* (Paris,
1921) p. 189.
[2] See R. Pipes, *The Social Democrats and the St Petersburg Labour Movement
1885-1896* (Cambridge, Mass., 1963) pp. 69, 73, 81–6, 93.
[3] Quoted in Trotsky, op. cit., p. 115.

were not in a position to enact statutes anyway. The Provisional Government worked its way through a mountain of decrees, reforms and legal documents, most of which had almost no effect on the public they were intended for. Many of them were never put into force before October.

The propaganda instruments of the Provisional Government were too slow-moving. They were also too conscientious. The Union of Zemstvos invited eminent personalities to lecture round the country on Russia's political reorganisation. Moscow gave 100,000 roubles for this purpose, Smolensk 80,000.[1] Men of this calibre attempted to educate their audiences rather than indoctrinate them; but there was no time for such methods, and the intellectual level of the propaganda was usually pitched too high. In the rural areas, 'the more conscientious the writers in their endeavours to present the subject lucidly, the more capable and cultured they were, the worse was the result. A stone was offered where bread was asked for.'[2]

The relationship between middle-class propagandists and their audiences was hardly more fruitful where more educated strata of the population were concerned. Bernard Pares found himself involved in the League of Personal Example, a band of liberals who travelled round Russia expounding their point of view. His general impression of the campaign was that

'we felt that our meetings did not make much difference to things; we could always get a good hall for nothing; it was always crammed; people always clapped vehemently; as a rule, the other side did not show up; and at the end, they all went off and no doubt simply asked themselves how soon we should have peace. The bourgeois were particularly annoying in this respect; they seemed to have no initiative . . . we should have felt happier if people had sharper convictions, whatever they were, and had stood up more vehemently for them'.[3]

Bernard Pares was a relatively neutral agent in that he was a foreigner, but the Provisional Government's propaganda cam-

[1] P. J. Novgorotsev, 'Universities and Higher Technical Schools', in *Russian Schools and Universities in the World War* (New Haven, 1929) p. 226.
[2] From a survey of Russia made in May 1917 and based on the data of the Provincial Section of the Provisional Government. Quoted in Vulliamy, op. cit., p. 261.   [3] Pares, *My Russian Memoirs*, p. 458.

paign suffered greatly from the fact that many of its representatives in local government, or 'commissars', as they were called, were highly unpopular in their areas. Only too often they were appointed after February rather than elected by popular vote, and they tended to be drawn from those ranks of society which were too closely associated with the old regime. As the year went by they became increasingly out of touch with what was going on in the minds of the local inhabitants. The teachers they appointed held right-wing views and cost too dear for the peasants, or so the latter claimed. 'Wait until the soldiers come back from the front', they threatened, 'they will teach us for nothing.'[1]

More often than not, the political parties trained their propaganda guns on each other rather than on the Russian people. In this vicious battle the truth was usually submerged completely, as Lenin observed in April, though his party was perhaps the most to blame in this respect: 'A popular method always used by the bourgeois press in every country with unerring effect is to lie, scream, raise a hullabaloo, and keep on reiterating lies on the off-chance that "something may stick."[2] A running fight went on throughout the year. In July the Provisional Government accused Lenin of being a German spy, quoting a false document to support their case. Petrograd was plastered with leaflets on the subject. Thus although the question of indirect German financial aid to the Bolsheviks was not of overwhelming importance in itself, it did lead to the slander against Lenin which temporarily eclipsed Bolshevik influence in July and August.

The tables were turned in September after the Kornilov episode. The Bolsheviks managed with some success to tar the Provisional Government with the brush of counter-revolution. After the October coup even the rival left-wing revolutionary parties were falsely accused of collusion: 'Comrades! Do not believe a single word of the Kornilovites who call themselves S.R.s and Mensheviks.'[3] As for the October coup itself, Trotsky tries to make out in his history of the revolution that the Bolsheviks only acted purely in self-defence to prevent another

[1] *Krasnyi arkhiv*, vol. xv, p. 56.
[2] Lenin, *Collected Works*, vol. 24, p. 118.
[3] Sidorov, *Oktiabr'skoe vooruzhennoe vosstanie v Petrograde*, p. 904.

F

attempted counter-revolution, staged on this occasion by Kerensky and the Provisional Government: 'To assure the publication of the Bolshevik press with the help of armed forces, or to retain the *Aurora* in the waters of the Neva – "Comrades, is that not self-defence? – It is defence!" If the Government intends to arrest us, we have machine guns on the roof of Smolny in preparation for such an event. "That also, comrades, is a measure of defence." '[1]

THE INSTRUMENTS OF PROPAGANDA

In many ways it could be argued that the spoken rather than the written word was more influential as an instrument of propaganda in 1917. Goebbels for one was convinced of this: 'Modern propaganda is based largely on the effect of the spoken word – revolutionary movements are not the work of great writers, but of great orators.'[2] Perhaps the most penetrating form of propaganda is a speech embodying a commonly held argument which is so successful that it is repeated from mouth to mouth and through other propaganda media. Goebbels elaborates further on this point:

> 'It is a mistake to assume that the written word is more effective because it reaches through the daily paper a wider public. Though an orator in most cases can reach only some thousands of listeners, whereas the writer succeeds in reaching some tens and thousands of readers, the spoken word influences not only those in the immediate audience, but is disseminated by word of mouth a hundredfold and sometimes a thousandfold.'[3]

Oratory was particularly valuable in Russia, where less than one person in three was able to read. The press was confined to toughly 20 per cent of the population; the telegraph and telephone were used almost exclusively by this same twenty per cent; and the railways did not penetrate into the depths of

---

[1] Trotsky, op. cit., p. 348. It is interesting to note that Trotsky singles out Kerensky's ban on the publication of *Rabochii put'* (*Pravda*) on 23 October as the act of provocation that finally set off the Bolshevik coup.

[2] Goebbels, op. cit.

[3] Ibid.

rural Russia, where most of the other 80 per cent lived. The Russian peasant had been nurtured for centuries on a strong oral tradition which could not be swept aside overnight in 1917. In general, oratory may be considered to be a stronger weapon of persuasion than the press, even when taken out of the special context of the Russian Revolution. The three great forces of human contact are men's lips, ears and eyes, and all of them are given free rein in public discussion. Oral propaganda can be tailored to fit a particular audience, and refashioned at a moment's notice according to the audience's immediate response. Contact is thus both flexible and swift – two qualities that were of immense political value in 1917.

The more astute party leaders were well aware of the power of oratory in the revolution. Kerensky rose to fame in 1917 mainly through his considerable talents as a public speaker. In the following passage he puts his finger on the reasons for the particular significance of oratory in the Russian revolution:

> The new Government had no physical means of imposing its will, and the only instrument of persuasion at its disposal was the spoken word. As Milton once pointed out, words are a great force which can be used for either creative or destructive purposes. During the early days of the Revolution, the spoken word played a quite extraordinary part, both for good and for evil.
>
> For the new Government trying to create order out of chaos, it was vital to take account of this potent weapon and exploit it for constructive purposes. It was not enough to write and publish high-minded manifestos and articles in the press. It was not enough to build up a new administrative machinery. It was also necessary, by constant use of the spoken word, to counter the forces of destruction and to instil in people a sense of their individual responsibility to the nation as a whole'.[1]

In the absence of success in other ways, Kerensky came to rely too heavily on his personal gift of oratory as 1917 went by. Dramatic speeches were peculiarly well suited to the emotional political climate just after the February revolution. Kerensky was in great demand by both the Soviet and the Provisional

[1] *The Kerensky Memoirs*, p. 229.

Committee of the State Duma. When Sukhanov was trying to get together an armed detachment to guard the Soviet's newly acquired printing press, he saw that he would have 'to carry on not individual agitation among the "thinkers" but a "mass" agitation among the ignorant and uncomprehending. I considered this business completely hopeless for myself. . . . I went off in search of Kerensky, the only man able to settle the matter at one stroke, by a single propaganda speech to the soldiers in the Catherine Hall.'[1]

As the year went by and the Provisional Government every day faced new problems which it could not resolve, 'Oratory became a substitute for action by Kerensky', as E. H. Carr has aptly put it. Listening to one of Kerensky's innumerable propaganda speeches to the military, the commander of the Petrograd district pondered sadly: 'There was a thunder of applause, but I very well knew that when, in the evening, the delegates would try to explain to the other soldiers in the barracks what Kerensky had said, they would never be able to do it, and would surely never revive the enthusiasm with which Kerensky had electrified them for a few moments. Even if any one of them did succeed, the effect would be immediately spoilt by the local Bolshevik who would simply inquire: "Did he tell you when the war would be over?"' The commander concluded: 'Unfortunately he [Kerensky] forgot that the effect of his speeches did not last long, and that when a crowd of soldiers had enthusiastically cheered him, that did not mean that when, a week later, those same men had to launch an attack they would remember his beautiful sentences.'[2]

Perhaps the most eloquent testimony to the power of words in 1917 was Trotsky's oratory. On 23 October the Peter-Paul fortress on the Neva, the burial place of the Tsars and prison for countless would-be revolutionaries in Russian history, was stormed and won over to the side of the Soviet, not by force of arms, but by the persuasive words of Trotsky.[3]

Trotsky's techniques were echoed throughout revolutionary Russia by thousands of Bolshevik supporters in 1917. Other men were less gifted, but they were a great help to the cause in

[1] Sukhanov, op. cit., p. 91.
[2] Polovtsov, op. cit., p. 223.
[3] See *Proletarskaia revoliutsiia*, no. 10 (1922).

the remote provinces, unused to the sophistication of the written word. Many of them were also possessed with amazing energy. Returning from Siberian exile in March, a Bolshevik agitator gave more than a hundred speeches on the railway journey from Irkutsk to Saratov. By the end of the trip he and his colleagues had lost their voices, so that they were reduced to 'hissing at each other like boa constrictors'.[1]

The widespread use of propaganda slogans in 1917 was an interesting phenomenon. Slogans are like frozen oratory; they stand halfway between the spoken and the written word, acting as shorthand signs to sum up a wider concept. Being short and simple, they were well adapted to the low political intelligence of the Russian nation. They could convey to the general public a vulgarised notion of the subtle differences between the political parties. Even educated men like the commander of the Petrograd military district had to rely on slogans in the early days after February:

> As I had not the slightest notion of the different political shades of the revolutionary parties, I turned to . . . an A.D.C. . . . and asked him if he knew the difference between a Socialist-Revolutionary and a Social-Democrat. He replied: "No, sir, but I shall find out", and disappeared. He returned in ten minutes and reported: "The slogan of the Socialist-Revolutionary is 'Land and Freedom'. That of the Social-Democrat is 'Proletarians of all countries unite'." I thanked him for his quick work and was satisfied for the time being with this elementary knowledge.[2]

One is reminded of Goebbels again, who said that slogans should characterise events: 'Words stand between people and events and people's reaction to events could be potently affected by words.' This was especially true of provincial Russia, which did not have direct experience of the events in Petrograd, and so relied on other men's words in order to keep in touch with the distant revolution. For lack of time and money, slogans were often the way in which political information was passed from the centre to the rest of Russia. The Petrograd Bolshevik Committee kept up a constant supply of slogans to its local

[1] V. P. Antonov-Saratovsky, *Pod stiagom proletarskoi bor'by* (Moscow, 1925) pp. 90–1.   [2] Polovtsov, op. cit., p. 193.

counterparts, as did many other organisations in the capital, particularly the left-wing ones. Thus railway workers in far off Krasnoiarsk on the Trans-Siberian line were fed with slogans retailed to them by Vikzhel like 'Down with the imperialist war!' and 'Hurrah for the first of May!'[1]

Slogans written out in large letters on banners seem to dominate filmed records of demonstrations and street processions in 1917. Anyone who has seen film sequenes of the revolution in Petrograd will be aware of the important role they played. They were the most appropriate way of proclaiming the political identity of a motley group of people. Their symbolic significance in the war of persuasion was like that of a flag in battle, and skirmishes often broke out between rival groups for the possession of each other's banners.[2] The sheer number and variety of banners on the city streets indicated just how many fragmentary political and social factions existed in 1917. Bernard Pares noticed their slogans on his walks through the capital after the February revolution:

> There were marvellous street placards. Every imaginable idea or fad was advertised. Associations were formed to follow up the Russian revolution with a Russian reformation. There were numerous little cliques which took high-sounding titles and regarded themselves as the saviours of the country. They indulged *ad infinitum* in the deplorable Russian habit of putting on paper schemes for the government of the whole world. One placard announced the United States of the World, to which was appended the statement: 'Original subscribers become life members'. Particular attention was given to education. All sorts of inappropriate bodies, such as the crew of a ship, formed what they called 'universities', really centres of university extension. Amidst the orgy of fancies I remember coming across a placard, 'The Land of the Happy Peasantry'; this, on examination, proved to come from an organisation for propagating in Russia the excellent agricultural methods of Denmark. The illiterate were begged to learn to read and write as quickly as possible. Of course

[1] Sidorov, *Aprel'skii krizis*, p. 50.
[2] For an interesting example of this in the July Days, see Znamensky, op. cit., p. 97.

many of the placards were Social-Democrat, and called for the education of the proletariat. One strange poster bore the heading, 'Self Organisation'. Apparently Russia was to be saved by a general dispatch of post-cards to a common anonymous address. I visited and addressed one typical, tiny newly-formed group; they were out to 'save the country', but none of them seemed to know or care what was being done by any other organisation.[1]

The frequent political posters that appeared on the walls of Petrograd or were thrown indiscriminately to passers-by from slow-moving vehicles were only a fraction less superficial and ephemeral than slogans written up on banners. But like the slogans, they served a useful if short-lived purpose. They were issued at crucial moments of crisis by contesting political parties. Leaflets and brochures were more substantial than posters, but not as effective as newspapers which could drive home their message in successive issues. Enormous quantities of pamphlets were produced in 1917. Well before the fall of the Tsarist regime Lenin had looked to these forms of propaganda as 'the first swallows of the proletariat's revolutionary initiative'.[2] In the Museum of the October Revolution in Leningrad stands a glass-cased machine which Lenin used on many occasions after his return to Russia in April. It is a Roneo duplicator, on which he reproduced many of his proclamations and letters for distribution in the form of leaflets.

The film and the theatre were two potential instruments of propaganda which lay ready to hand in 1917. Russia's European cities were well provided with theatres. At the turn of the century she had given the world Stanislavsky, one of the most brilliant producers of all time. By 1917 Russia also had a thriving cinema industry. About five hundred films were made a year and shown in 1,045 cinemas through the country.[3] But when the revolution came, events were too fast-moving to allow any party the time to harness the theatre or the film industry to its propaganda campaign. In the more leisurely

[1] Pares, op. cit., p. 423.
[2] Lenin, op. cit., vol. 9, p. 82. Quoted in E. S. Petropovlovsky, *Listovki kak istochnik pri izuchenii istorii KPSS* (Moscow, 1966) p. 7.
[3] See N. A. Lebedev, *Ocherk istorii Kino SSSR* (Moscow, 1947) pp. 33–5. and T. Dickinson and C. De La Roche, *Soviet Cinema* (London, 1948) pp. 9–11.

French revolution the stage was often used by the Jacobins as a platform for their political views. Free tickets were distributed, and the theatre was wielded as 'a school of morals and a burning hearth where souls can constantly be retempered in republicanism'.[1] As for the cinema, Lenin had prophesied in 1907: 'When the masses take possession of the film and it comes into the hands of true supporters of socialist culture, it will become one of the most powerful means of educating the masses.'[2] As an instrument of mass propaganda, the Soviet cinema eventually came into its own after 1917 under the directing genius of Eisenstein.

THE TARGETS OF PROPAGANDA: THE ARMY

Since it would be impossible within the scope of this essay to cover all those areas of Russian society that were the main targets of political propaganda in 1917, two only have been selected for closer study, the Army and the peasants.

A general point should be made at the outset. In the Russian revolution the instruments of propaganda were many and varied: the sheer output of material was prodigious by any standards. As in nature, however, a great number of seeds carried on the wind never reached their target. This element of wastefulness in all propaganda is summed up beautifully in the New Testament parable of the sower. Russia was no exception. There were many sowers in competition with each other, and the ground was often stony. No one realised this better than Lenin. When his Decree on Land was distributed to soldiers after the October coup so that they would act as unpaid carriers of propaganda on their way back to the villages, Lenin is supposed to have ordered that they each be given an old calendar as well. This was intended to deter them from using the decree copies as cigarette papers – the calendars would do just as well.[3]

Many different propaganda agents were at work in the ranks of the Army. Just before the February revolution even the Tsarist

---

[1] Quoted in C. Brinton, *The Jacobins* (New York, 1961) p. 82.

[2] *Lenin, Stalin, partiia o kino* (Moscow, 1938) pp. 7–8.

[3] V. D. Bronch-Bruevich, *Na boevykh postakh fevral'skoi i oktiabr'skoi revoliutsii* (Moscow, 1931) p. 115.

Minister of War was roused to take vigorous measures to step up governmental activity. He was frightened into it by an anonymous circularised 'letter' from the front giving sophisticated proposals on how the military should organise the approaching revolution. Commanding officers were therefore ordered to conduct propaganda talks with their junior officers and N.C.O.s, while Army priests were given a list of suitable themes for inclusion in their sermons to all ranks.[1] It was far too late. On 19 February the commander of the northern front observed that 'soldiers are beginning to feel the effects of the collapse in the rear', and went on to stress that the food supply and the chaos on the railways were most to blame for the dissension spreading amongst the ranks.[2] This silent propaganda was much more telling than the eloquence of Tsarist agents.

Foreign powers were also involved in the propaganda campaign both before and after the February revolution. The Allies were determined that Russia should remain a strong military force on Germany's eastern front, whatever changes occurred in her domestic political situation. Britain and France frequently applied pressure on the Tsarist and Provisional Governments, though it was done in a very clumsy way.[3] Propaganda at the lower levels among the Russian population was handled even worse. Apart from a few film shows at the British Embassy about the Allied war effort on Germany's western front, British activities centred on the propaganda office in Petrograd as described by Hugh Walpole, who was employed there:

I went up in the lift to the Propaganda office and found it a very nice airy place, clean and smart, with coloured advertisements by Shepperson and others on the walls, pictures of Hampstead and St Albans and Kew Gardens that looked strangely satisfactory and homely to me, and rather touching and innocent. There were several young women clicking away at typewriters, and maps of the Western Front, and a colossal toy map of the London Tube, and a nice English

[1] *Krasnyi arkhiv*, vol. 17, pp. 38–44.
[2] Ibid., p. 49.
[3] For a full treatment of this subject, see the excellent book by R. D. Warth, *The Allies and the Russian Revolution: From the Fall of the Monarchy to the Treaty of Brest-Litovsk* (Durham, N.C., 1954).

library with all the best books from Chaucer to D. H. Lawrence and from the Religio Medici to E. V. Lucas's *London*.

Everything seemed clean and simple and a little deserted, as though the heart of the Russian public had not, as yet, quite found its way there. I think: 'guileless' was the adjective that came to my mind, and certainly Burrows, the head of the place – a large, red-faced, smiling man with glasses – seemed to me altogether too cheerful and pleased with life to penetrate the wicked recesses of Russian pessimism'.[1]

This little bit of Kensington in Barbary 'later developed under Hugh's influence into something grievously like a joke'.[2] Colonel Robins, an American who saw rather more of the Russian front lines in 1917, reported back to an investigating committee of the Senate:

The Allied propaganda at that hour, Senator Overman, was this: pictures and written words about how great France is, how tremendous England is, how overwhelming America is. 'We will have 20,000 airplanes on the front in a few weeks. In a few months we will have 4,000,000 soldiers. We will win the war in a walk.' The peasant moujik said: 'Oh, is that so? Well, if the Allies are going to win the war in a walk, we who have been fighting and working a long time will go back and see the folks at home'; and the real effect of the Allied propaganda was to weaken the morale instead of strengthening it, if I am any judge of the facts'.[3]

German propaganda was undoubtedly more effective in Russia than Allied bungling. This was mainly due to the fact that the Germans were trying to break down the morale of the Russian soldier rather than to build it up, and it was a much easier task to achieve, given the terrible conditions in which the Russians fought. Also the German aim coincided with that of the Bolsheviks in their role as 'defeatists' and internationalists. This proved to be a dynamic combination. Germany

[1] Quoted in R. Hart-Davis, *Hugh Walpole, A Biography* (London, 1952) p. 156.
[2] Ibid., p. 152.
[3] Quoted in H. D. Lasswell, *Propaganda Technique in the World War* (London, 1938) p. 120.

supplied money through indirect channels for Bolshevik propaganda. The funds were large, as has already been seen.[1] Money came from other sources for other purposes, though admittedly on a lesser scale. A single individual, Colonel W. B. Thompson of the American Red Cross, spent a million dollars of his own money in an effort to stave off the defection of Russia.[2] All German propaganda in Russia had to be indirect as long as the war continued. Besides sending funds through Denmark and Sweden, Germany also realised the value of helping 'defeatist' Russian revolutionaries to return to their own country. As a result, Lenin and a number of less important figures were dispatched like a 'plague bacillus' sent to infect Russia, as Winston Churchill put it.[3]

The Provisional Government fared little better than the Allies in their shared aim of boosting the Army's morale. The task was difficult in itself, and the Provisional Government did not improve the situation by its slow and maladroit methods. Time and again in 1917 we find officers at the front telegraphing to Petrograd for Provisional Government commissars to come, not in order to start a propaganda campaign of their own, but to counteract earlier, more successful Bolshevik propaganda in the trenches.[4] The position was no better in Petrograd itself. The advice given by a government official to the commander of the troops in the capital on how to address crowds was entirely defensive, and irresponsible as well:

Remember the advice I gave you all at the beginning of the revolution: never argue in front of a crowd. If there is a Bolshevik speaker, he will always have the better of you

[1] Cf. p. 120 above. More information on this may be found in Z. A. B. Zeman (ed.), *Germany and the Revolution in Russia, 1915–1918* (London, 1958) esp. pp. 4, 16–18, 75, 93.

[2] Lasswell, op. cit., p. 122.

[3] German intentions were kept secret at the time, but are now revealed in the published archives of the German Foreign Office. A German agent in Copenhagen commented on the successful dispatch of Sasonov, another Russian 'defeatist': 'Am 26 d.M. [March 1917] sind unter anderen auch Sasonov und seine treue Gehilfin, Frau Rubinstein nach Russland abgereist. Sasonov glaubt, dass ihn seine Partei hauptsächlich diese Rolle zugedacht ist, so ware dass fur uns ein grossen Gewinn.' Letter in the German Foreign Office Archives, L.831/L243062.

[4] For one of many instances, see *Krasnyi arkhiv*, vol. 58, p. 51.

because he can offer the crowd things which you cannot offer, so he will always be more popular. Don't argue, but find a way of rendering your opponent ridiculous. If you say that you agree with all he is saying, but that you would like to know why he has not returned to you the five roubles he borrowed from you last week, the crowd will laugh, and the effect of his speech will be nil; so don't forget the five-rouble stunt. It is, of course, better still to ask the orator why his wife is unfaithful to such a clever fellow. That will ruin him for a long time. Make him look ridiculous anyhow'.[1]

Ironically enough, right-wing elements in the Provisional Government and outside it served only to weaken the propaganda campaign when in the summer of 1917 they attempted to buttress its main aim of keeping morale high among the troops. These elements were headed by Kornilov for the military, and the members of the civilian Society for the Economic Rehabilitation of Russia. Amongst the Society's leaders were A. Putilov, the owner of the famous Putilov works in the capital, and A. I. Guchkov, who had been Minister of War until May. Putilov later stated that even in the early days of the Society, four million roubles were raised. 'As is well known', Putilov said, 'one cannot conduct propaganda without money.'[2] Early in August Kornilov and General Denikin, the new commander of the south-western front, decided to take new measures in order to restore morale in the Army. According to Kerensky, 'Their policy toward the commissars and Army committees [the propaganda organs of the Provisional Government] changed abruptly. Commanders who considered a collaboration with their organisations necessary were given the cold shoulder and were replaced by die-hard advocates of the former regime.' This naturally cut off the officer corps from their political advisors, and antagonised further the other ranks, who by this time could scarcely tolerate liberal officers, let

---

[1] Polovtsov, op. cit., p. 195.

[2] *Posledniia novosti* (Paris) 20 Jan. 1937. This right wing did not put its funds to such good use as the Bolsheviks. We know from the German archives that the Bolsheviks overspent their German funds (see Zeman, op. cit., pp. 16-18), but 2·7 million roubles of the Society's four million were not spent, and were lost in the process of the nationalisation of the banks by the Soviets (see *Posledniia novosti*, 24 Jan. 1937).

alone right-wing ones. Kerensky goes on to assert that 'the campaign against the elected Army organisations and commissars was waged – and I know this for a fact – by those very officers' organisations and groups which shortly after became the nucleus of the military conspiracy [the Kornilov affair]'.[1]

In the Soviet period the Bolsheviks were to copy the system of political commissars attached to leading military units. This system was first set up by the Petrograd Soviet on 19 March, and taken over by the Provisional Government after Kerensky's appointment as Minister of War in May. On 16 April Kerensky's predecessor, Guchkov, introduced elected Army committees and disciplinary courts, 'guaranteeing every soldier the exercise of his civil and political rights'.[2] Some of them were later to turn sour on Kerensky, as the soldiers veered further to the left wing. In addition the Provisional Government set up commissions to settle disputes between officers and men, and Army schools to tackle the illiteracy problem in the ranks and to inculcate political propaganda at the same time. Finally in September Kerensky proposed that central government departments should form commissions which would investigate conditions at the front, report back to Petrograd and then help to put through military reforms.[3] All in vain. By September such cumbersome methods were doomed to failure before they got off the ground. Bolshevik propaganda was sweeping everything before it.

The Bolshevik Military Organisation in Petrograd worked in close liaison with *Pravda* and edited *Soldatskaia pravda*, trying to co-ordinate propaganda disseminated in the Army. It kept in touch with the front by sending out special commissions to investigate complaints. In this way the Bolsheviks undermined the official military authorities, and the soldiers learnt to look to them rather than to their local committees to settle their disputes. The agents of high-level Bolshevik propaganda were relatively thin on the ground at the front, especially in the spring of 1917. After all, there were only about 30,000 members of the Bolshevik party as a whole in February, though the figure rose to about 76,000 in April. But the military authorities ob-

---

[1] *The Kerensky Memoirs*, p. 297.
[2] *Vestnik vremonnogo pravitel'stva*, 20 Apr. 1917.
[3] *Krasnvi arkhiv*, vol. 60, p. 154.

served that in extremist propaganda compaigns 'a small group forms the energetic and active part'.[1] The quality of Bolshevik agents was certainly far higher than those of the Provisional Government, or of the S.R.s or Mensheviks. Names that were later to become famous were on the Bolshevik lists. K. Voroshilov was working in Lugansk, M. Frunze was on the western front, and L. Kaganovich in Saratov. Helpers were few, but they were carefully placed at the nerve centres of the body military. At a conference of the Petrograd Bolsheviks in the early days of October, Lenin directed agitators to all the most important naval and Army centres near the capital, in order to prepare them for the possibility of a quick general uprising against the Provisional Government. Men were sent out to the fleet at Helsingfors, Kronstadt, Reval, and to military units to the south and west of Petrograd.[2]

The content of Bolshevik propaganda was of course easier to instil into the military than Kerensky's propaganda because the Bolsheviks' 'defeatist' ideas more often than not coincided with the soldiers' own feelings. Also in the anarchical mood prevalent in the revolution it was simpler to promote ideas designed to shake the existing regime rather than to mobilise the Army for organised action of any kind. One of the chief flaws in the propaganda of the Provisional Government and the Allies was that it rarely filtered down below the level of the N.C.O. The Bolsheviks, on the other hand, generally ignored the military authorities and burrowed underneath them, applying their energetic tactics to the lowest ranks. Here were the men who suffered most from the war and were more likely to adopt a defeatist attitude. Without them the war could not go on. Some of them could be relied on to act as amateur propaganda agents for the professional Bolsheviks, who were already overworked.

One of the most effective ways of contacting soldiers of this kind was through the many Army congresses that were called in 1917. Guchkov and Kerensky gave long, emotional speeches at the first congress of delegates from the front held at the end of April. Again, on 1 June, Kerensky returned specially to Petrograd for the All-Russian Congress of Soviet and Front

---

[1] Ibid., p. 153.
[2] Mel'gunov, op. cit., p. 19.

Line Organisations which opened on 3 June. His aim was to gain support from the lower ranks for the Russian military offensive which was to begin on 18 June. There were 822 voting delegates at the Congress, of whom only 105 were Bolsheviks, but in the event over 200 delegates opposed the renewal of hostilities at the front, since the Menshevik Internationalists and the left-wing Socialist Revolutionaries supported the Bolsheviks. Lenin prevented the Congress from functioning normally by staging a demonstration of soldiers and workers shouting 'Down with the ten capitalist ministers'.[1] A few days later the Bolsheviks opened their own military conference in the capital. Its members represented forty-three Bolshevik organisations at the front and seventeen from the rear. Between them these organisations were spreading propaganda among 500 regiments in the line and thirty city garrisons.[2] Reverberations from this conference were felt all along the Russian fronts when delegates returned to the trenches with fresh propaganda methods and news items from Petrograd.[3] Large meetings of this kind were frequently held in Petrograd and behind each front, but there was also a daily traffic to the capital by individual soldiers or by small groups. A Soviet scholar has estimated that the Bolshevik Military Organisation received over 300 delegates a day from units in the active Army.[4]

Two general orders issued by the Petrograd Soviet probably had a more shattering effect on morale at the front and the spread of propaganda amongst the rank-and-file than all the wiles of Bolshevik agents. On 1 March Order No. 1 provided for the establishment of 'committees from the elected representatives of the lower ranks' in military units. Arms of every kind were to be kept at the disposal of the committees and not handed over to the officers; saluting off duty was abolished. The effect was immediate, as the Supreme Commander complained to the Minister of War in a telegram of 5 March:

Unless the Government issues in all haste to the troops under military command an unequivocal and convincing appeal

[1] *The Kerensky Memoirs*, pp. 283-4.   [2] *Krasnyi arkhiv*, vol. 84, p. 136.
[3] For an example of this on the distant Rumanian front, see *Krasnyi arkhiv*, vol. 58, p. 88.
[4] E. Erykalov, *Krasnaia gvardiia v bor'be za vlast' sovetov* (Moscow, 1957) p. 19.

for order, and unless it provides for the cessation of the occurrences taking place in the rear of the armies . . . the commanders-in-chief cannot vouch for the maintenance of order and discipline; this situation would unfailingly result in defeat. Literally speaking, every moment lost threatens a fatal catastrophe. For the good of the cause, any modification of the existing rules and military regulations made within the Army other than by the Supreme Commander and without his consent, is inadmissible.[1]

This warning was not heeded. Under strong pressure from the left wing, Kerensky later published Order No. 8, issued by the Soviet, on the rights of servicemen. Guchkov, the Minister of War prior to Kerensky, had refused to pass it. Item 3 read as follows: 'Every serviceman when off duty has the right freely and openly to express or profess orally, in a written or printed form, his political, religious, social and other opinions.'[2] The door for propaganda was wide open.

The combined effect of these orders, Bolshevik propaganda and the breakdown of supplies was catastrophic. Dissension and extremist political views spread like a forest fire along Russia's protracted fronts, stretching on her western flank from the Baltic to the Black Sea. By early summer the soldiers were waging their own crude propaganda campaigns, carrying the infection from one sector of the front to another. Five hundred men and one officer on the northern front took it into their heads to march over to the trenches of a neighbouring division waving a large placard bearing the slogan 'Down with the offensive!'[3] Other units proceeded in a more organised manner, formally electing agitators to go round adjoining areas.[4] Reserve units in the rear had more leisure to embark on long-term projects. The committee of the 3rd Infantry Reserve Regiment procured 55,000 roubles for setting up its own printing press. The 1st Machine Gun Reserve Regiment, which played a prominent role in the attempted July uprising in Petrograd, took 10,000 roubles from regimental funds in order to build up its library with suitable political literature.[5]

[1] *Krasnyi arkhiv*, vol. 5, p. 227.
[2] *Vestnik vremennogo pravitel'stva*, 14 May 1917, p. 1.
[3] *Krasnyi arkhiv*, vol. 58, p. 90.
[4] Ibid., p. 91.   [5] Ibid., vol. 60, p. 154.

The greatest propaganda travellers were the sailors. The receptive audience that Il'in-Genevsky discovered at Helsingfors when he went there in March to establish the Bolshevik press was soon providing money for sailors to go inland from the Baltic ports to the nearby fronts. After bombarding the soldiers with defeatist telegrams, the Central Committee of the Baltic Fleet sent many delegations to other war centres, some of them as far away as the Black Sea ports. Sailors on leave were encouraged to act as voluntary agitators among their military colleagues.[1]

The results of Bolshevik propaganda were not spread evenly over all the fronts. The northern and western fronts were the most affected. They were the closest to the extremist influences of Petrograd and the Baltic Fleet, and bore the brunt of the German war effort. In the elections for the Constituent Assembly after the October Coup, the Bolsheviks received over a million votes on these two fronts, whereas the S.R.s, who beat their rivals in the country as a whole, only got 420,000 votes.[2] The least affected front was in the Caucasus, opposing the Turks. It was a long way from the centres of Bolshevik influence, but near to 'defensist' Menshevik strongholds. In September only the Caucasus of all the fronts was found to be in a condition fit for fighting.[3] The débâcle of the Russian Army was complete. The role of Bolshevik propaganda was important in the breakdown of the Army, but it was nevertheless/ a subsidiary role. The disruption of supplies and the mismanaged war were more effective in reducing the morale of the soldiers. What was far more important was the fact that by the time of the October coup the Bolsheviks were able to carry through their decisive struggle for power in Petrograd and Moscow with little fear of hostile obstruction by the great majority of military units at the front. In the short space of eight months Lenin's propaganda campaign could not hope to achieve its ultimate aim of winning over the Army so that it could be used as a Bolshevik instrument of coercion; but it succeeded in neutralising the military to such a degree that Petrograd could be taken in October by a minute and mainly

[1] *Protokoly i postanovlenii tsentral'nogo komiteta baltiiskogo flota, 1917–1918,* ed. D. A. Chugaeva (Moscow, 1963) pp. 9, 23, 77.
[2] *Krasnyi arkhiv,* vol. 84, p. 137.   [3] Ibid., p. 166.

amateur force, concentrating on the control of communications. The Army was scarcely involved.

THE PEASANTS

Bolshevik propaganda met with less success among the peasantry. The peasants' traditional champion among the revolutionary parties, the S.R.s, gained 410 seats out of a total of 707 in the Constituent Assembly. The Bolsheviks won only 175. In the nation-wide voting, the influence of the submerged rural population was bound to tell. Before 1917 the Bolsheviks had devoted most of their energy to the working class in the cities of European Russia, whereas the S.R.s over a longer period had built up large followings in the rural areas. During the revolution Lenin skilfully adopted many of the details in the S.R.s' agrarian programme, and appealed to the peasantry by constantly repeating that they should seize the land, and ignore their mortgages and the slow-moving reforms proposed by the Provisional Government. But this did not allow the Bolsheviks to wrest control from the S.R.s on a sufficiently wide basis.

There was another factor which checked all political propaganda – the peasants' ignorance and backwardness. When parish committees were set up in the rural areas after February, the agents of the Provisional Government were appalled by reactionary attitudes in the countryside. 'The results of some of the elections were staggering. For instance, in one of the sub-districts of the Smolensk guberniia, the committee was composed of such incongruous members as two uncompromising monarchists; the local psalm-reader, who instigated the peasants to extortions and violence; and a dissipated squire, now an innkeeper, a man without honour or convictions.'[1]

Hopes for the political future of Russia, symbolised by the Constituent Assembly, were no brighter.

Generally speaking, the peasants have no ideas concerning the Constituent Assembly; in some villages its existence is unknown, notably to the women. The peasants do not discuss political questions with them, with the result that a large proportion of the rural inhabitants know absolutely nothing

[1] *Report of the Provincial Section attached to the Provisional Committee of the State Duma*, quoted in Vulliamy, op. cit., p. 243.

as to their future. The peasantry have formed absolutely no opinion of their own about the Constituent Assembly; that is a fact which must be taken into consideration. Intensive and urgent instruction is required to cope with this problem, not by means of pamphlets, which the people, who are almost entirely illiterate, do not understand, but by word of mouth, meetings and discourses. The peasant can follow an argument only when he himself takes part in it by asking questions; never when he is listening to an impersonal oration. He himself, Petr, Ivan, Sidor, must be addressed in person'.[1]

This extract points up the importance of oratory as a weapon of propaganda among the peasants. It also helps us to understand why Lenin watered down the intellectual content of Bolshevik propaganda so drastically in 1917. This technique held dangers for the future, because the less palatable or difficult aspects of the party's agrarian programme were shelved in 1917. When they were brought to light in the Soviet period, they were not to the taste of the peasants, who resisted them stubbornly.

Another reason for the weakness of Bolshevik propaganda in the countryside was the enormous size of Russia compared with the relatively small number of party activists, particularly in the rural districts. The proletariat and the Army, the other two main targets of Bolshevik propaganda, were concentrated within much smaller areas, and Lenin skilfully placed his men at key points in them. No such points existed on the immense rolling steppes of Mother Russia. The February revolution coincided with the season of spring floods in the European part of the country, when the universal mud slowed up all forms of transport except for the railways. The state of the transport network throughout 1917 needs no further comment, though this cry from the heart by a woman delegate in the Nizhnii-Novgorod guberniia may serve as an epitaph: 'The means of communication are appalling, there is not a horse available for hire – they are all out on field work. We are obliged to walk from village to village, carrying stacks of books and newspapers. . . .'[2]

Since the Bolsheviks were lacking in recruits from the

[1] Ibid., p. 237.   [2] Ibid., p. 264.

peasantry, they tried to compensate for this by using peasants in soldiers' uniforms and workingmen's clothes as their propaganda agents in the countryside. Uprooted peasants formed the backbone of the Tsarist Army. It has been estimated that in fifty Russian guberniias 47·4 per cent of all able-bodied men, the great majority of them peasants, were recruited for the war.[1] At the front the peasants were subjected to physical hardship and political propaganda. A few of them learnt to think for themselves in 1917. When they went home on leave, or defected as the year wore on, they acted both consciously and accidentally as agents of extreme social and political views which often coincided with those of the Bolsheviks. Their influence had a galvanising effect in the villages, since a 'community's traditional elders tend to lose much of their pre-eminence to individuals whose position allows them to act as pipelines to the great world outside – provided that they have not become alienated from the local community'.[2]

Lenin made good use of the ties between the Army and the peasantry. He urged: 'In order that the peasants in the localities can take all the land from the landowners at once . . . it is necessary for the soldiers to help the peasants.'[3] Wherever it could be engineered, Bolshevik activists at the fronts and in the Navy organised the dispatch of agitators. In September the Bolshevik committee in Helsingfors sent out a hundred agitators to rural areas: two were sent to each guberniia with an allowance of ten roubles a day donated by the sailors. Before setting out, the volunteers were subjected to a course of three lectures in the party programme.[4] The results of these techniques could be impressive. Saratov on the Volga had been one of the prime centres of S.R. influence before 1917, but before October the Bolsheviks won a lead over their rivals, chiefly owing to the activities of soldiers back from the front lines.[5] On other occasions agitators had a rough reception, as in the case of a Bolshevik sailor who reported that 'the peasants wrote

[1] P. I. Liashchenko, *Istoriia narodnogo khoziaistva SSSR*, vol. II (Moscow, 1948) p. 643.

[2] W. Schramm (ed.), *The Science of Human Communication* (New York, 1963) p. 100.   [3] Lenin, *Sochineniia*, 2nd ed., vol. 20, p. 171.

[4] *Perepiska . . .*, vol. I, p. 187.

[5] O. Radkey, *The Sickle under the Hammer: The Russian Socialist Revolutionaries in the Early Months of Soviet Rule* (New York, 1963), pp. 268, 270, 273, 278.

to the public prosecutor saying that I was engaged in blasphemy and Bolshevik propaganda'. The prosecutor sent out six men to arrest him.[1]

The Bolsheviks used city workers as agitators among the peasants, in the same way as they used the soldiers and sailors. Social conditions in Russian industry in 1917 were in some respects reminiscent of the situation prevailing in England during the late eighteenth and early nineteenth centuries, when large numbers of peasants were being drafted into the industrial towns. Even as late as 1917 many of those who worked in the city factories of Russia had not been born in the urban areas, and if they had, they usually inherited peasant traditions from their parents. Shortly after the turn of the century 70 per cent of all factory workers were employed away from the main centres of population.[2] In 1917 many factory workers returned to their villages for part of the year, usually to help at harvest time, as they had done in previous years.

The Bolsheviks seized upon these useful contacts and developed them to their own advantage. Factory workers converted to their cause were sent to the country in considerable numbers, particularly from Petrograd and Moscow. The Secretariat of the Bolshevik Central Committee supervised a large part of the activities, often working through the *zemliachestva*. These were societies of individuals hailing originally from the same rural areas as each other. Workers from the giant Putilov factory, always to the fore in matters of self-organisation during 1917, first organised themselves into new societies of this kind in the middle of the year. In the second half of the year twenty guberniia societies and thirty-three based on the smaller administrative area of the *uezd* were formed; nineteen others were established at the *volost* level.[3] These societies had their own Bolshevik fractions which fought tooth and nail for better representation.[4] Altogether the *zemliachestva* were

[1] *Golos pravdy*, 29 Nov. 1917.

[2] T. von Laue, 'Russian Peasants in the Factory 1892–1904', *Journal of Economic History* (1961) p. 212. This article gives a balanced estimate of the ties between the peasantry and the factory workers.

[3] A. G. Egorova, *Profsoiuzy i fabzavkomy v bor'be za pobeda Oktiabria* (Moscow, 1960) p. 183.

[4] T. Trenogova, *Bor'ba petrogradskikh bol'shevikov za khrestianstvo v 1917 g.* (Leningrad, 1946) p. 82.

thought to include over 30,000 workers.¹ They took up a wide
variety of activities. In their desire to show their unity with the
peasantry, some of the left-wing ones turned away from armaments production, once they had got rid of their managers, and
made agricultural machinery instead. This they sent off to their
local areas as a sign of their fraternity and of their rejection
of the war. In the words of the steelworkers' press organ,
'Each plough sent by a worker's committee not only turns
over the peasant's land, it loosens the ground for sowing the
idea of socialism in the heart and consciousness of the village
toiler'.²

The societies sent out circular letters to their local contacts,
urging the need for political agitation. They were helped in the
campaign to bombard the provinces with literature by the
central Bolshevik military organisations. Between 24 March
and 15 June alone, the Moscow bureau dispatched about
400,000 leaflets, newspapers and books to the villages and to
the front.³ The Secretariat of the Bolshevik Central Committee
in Petrograd acted as the supreme co-ordinating office. To it
were addressed the bulk of letters from the country, demanding
help of all kinds. Here is a typical exchange of letters:

15 October 1917
. . . First of all we send you our warm greetings and wish you
all the best. . . . At the present time we are in the Nevel'sk
district of the Vitebsk guberniia and are conducting propaganda campaigns in the sub-districts of Kubetsk, Dalyssk,
Trekhalevsk and Rykshinsk, where the peasants formed a
good impression of our Bolshevik party. These peasants asked
us to collaborate with them as closely as possible to get the
'leading figures' – the Kadets, the 'defensists' and the S.R.s
out of their positions in the guberniia, the districts, and on
the sub-district zemstvos. So we urgently ask you to send
party helpers to the guberniias, the districts and district
zemstvos – Our heartfelt thanks for the copies of *Rabochii
put'*. We received five numbers free of charge, thanks to

¹ *Velikaia oktiabr'skaia sotsialisticheskaia revoliutsiia-khronika sobytiia*, vol. 1
(Moscow, 1957) p. 632.
² *Moskovskii metallist*, 1 Oct. 1917.
³ Egorova, op. cit., p. 180.

your cooperation. Till we meet again. We're waiting for
your reply.

With respect,
Fedorev the sailor, and Repinsky, agitators
from the 'Skorokhod' factory

20 October 1917
Dear Comrade

Thank you very much for your letter to hand concerning
your business in the Vitebsk guberniia. You ask us to send
agitators to the guberniias, districts and sub-districts of
Russia. Every day comrades from different factories and
plants come to us and then travel to all parts of Russia. We
are sending to them and to you *Derevenskaia bednota* (*Village
Poverty*), a newspaper that has just come out, and we hope
that it suits you. We would like to make you regular subscribers, but we have very little money, and the demand for
this paper and other literature is great, so great in fact that
we cannot satisfy it.

With comradely greetings,
The Secretary of the Central Committee[1]

The *zemliachestva* societies kept a strict control over their
agents in the countryside, and the societies in turn were carefully supervised by the Bolsheviks, as this advice from the
Kronstadt Soviet shows: 'If an agent turns out to be incapable
or inactive ... the *zemliachestva* must recall him at once and
substitute another in his place.'[2] The routine work of an
agent of this kind often got him into difficulties. An agitator
from the Putilov factory who went to a grain-growing area of
Belorussia near his original home began by stirring up discontent among the peasants, but this incurred the anger of the
landowner, who got the local civil servants on to his side. So
the agitator with the help of a sailor went to a food-supply
committee, intercepted peasants who arrived with sacks in the
hope of getting grain, and encouraged them to raid the landowner's supplies instead. Then in another meeting he repeated
the gist of a speech he had heard Lenin give against the war.
The landowner appeared and announced that Lenin was a

[1] *Perepiska* ..., vol. 1, pp. 367–8, 385–6.
[2] *Izvestiia kronshtadtskogo soveta*, 8 June 1917.

German spy, and that he had been arrested. The rich peasants and the miller supported the landowner, but they were shouted down by the agitators with the help of the poorer peasants.[1]

Bolshevik methods were more often than not unscrupulous, but they were clearly making inroads into peasant apathy and ignorance by the time of the October coup. In most revolutions in history, political factions initially have found it difficult to stir up the peasantry. The Jacobins tried to do it in the French revolution by adopting a paternalistic attitude and planting symbolic 'Trees of Liberty'.[2] At least the Bolsheviks probed deeper than that. Once roused, however, both the French peasant and the Russian *muzhik* raged wildly, with an extremism that chilled the most hardened revolutionaries.

POLITICAL RUMOURS

The peasant *jacqueries* that broke out in Russia with increasing violence after the spring of 1917 are a good example of those social disturbances in the revolution which were only partly instigated by political propaganda, and were not regulated by it once they had been unleashed. So far our attention has been concentrated on the deliberate propagation of ideas and information by political agents; but it must not be thought that when propaganda did sink in, it always had the desired effect on the public mind. More often than not it was adopted in a garbled form, and had repercussions unforeseen by those who had promulgated the original ideas.

Rumours of every conceivable kind were spread about during the Russian revolution. Given the frequent lack of more reliable political information, rumours provided a substitute. They were already rife before February, when the Tsarist censorship was an additional obstruction to the circulation of news. Trotsky describes its effects in November 1916, when the Duma met for the last time. 'The Government was almost without defenders. It answered in its usual way: the speeches of the Duma orators were forbidden publication. The speeches therefore circulated by the million. There was not a government department, not only in the rear but at the front, where

---

[1] *V bor'be za oktiabr' v Belorussii* (Moscow, 1957) pp. 146–9.
[2] Brinton, op. cit., pp. 83–4.

the forbidden speeches were not transcribed – frequently with additions corresponding to the temperament of the transcriber.'[1]

Lack of information leads to wild speculation and fear. 'Your electric telegraph is a great alleviator of anxiety', as Joseph Conrad put it. Private individuals at the centre of affairs, let alone the rural millions of Russia, were cut off from accurate news. The poet Alexander Blok, who lived in the capital, comments in many places in his diary for 1917 on the number of rumours flying round the city. He also observed that his correspondence was delayed considerably in the post, so that direct information from the provinces was slowed down.[2]

The nervous mood of the population contributed to the prevalence of rumours. The mismanaged war and the revolution which followed it created an atmosphere which bordered on panic in some quarters. The very real threat to people's means of subsistence, their property (if they had any) and their lives awoke fears that were only too often substantiated. Commenting on food riots in August, a leading newspaper observed: 'Intense discontent, irritability, heightened nervousness, and suspicion are favourable psychological ground for all sorts of rumours, and the mob falls under the power of irresponsible agitators who conduct all sorts of violent agitation against the Jews, against the bourgeoisie, and against the intelligentsia.'[3]

In times of great trouble men's sense of balance leaves them, and they run to a strange kind of apocalyptic optimism. Many political rumours were founded on such optimism in 1917. Just after the February revolution there was a widespread notion that a similar revolution had taken place in Berlin and that the Kaiser had been deposed.[4] In the July Days sections of the Petrograd population were convinced that the Soviet had taken sole governmental power into its hands.[5] Some untruthful rumours were knowingly planted by the authorities in an effort to pin the blame for catastrophe on someone other than themselves. All the political parties indulged in this, and the military were not exempt from it either. When the enemy broke through

[1] Trotsky, op. cit., p. 27.
[2] Alexander Blok, *Sobranie sochinenii*, vol. 7 (Moscow, 1963) pp. 265, 275, 283.   [3] *Russkiia vedomosti*, 24 Aug. 1917.
[4] For an example of this, see Sukhanov, op. cit., p. 151.
[5] *Russkiia vedomosti*, 4 July 1917.

on Russia's south-western front in July, the official commiqué from staff headquarters blamed the defeat on the influence of subversive Bolshevik propaganda. The truth was that several hundred enemy field-guns triumphed over six Russian guns.[1]

In the chaotic conditions brought on by the war and the revolution, it was very hard for persons in authority to perceive the truth. It was even more difficult for the common mass of humanity caught up in the political whirlwind. Unable to analyse the cause of their hardship, men took to blaming a whole sector of the community, and invented rumours to back up their vain notions. Stereotyped views of what was happening went to ludicrous extremes. In the trenches everything was blamed on 'treason'. 'People whispered it or roared it at the tops of their voices, but everyone repeated it, from transport soldiers to generals. Even the wounded, asked how they got their wounds, shouted angrily: 'Treason!'[2]

Another reason for false rumours were the garbled interpretations put on propaganda handed out by the politically educated, and distorted into all kinds of nonsense, like this gem picked up by Bernard Pares:

Any day the streets would bubble up into little group meetings. These would become larger and larger until there was some kind of an explosion; then there would be a lull, and it would begin over again. Politically speaking, one could tell the temperature each day by walking down the Nevsky; even the staff of our Anglo-Russian Hospital, who did not know any Russian, could gauge the political weather pretty accurately. Most of these groups were very simple and primitive. You would stop to listen, and you would hear a muzzy-looking man dreamily denouncing something, and be quite unable to see what he was after. Then perhaps you would understand and smile and pass on. Here was an orator demanding immediate peace 'Bez aneksiy i contributsiy', which really meant 'Without annexations and contributions', but neither of these were Russian words: and the speaker himself imagined that 'Aneksia' was an extra daughter of Nicholas II, who on no account should be allowed to come to the throne, and that 'Contributsia' was a town in the

---

[1] *The Kerensky Memoirs*, pp. 293–4.   [2] Paustovsky, op. cit., p. 132.

Archangel Government (probably Murmansk), seized by the English, which they could not be allowed to retain'.[1]

The power of rumour was such that lies about Rasputin and the Empress were well known in the furthest corners of Russia, where serious items of correct news rarely penetrated. How did rumours spread in 1917? In his analysis of *La grande peur* in the French revolution, G. Lefebvre found that there were specific centres from which rumours and panic radiated. The Ottoman Sultans well knew how to stamp out rumours: when dangerous ones were abroad, they closed the coffee houses and the public baths in Constantinople. In Petrograd rumours spread in those places where different elements of the population came together and exchanged information. Blok noticed that the rough-and-ready refreshment buffets outside the meeting hall of the Soviet were places of this kind.[2] Here men from the front gossiped with peasant delegates from the countryside. The countless congresses and conferences held in the capital during 1917 were also excellent generators of rumour, which was carried by returning delegates to the rest of Russia.

Railway stations and compartments served the same function. Travelling into Petrograd from a nearby village in July, the daughter of the man who was hiding Lenin in his flat listened eagerly to the conversation in her carriage, 'The events in Petrograd overshadowed all other interests. People dressed and thought differently and were strangers to each other, but all of them talked and quarrelled about one thing – what was happening in the Capital? "The Bolsheviks, Lenin!" could be heard in several corners of the carriage. "The Bolsheviks have been driven out ... Lenin has fled ... shot. ..." "He's fled, I know for certain. ... He's hiding in the Kronstadt." ... "No, he's been taken out on a minesweeper. ... A chap I know told me himself." '[3]

The most effective carriers of rumour to the depths of provincial Russia were deserters from the Army. In 1917 half a million British soldiers were killed or wounded at Passchendaele, but there was virtually no desertion. Russian peasant

[1] Pares, *My Russian Memoirs*, p. 427.
[2] Blok, op. cit., p. 263.
[3] A. Allilueva, *Memoirs* (London, 1946).

soldiers trekked back to their distant villages over a contiguous land surface, but the English Channel cut off potential British deserters from their homeland. In any case morale was far lower in the Russian Army. By 9 April already it was estimated that up to two thousand deserters were travelling on the south-western railways every day.[1] The civil authorities did not improve matters by allowing soldiers to wear civilian clothes off duty, with the result that they could not be identified, and by being remarkably lenient at first to deserters, letting them off punishment provided they reported for duty by 15 May.

In the same month, however, the Provisional Government issued a special law for keeping deserters off the railways,[2] where they used force to commandeer carriages for their use, and generally behaved in an obstreperous manner. Their arrival in the garrisons of the capital led to a great lowering of morale through their malignant influence. By July the barracks were said to be full of men without proper military documents.[3] The deserters' impact on the rural areas was even greater, as has already been seen with regard to serious political propaganda. More often they spread wild rumours about the state of the war which inflamed the peasants. By midsummer large numbers of deserters were causing trouble as far east as Kazan',[4] and they travelled even further afield than that. Approximately two million of them were dispersed all over Russia by October.

The subject-matter of many rumours was connected with the war. Their political importance was great, not because they were true – they were usually incorrect – but because of the harm they caused to the person or authority involved, and the damage they caused to the confidence of those who listened to them. That is why before the revolution Rasputin's activities in themselves did less damage among the general public to the reputation of Nicholas II and the Empress than the rumours which linked their three names together in all kinds of vile insinuations. After the murder of Rasputin in December 1916, Alexandra's name continued to be dragged through the mud. It was not a scheming commoner but the sister of a Guards

---

[1] According to *Den'*, 9 Apr. 1917.
[2] *Sobranie uzakonenii*, I, 1, no. 711.
[3] Mel'gunov, op. cit., p. 22.
[4] *Krasnyi arkhiv*, vol. 14, p. 215.

officer who spread the well-known rumour that Alexandra was exchanging telegraphed messages with Berlin.[1] According to Baroness Buxhoevden, who took a more sympathetic view, 'Such gossip would never have been listened to for a moment had not the whole country's nerves been strained to such a pitch that nothing seemed too wild to be thought possible. . . .'[2]

The rumour concerning Lenin's links with Germany was just as damaging politically, and was supported by the Provisional Government. Some tongue-waggers even had it that Lenin and Kerensky were really hand in glove, and that both of them were German agents.[3] Other war rumours stopped at nothing. Kaiser Wilhelm expired in March, Lenin fled to Germany in July, Petrograd was going to be bombarded on a huge scale, etc.[4] Perhaps the most alarming aspect was that these panic-stricken notions were believed by well-informed men. In 1917 even Bernard Pares believed that Order No. 1. had really been put out by the Germans at some date prior to the revolution.[5] During the Russian revolution the habit of spreading rumours was trapped in a vicious circle. Anxiety led to rumours, which in turn caused more nervousness. Men adopted extremist opinions and could no longer trust any authority, whether royal, civil or military. The Provisional Government suffered in consequence, being one of the main scapegoats. The Bolsheviks usually tended to profit, since they held no responsibility until October.

[1] E. M. Almedingen, *The Empress Alexandra 1872–1918: A Study* (London, 1961) p. 179.

[2] Baroness S. Buxhoevden, *Life and Tragedy of the Empress Alexandra* (London, 1928) p. 225.

[3] Radkey, op. cit., p. 263.

[4] Mentioned in D. Francis, *From the American Embassy* (New York, 1921) pp. 70–2, Il'in-Genevsky, op. cit., p. 80, and Blok, op. cit., p. 298, respectively.

[5] Pares, op. cit., p. 417.

6 Petrograd and the Provinces

> The great Russian Revolution is bigger, more sublime, and on a wider scale than the Petrograd adventure of the Bolsheviks. Our revolution is a national revolution.
>
> From the Proclamation of the Socialist Revolutionaries of the Right. *Delo naroda*. 28 Oct 1917

Virtually all the major accounts of 1917 in English to date deal almost exclusively with events in Petrograd, paying occasional attention to other parts of European Russia. An admirable exception has been provided by Dr John Keep, who has written a fascinating account of the reception of the October coup in the provinces.[1] In this essay other neglected aspects of the hiatus between the capital and the rest of the country are taken up which refer to the period prior to October. As an introduction to these aspects it would seem useful in the first place to mention some of the well-established considerations on this subject.

Historians of every political hue have tended to equate the Petrograd-centred events with the Russian revolution. Because they were initially successful in Petrograd above all, the Bolsheviks have preferred since 1917 to concentrate on the political course of events in the capital in order to justify their claim to have inherited the cloak of sovereignty from the old regime. Non-Bolshevik Russians writing on the revolution in exile were nearly all related originally to the political and cultural life of Petrograd, or, to a lesser extent, of Moscow.

[1] John Keep, 'October in the Provinces', in R. Pipes (ed.), *Revolutionary Russia* (London, 1968) pp. 180–216.

Non-Russian observers of the vast continent have also until very recently been apt to assume that the northern and western parts of European Russia were the only areas worth including in their accounts. In the same way the eastern states of North America stood so long for the whole of the United States in European eyes.

From its first to its last day, the revolution was centred on Petrograd, yet the capital was not a sensitive barometer of the political climate in the rest of Russia. In February it was probably the nearest to being so, since although the revolution was touched off, organised and completed in Petrograd with scant reference to other areas, at least these activities were welcomed and usually copied throughout the country. Nevertheless Trotsky remarked that the February revolution 'was carried out upon the initiative and by the strength of one city, constituting approximately about 1/75 of the population of the country. You may say, if you will, that this most gigantic democratic act was achieved in a most undemocratic manner. The whole country was placed before a *fait accompli*. . . . This casts a sharp light on the question of the function of democratic forms in general and in a revolutionary epoch in particular.'[1]

In February the Empire acquiesced in the destruction of the old regime. It was easier to agree on how to pull down a political edifice than to construct a new one. By the summer of 1917 left-wing opinion in Petrograd was racing so far ahead of other social and geographical groupings in Russia that even Lenin restrained the attempt at an armed uprising in the capital in July. The time was not ripe, and the July disturbances 'threatened to create an abyss' between the population of Petrograd and the remainder of Russia.[2] By September the Bolsheviks commanded a majority in the Petrograd Soviet, but in the all-Russian elections to the Constituent Assembly which began on 25 November (New Style), the voting gave the Bolsheviks only 175 of the 707 members. 410 of them were Socialist Revolutionaries, who dominated popular opinion in the country as a whole. In the October coup d'état the Bolsheviks abandoned quasi-legal methods of persuading the Dual

---

[1] Trotsky, op. cit., pp. 134–5.
[2] An expression used at the time by the Executive Committee of the Petrograd Soviet. *Krasnyi arkhiv*, vol. XIII, p. 2.

Government in the capital to accept their policies. Instead they resorted to force, applying it to vital points within Petrograd, and at the same time ensuring their control over all forms of communication between Petrograd and the rest of Russia.

During the armed uprising the Bolsheviks claimed that they were not carrying out a coup in one corner of a continent without heeding voices from outside. They declared that they were appealing to and relying on the Second Congress of Soviets, which assembled at the time of the coup and represented the large network of Soviets thrown up by the revolution throughout the country. It is true that more than any other party the Bolsheviks had brought their policies to the notice of a wide public beyond the capital, but their vigorous propaganda campaign had not overcome the S.R.s' lead by October. It so happened that a majority of the delegates to the Second Congress of Soviets who were already present on 25 October were Bolsheviks, but this did not represent national opinion accurately, as the voting for the Constituent Assembly was to show. Nor was the Second Congress so well attended as the First, Third or Fourth Congresses: in this way too, it was unrepresentative.[1] Besides, the Second Congress only included workers' and soldiers' deputies, and so was totally unrepresentative of the non-soldier peasants.

What is more important, the Second Congress of Soviets did not assemble until the success of the Bolsheviks' armed coup was assured. The Congress in October, like the rest of the country in February, was confronted by a *fait accompli*. When the Congress met, the non-Bolshevik delegates on the left wing naturally demanded that a coalition Government of the left be formed following on the armed uprising. Trotsky's reply to this request deserves close study. He said:

> The insurrection of the masses stands in no need of justification. What is taking place is not a conspiracy but an insurrection. We moulded the revolutionary will of the Petrograd

[1] The total membership of the Second Congress of Soviets can only be approximately determined, but the figure was about 900 at the time of its dispersal. At the start of the Congress there were about 690 delegates, of whom 390 were Bolsheviks or Bolshevik supporters. At the First Congress in July 1917 there were 1,090 delegates; at the Third Congress in January 1918, 942; and at the Fourth Congress in March 1918, 1,204 delegates.

workers and soldiers ... The masses gathered under our banner, and our insurrection was victorious. But what do they (the other socialists) offer us? ... To give up our victory, to compromise, and to negotiate – with whom? With whom shall we negotiate? With those miserable cliques which have left the Congress or with those who still remain? But we saw how strong those cliques were! There is no one left in Russia to follow them. And millions of workers and peasants are asked to negotiate with them on equal terms. No, an agreement will not do now. To those who have left us and to those proposing negotiations we must say: You are a mere handful, miserable, bankrupt; your role is finished, and you may go where you belong – to the garbage heap of history!'[1]

Trotsky refers to the 'masses' who supported the Bolsheviks, and to the 'millions of workers and peasants' on their side, but in the same breath he admits that the Bolsheviks 'moulded the revolutionary will of the *Petrograd* workers and soldiers', as if they and the massed millions were synonymous. He refers to the S.R.s and the Mensheviks as 'miserable cliques' for whom 'there is no one left in Russia to follow. . . .' This was soon proved to be a gross exaggeration.

Students of 1917 are well aware that in its early stages the 'Russian revolution' starting on 25 October was neither all-Russian nor a revolution. It was virtually a Petrograd coup d'état. The coup was then slowly turned into a nationwide revolution in the course of a protracted civil war. In order to do this, the Bolsheviks relied on three supports: their control over vital points in the communications network throughout Russia, and their influence over the local population. Both of these props had been built with great care prior to the October coup. Indeed most of the party's energies had been applied here. But the tasks had remained unfinished, especially the second one. Therefore a third support, the Red Army, took on increasing importance, as it developed out of the diminutive Red Guard. The civil war made it supreme.

The course of events in Petrograd between February and October tended to become more and more estranged from the revolutionary tide in the rest of the country. In grasping power

---

[1] Sukhanov, *Zapiski o revoliutsii* (Berlin, 1922–3) vol. 7, p. 203.

G

by force in one very special city of Russia towards the end of the year, the Bolsheviks showed tacitly that they had lost patience with their brilliant propaganda campaign, which was moving too slowly for them. Instead they relied on a little armed might, first in Petrograd and then in some other cities, and on their carefully prepared control over all channels of communication throughout the remainder of Russia. The passivity of most of the population, the earlier successful Bolshevik penetration of some elements, and the general sense of exhaustion left by war and revolution, then gave the Bolsheviks a short lull. In a few months they consolidated their hold on the heart of European Russia by the use of both force and persuasion, so that when the civil war began in earnest round the periphery of the Soviet bastion, the new regime was able, after four years of armed opposition, to survive. The civil war was the natural boomerang effect of the Petrograd coup of October 1917. It was the fierce clamour of that part of the Russian nation which the Bolsheviks had neither persuaded during 1917, nor intimidated by force in October or afterwards, into joining their cause.

THE UNIQUENESS OF PETROGRAD

Petrograd had the usual features of any capital which made it unique in some respects. It was the political, social, legal and economic centre of the Empire, although Moscow was a close competitor in the last sense. It was to Petrograd that all the major political exiles flocked without exception after February. The capital's political sophistication extended to experience of revolutionary situations. In 1905-7 many social groups in the city beyond high-ranking statesmen had a taste of what this was like.

The social élite of the Empire was based on the Tsarist court in Petrograd, but the same city also included the largest concentration of Russia's proletariat. The contrast between Petrograd's political and social brilliance and the abject state of the provincial population was more marked than in any other European country in 1917. All visiting foreigners remarked on the startling difference. It was easily apparent on the streets of the capital itself, where illiterate peasant workers mixed with persons of an elegance unsurpassed anywhere else in the

world. Contrasts of this kind, and the great gulf set between
Petrograd society and provincial Russia, were superficial reflections of those deeper political, economic and social injustices
that had finally led to the February revolution. Peter the Great's
window on Europe for two centuries had not succeeded in
letting enough light through to the interior of the Eurasian land
mass that lay behind it.

The distinctive qualities of Petrograd that set it further apart
from the rest of the hinterland than was the case with other
European capitals were mainly the result of its peculiar geographical and economic characteristics. In 1917 no other
capital city in the world was so strangely placed as Petrograd.
Built on a marsh at the extreme north-western edge of the vast
continent over which it ruled, Petrograd on one side faced the
Baltic, a sea that Russia could never dominate, on another the
rebellious Grand Duchy of Finland, and on the third Lake
Ladoga, which effectively blocked the way to the north-east
and east. The only manner in which roads and railways could
penetrate into the city was from the south and south-west.
During 1917 Petrograd was more than usually difficult of
access, owing to the chaotic transport situation. It was hard for
delegates to get to the innumerable congresses that were summoned. Travel was a hazardous affair, and not least to the
capital. First-hand information about what was going on in
Petrograd from persons who had been there was not easy to
come by in the provinces.

Petrograd's isolated position, far away from the nation's raw
materials and wheatfields, made it one of the chief victims of
the general supply crisis in 1917, as has been seen. The inefficient rationing system that was introduced only led to a
thriving black market and heightened class antagonism, since
the rich could still buy anything they pleased, at a price. The
shortage of raw materials led to suspicions of sabotage either by
employers or employees. Whichever was true, the result was
that factory workers were rendered idle and restless, adding to
the street crowds that were probably far greater in volume than
in any other Russian city.

Petrograd was in a very exposed situation with regard to the
war. Indeed, after the fall of Riga to the advancing German
Army on 21 August, the Provisional Government decided to

treat the capital as part and parcel of the military zone of Russia. The Petrograd Military District was put under the jurisdiction of the Supreme Commander, and a cavalry corps was sent to the capital to be at its disposal. The weight of Germany's armies menaced the Provisional Government across an easily traversed plain. Petrograd's vulnerability in the war heightened the anxiety of its population, which, in combination with rising panic caused by lack of supplies and the troubled political horizon in general, contributed to the peculiarly extremist views adopted by left-wing supporters in the city by the autumn of 1917.

Being so near to the military theatre, Petrograd contained a large number of soldiers in its swollen garrisons. In February there were about 160,000 in the city,[1] and this figure was increased during the following months by men on leave, the wounded, and, more important from the political point of view, by deserters. Then there were the sailors, in even closer proximity to Petrograd than the military, and with far more time on their hands owing to the relative inactivity of the Baltic Fleet. Their extremist views had a considerable effect on the political climate in the capital. The Kronstadt Soviet, which was the first in the country to have a Bolshevik majority, was under the sailors' control. The abortive armed uprising in the July Days was engineered by them to a great extent. Sailors were used by the Bolsheviks to disperse the Constituent Assembly when it finally met.

Petrograd found itself in a special situation in another respect. Russia's wartime access to Western Europe lay exclusively through the northern routes via Finland and neutral Sweden. A large proportion of revolutionary, and especially Bolshevik, literature, arms and personnel was funnelled into Russia through this narrow channel during the war years. Petrograd lay directly across its path, and was the first target. Lenin was but the most famous of a flood of returning political exiles who entered Russia via the Finland Station in 1917.[2]

Of all Petrograd's distinctive features, the size and nature of her industrial population was perhaps the most striking. Prior to 1917 Russia had been caught in the throes of a dynamic but erratic industrialisation process which was accompanied by a series of booms and depressions. The social repercussions were tremendous. In the late nineteenth and early twentieth centuries the cities of European Russia, Petrograd and Moscow in particular, were expanding at a rate and in a way that Britain had not experienced since the early nineteenth century. The rapid but unsteady influx of peasants into new industries created enormous social problems that the Tsarist bureaucracy was unwilling and unable to solve.

Class antagonism in the capital increased acutely towards 1917. Nicholas II's winter residence lay in the heart of Petrograd, together with the court circles that in some ways were scarcely less feudal than those which surrounded Louis XVI at Versailles, situated more discreetly some distance outside the capital. Paris at the time of the French political revolution had not yet submitted to industrial revolution. Approximately 400,000 factory workers lived in the Petrograd guberniia in February 1917. Together with 160,000 soldiers in the city itself, they made up a formidable social group among the lower classes; and these were the two sections of the population that were the most receptive to Bolshevik propaganda. The literacy rate in the capital was unusually high. In February 1917 factory inspectors reported 432,000 strikers throughout the country; 200,000 of them were in Petrograd.[1] The total population of the city itself only amounted to about two millions.

During the war years the working conditions of the Petrograd proletariat were among the worst in the country. Wages rose between 1914 and 1917, but even more so did the cost of basic foodstuffs and other essential goods, which were the most expensive in the Empire. They went up from four to five times in price in three years.[2] Rents in the overcrowded capital increased two- or threefold.[3] Many of the factories in Petrograd

---

[1] V. L. Meller and A. M. Pankratov (eds) *Rabochee dvizhenie v 1917 godu* (Moscow, 1926) pp. 20–2.

[2] P. I. Liashchenko, *Istoriia narodnogo khoziaistva SSSR*, vol. II (Moscow, 1956) p. 647.

[3] I. P. Leiberov, *Statechnaia bor'ba petrogradskogo proletariata v period pervoi mirovoi voiny*, in *Istoriia rabochego klassa Leningrada* (Moscow, 1963) p. 164.

were engaged in production for the war. Under increasing pressure, work standards declined. The number of accidents went up by two and half times after 1914,[1] and the usual working day lasted as long as from twelve to sixteen hours.[2] Such atrocious conditions led to strikes during the war years, even though they were strictly forbidden. Petrograd workers headed the agitation. According to a Soviet scholar, a total of 633 strikes occurred in the capital between 1 August 1915 and 31 August, 1916.[3] Even more significant than the number of strikes were the first tentative connections between the workers and elements in the military garrison. The earliest known example of this in the war period took place in August 1915.[4] The example was repeated in the series of strikes that disturbed Petrograd again from January to March 1916. The Bolsheviks organised a strike committee in September 1915 to co-ordinate strikes in the city and also to link up with disturbances in other European cities of Russia. In the same month Petrograd strike leaders considered setting up a workers' Soviet in the capital. Lenin warned the Bolsheviks among them against it, since he thought the time was not yet ripe.[5]

The composition of the factory workers in the capital changed during the war. Mobilisation emptied the plants of 40 per cent of all workers in 1914.[6] The loss was soon made good, partly by new recruits from the countryside, and by women from the city. As a whole they were less revolutionary in temperament than the men they replaced at the work-benches. But they were joined by large numbers of evacuees from the factories of Poland and the Baltic provinces. When the factories of Riga were evacuated in July 1915, to take one example among many, only 3 per cent of that city's metalworkers stayed on. The total population was reduced from five hundred to two hundred thousand. A large proportion of those who left Riga went to Petrograd. The political awareness of the highly industrialised

---

[1] *Naemnyi trud v Rossii*, pt i (Moscow, 1927) pp. 131–4.
[2] Leiberov, op. cit., p. 164.
[3] Ibid., p. 177. This figure should be regarded with caution.
[4] *Voprosy istorii KPSS*, no. 5 (1960) p. 72.
[5] Lenin, *Sochineniia*, vol. 35, p. 162.
[6] A. Lomov, *V mire konkurentsii*, in *Pod starym znamenem* (Petrograd, 1917) pp. 98 ff.

populations of Warsaw, Riga and other cities was acute even before 1914, as the size and influence of the local left-wing parties showed. Their influence soon began to tell in Petrograd. The Lettish Central Committee of the Social Democrats ordered evacuees to get in touch with their Russian counterparts on arrival in the capital.[1]

The peculiar size of Petrograd's factories distinguished its proletariat from workers in all other Russian cities except Moscow, and even there the number of large plants did not approach those in the capital and its neighbourhood, where by 1917 355,000 employees were crammed into 140 large factories.[2] This made for terribly crowded working conditions, leading to discontent. It also made for large and powerful workers' representative committees. The most famous instances of revolutionary activity in big plants of this kind came from the Putilov works, the largest in Petrograd. Seventy per cent of all Russia's armaments were produced in the Putilov giant. Prior to 1917 many of the strikes in Petrograd had been organised by metalworkers, often at the instigation of Putilov workers, who encouraged demonstrations in other metal factories to link up with their own. In 1917 the Putilov plant formed the backbone of the Workers' Soviet and the Red Guard. Its ties with the soldiers' garrisons, facilitated by the military nature of its production for the war effort, were of crucial political significance in 1917. One of the vital differences between the 1905 and 1917 revolutions in the capital lay in the fact that in the first revolution the military did not connive with the factory workers against the authorities.

The gulf that separated the social and political consciousness of city workers in large factories from that of workers in smaller plants outside Petrograd and Moscow may be illustrated by an amusing incident related by Bernard Pares:

Of another factory in the Ryazan Government I am told, at second hand, the following story. Some sixty strikers came from Moscow. 'You must strike,' they said. 'Why?' asked

[1] See Ia. Kaimin', *Latyshkie strel'by v bor'be za pobedu oktiabr'skoi revoliutsii* (Riga, 1961). At several points in previous essays the revolutionary actions of non-Russian nationals, mainly from the Baltic area, have been noted with regard to the manipulation of communications in Petrograd.

[2] Lomov, op. cit.

the workmen, 'We see no reason.' 'Why, because everyone else is striking.' 'Then what for?' 'For an eight-hours day, and, if you don't, we will burn your factory.' To this the workmen said, 'No,' and the agitators passed on to a neighbouring factory, which they did actually set on fire. At this the men in the first factory struck, apparently because they realised that the burning of the factory would deprive them of a livelihood. They were asked what they struck for; they replied: 'For an eight-hours day.' 'All right,' said the employer, 'I will give you an eight-hours day', and on examination it turned out that, on account of the slackness of trade, they were already working for less than eight hours. The men thereupon sent a deputation saying: 'Please let it be as it was.'[1]

This anecdote may be compared with Sukhanov's comment on the difference between Petrograd and provincial delegates at the Second Congress of Soviets in October 1917:

The hall was already full, still with the same grey mob from the heart of the country. An enormous difference leaped to the eye: the Petersburg Soviet, that is, its Workers' Section in particular, which consisted of average Petersburg proletarians, in comparison with the masses of the Second Congress looked like the Roman Senate that the ancient Carthaginians took for an assembly of gods. With masses like that, with the vanguard of the Petersburg proletariat, I think it really was possible to be enticed into an attempt to illuminate old Europe with the light of the Socialist revolution. But in Russia this incomparable type is an exception. The Moscow worker is as different from the Petersburg proletarian as a hen from a peacock. But even he, as familiar to me as the Petersburger, is not altogether benighted and homespun. Here at the Congress, however, the hall was filled with a crowd of a completely different order. Out of the trenches and obscure holes and corners had crept utterly crude and ignorant people whose devotion to the revolution was spite

[1] Sir Bernard Pares, *Russia between Reform and Revolution* (New York, 1962) pp. 416–17. This refers to 1905, but the story is typical of the situation in 1917 also.

and despair, while their 'Socialism' was hunger and an un-
endurable longing for rest. Not bad material for experiments,
but – those experiments would be risky.[1]

Both the Tsarist and the Provisional Governments were
aware of the special threat posed by the presence of a peculiarly
large and restive proletariat at the political centre of the
country. On several occasions they tried to soften its influence
by removing, or attempting to remove, the more dangerous
elements. After the demonstration of July 1914, the Tsarist
Government seized about a thousand Bolshevik party members
and expelled them from Petrograd.[2] At the same time thousands
of the more unruly factory workers were drafted into the Army.[3]
In 1917 middle-class support for the Provisional Government
drained away from Petrograd at an ever-increasing rate.
Trotsky reported that by the early autumn 'The flight from
raving and hungry Petrograd to a more peaceful and well-fed
province, on the increase ever since the July Days, now be-
comes a stampede. Respectable families who have not succeeded in getting away from the capital, try in vain to insulate
themselves from reality behind stone wall and under iron
roof.'[4]
     The Provisional Government tried to divest Petrograd of part
of the social groups that were hostile to it. The reason given was
the shortage of food and other supplies in the capital, and also
the proximity of German armies. Kerensky eventually contemplated evacuating the whole governmental machine to
Moscow. It was true that food was scarce in Petrograd, and that
factories were idle for lack of raw materials, but Kerensky's
motives were probably coloured by the consideration that the
removal of undesirable elements from the political point of view
would help to secure the safety of the Provisional Government.
In this context it is interesting to note that at a military conference held at staff headquarters a month before the fall of
Riga, Kerensky held a more pessimistic view with regard to the
defence of Petrograd than did his generals, although on all

[1] Sukhanov, *The Russian Revolution 1917*, p. 635.
[2] *Sotsial-Demokrat*, 12 Dec. 1914.
[3] Leiberov, op. cit., p. 165.
[4] Trotsky, op. cit., p. 337.

other points concerning the Russian Army the generals were more pessimistic.[1]

Kerensky took definite steps on 8 August to relieve Petrograd of subversive groups in connection with his wider aim of moving some government departments and industries out of the city. The military authorities in the city were instructed to check the credentials of all ranks under their command. Soldiers entering Petrograd without permission were to be expelled.[2] Kerensky was obviously aiming at deserters here. Further government orders prepared for the evacuation of plant and workers temporarily deprived of raw materials. They were to be re-established nearer the source of the raw materials.[3] These arrangements were never put into effect, but they would have removed a large number of unemployed and dissatisfied workers from the capital had they been implemented.

The proposed evacuation of Petrograd suddenly blew up into a major political question at the beginning of October. The Provisional Government was planning to evacuate most of the city's garrison and set it to guard the approaches to the capital against possible German attacks. On 9 October the Petrograd Soviet drew up a resolution protesting against the notion. According to S.P. Mel'gunov, some of the Bolshevik leaders decided on the same day to stage an armed uprising in the near future. Lenin now claimed that as Kerensky was about to move the entire Government to Moscow, he was giving up any real hope of defending Petrograd. The fall of Petrograd would be a fatal stab in the back for the Soviet and for the Bolsheviks in particular, given their great following in the capital. The Bolsheviks called for the patriotic defence of the city, and subsequent preparations for the armed uprising were carried out on the basis of this transparent pretence. At the Soviet Congress of the northern territories, held on 11 October, Trotsky declared that 'The Government may flee from Petrograd, but the Petrograd Soviet and the revolutionary population will not go away anywhere, they will fight, and, if need be, will die at their posts.'[4] These words sounded strange in the mouth of one of the revolution's leading defeatists.

[1] *Krasnaia letopis'*, vol. VI (Leningrad, 1923) pp. 19-51.
[2] *Sobranie uzakonenii i rasporiazhenii pravitel'stva*, no. 204 (1917) p. 1288.
[3] Ibid., no. 210 (1917) p. 1348.   [4] Mel'gunov, op. cit., pp. 33-4.

CENTRALIST AND NON-CENTRALIST THEORIES OF REVOLUTIONARY STRATEGY

The Bolsheviks reaped enormous dividends from the fact that their centralist theory of revolutionary strategy was worked out in practice in Petrograd, a city whose distinctive characteristics favoured them greatly in 1917. Before inquiring further into Bolshevik strategy, however, it may be useful to look very briefly at the ideas of their main protagonists on this subject. By tradition the Socialist Revolutionaries were non-centralist. As the heirs of the Populist movement in nineteenth-century Russia, they still looked to the peasantry for their main support, although for some years prior to the 1917 revolution they had been cultivating the city proletariat as well. But this change of emphasis had not altered their basic ideas on the future government of Russia. They advocated a loosely federated republic in which the autonomous units would have substantial control over their internal affairs. The S.R.s discovered in 1917 that they could not set their own house in order, let alone the structure of the Empire. O. H. Radkey, the author of an authoritative study on the S.R.s,[1] concludes that one of the main reasons for their failure in the revolution was their loose party organisation, leading to fatal splits on policy.

The S.R.s' original stronghold was on the Lower Volga, not in the capital nor in Moscow, though their strength in the latter city was considerable. Their support, like their political ideas and party organisation, was disjointed. The voting for the Constituent Assembly showed the numerical strength of their supporters, but they were scattered far and wide over the immensity of Russia. S.R. men did not occupy the vital centres of communication in the country as the Bolsheviks did, with their much better grasp of revolutionary strategy. The S.R.s were losing their hold in the localities even before October. One reason was that 'their peasant empire had rested on shallow foundations. A certain political tradition had been created, particularly in the black-earth region, but it had only relative and not intrinsic strength, being derived from the absence of any other tradition rather than from a tempering process in the

---

[1] See his *The Agrarian Foes of Bolshevism* (New York, 1958) and *The Sickle under the Hammer* (New York, 1963).

fire of competition.'[1] The success of Bolshevik propaganda methods was a second reason for the S.R.s' decline. Lenin's agrarian policy seemed to be virtually the same as the popular S.R. policy by the close of 1917: certainly the peasants could see little difference between them. By concentrating their propaganda on the military and winning over a large number of the peasant soldiers, the Bolsheviks were at the same time infiltrating into the peasantry proper. The Russian soldier, demobilised or deserting, 'went home – and shattered the matrix. He established his authority in the village and wrenched it out of the age-old ruts, imparting to it a leftward twist which served the Soviet power well for years to come. . . . When the S.R.s lost the soldiers, they lost the peasants too, and so the revolution.'[2]

After the February revolution the Provisional Government seemed to be the best placed to exercise central control over the rest of the country beyond Petrograd. It took upon itself temporarily the cloak of sovereignty cast off by the old regime, and for a few months at least commanded some measure of response from the provincial administrative systems; but in other ways it was at a disadvantage. The Kadet party, who formed the core of the first Provisional Government in February, were like the S.R.s in that their support came traditionally from the localities. Any liberal party atempting to curb autocratic central power in the Duma period of necessity appealed to regional counter-influences such as the zemstvo system. At the political centre in the capital they were almost as helpless as the revolutionary parties in the years 1905-17. The first concern of the Provisional Government after the February revolution was to keep the civil and military administrative machines functioning. The only way to do this in the short run was to make use of the old Tsarist system, and of some of its less hated manipulators. The Augean stables could not be cleansed in a day. In the localities Tsarist institutions and servants were symbols of repression and autocracy, and their continued unpopularity after February reflected on the prestige of the Provisional Government.[3]

[1] Radkey, *The Sickle under the Hammer*, p. 277.　　　[2] Ibid., pp. 278–9.
[3] In the first period after the February revolution the local population often confused the Provisional Government with the old State Duma. See Vulliamy, op. cit., p. 235.

The interest of the new regime in the localities also tended, paradoxically enough, to undermine its prestige in the provinces. Each ministry genuinely attempted to set into motion grandiose nationwide reforms in every sphere. Unwieldy committees were established which issued a flood of reports, censuses and general advice, but very little effective action was taken in any field before October. The task was enormous, and soon got bogged down in legal and administrative complications. As a result, the average Russian never felt the impact of this prodigious labour, nor indeed ever knew how solicitous the Provisional Government really was for his future welfare. This was partly the fault of the Government, which was extraordinarily inept at propagandising its broad reform aims and the steps it was taking to enforce them. The crux of the dilemma lay in the fact that the Government just could not have enforced the reforms even if they had materialised before October. Overwhelming evidence for the views expressed above is to be found in the collection of documents relating to the Provisional Government edited by Kerensky himself.[1] Another inhibiting factor was that the Provisional Government saw itself only as a caretaker of national sovereignty. The much delayed Constituent Assembly was to be the real legislator of the Russia of the future. Besides, the Provisional Government went through a series of disturbing coalitions in 1917, during which ministers rose and fell with an alacrity that was bound to hamper the running of the administration.

The Bolsheviks were not burdened with the enormous task of governing an impatient country involved in war and revolution at one and the same time. Free from involvement in immediate legal reforms and also from the blame attached to the reformers when changes were slow in coming, they were not compelled to disperse their energies over the whole range of central and local administration. Instead they directed their attention to capturing quick support for their very broad and eye-catching programme at the essential points of the body politic, especially Petrograd. No laborious committee and legal work was involved. This was politically unrewarding in any case. Their skill was channelled mainly into centrally con-

---

[1] R. P. Browder and A. F. Kerensky (eds), *The Russian Provisional Government 1917*, 3 vols (Stanford, 1961).

trolled propaganda activities, which paid handsome rewards.

It so happened that this pragmatic centralist approach of the Bolsheviks coincided with Lenin's centralist political theory formulated prior to 1917. In *What is To Be Done?*, written in 1902, Lenin called for a highly centralised party which would lead the revolutionary movement and not follow in its steps. The party was to act as the vanguard of the proletariat. In 1917 the leading and peculiarly extremist elements of the Russian proletariat and the élite of the Bolshevik party membership were concentrated in Petrograd. Events in the capital favoured the Bolsheviks in the revolution, so what was more natural than that Trotsky, writing with the benefit of hindsight in 1930, should link up Lenin's élitist theory with the idea of the leading role of Petrograd?

> If the capital plays as dominating a role in a revolution as though it concentrated in itself the will of the nation, that is simply because the capital expresses most clearly and thoroughly the fundamental tendencies of the new society. The provinces accept the steps taken by the capital as their own intentions already materialised. In the initiatory role of the centre there is no violation of democracy, but rather its dynamic realisation. However, the rhythm of this dynamic has never in great revolutions coincided with the rhythm of formal representative democracy. The provinces adhere to the activity of the centre, but belatedly. With the swift development of events characteristic of a revolution this produces sharp crises in revolutionary parliamentarianism, which cannot be resolved by the methods of democracy. In all genuine revolutions the national representation has invariably come into conflict with the dynamic force of the revolution, whose principal seat has been the capital. It was so in the seventeenth century in England, in the eighteenth in France, in the twentieth in Russia. The role of the capital is determined not by tradition of a bureaucratic centralism, but by the situation of the leading revolutionary class, whose vanguard is naturally concentrated in the chief city: this is equally true for the bourgeoisie and the proletariat.[1]

[1] Trotsky, op. cit., pp. 135–6.

Trotsky's ideas may be compared with something Lenin wrote as early as 1897.

> The Russian Social-Democrats must not dissipate their forces; they must concentrate their activities among the industrial proletariat, which is most capable of imbibing Social-Democratic ideas, in the most developed class intellectually and politically, and the most important from the point of view of numbers and concentration in the important political centres of the country.'[1]

At this point it might be profitable to examine Lenin's ambivalent attitude, as expressed in his speeches and writings in 1917, on the revolutionary role of Petrograd versus that of the rest of Russia. This also involves the wider question of whether the Bolsheviks claimed to represent the majority of the Russian population in 1917.

In April Lenin appeared to support the localities rather than the leading industrial cities as the prime movers of the revolution:

> In the Russian revolution we observe a certain bureaucratism in the centres, and a greater exercise of power wielded by the Soviets locally, in the provinces. In the capital cities the Soviets are politically more dependent upon the bourgeois central authorities than those in the provinces. In the centres it is not so easy to take control of production; in the provinces this has already been carried out to some extent. The inference is – to strengthen the local Soviets. Progress in this respect is possible, coming primarily from the provinces.'[2]

From this argument Lenin deduced that it was necessary to 'gather local experience for prodding the centre: *local areas* became a *model*'.[3] In the same month Lenin wrote elsewhere, 'We are not Blanquists, we do not stand for the seizure of power by a minority'.[4] And in May he stated that 'the transfer of all state power directly to the majority of the population alone can save the peoples'.[5]

[1] Lenin, *The Tasks of Russian Social-Democrats* (1897).
[2] Lenin, *Collected Works*, 4th ed., vol. 24, p. 254.
[3] Ibid., p. 256.   [4] Ibid., p. 40.
[5] Ibid., p. 374.

This non-centralist approach was probably based on two tacit assumptions: first, that the 1917 revolution, like that of 1905, would gather its main impetus from the localities, and second, that the vacillating Petrograd Soviet of March and April was no match for the Provisional Government in Petrograd. Already in April Lenin was changing his mind. In his *Tasks of the Proletariat in Our Revolution* he observes:

> From the point of view of science and practical politics, one of the chief symptoms of every real revolution is the unusually rapid, sudden, and abrupt increase in the number of 'ordinary citizens' who begin to participate actively, independently and effectively in political life and in the organisation of the state.
>
> Such is the case in Russia. Russia at present is seething. Millions and tens of millions of people, who had been politically crushed by the terrible oppression of Tsarism and by inhuman toil for the landowners and capitalists, have awakened and taken eagerly to politics. And who are these millions and tens of millions? For the most part small proprietors, petty bourgeois, people standing midway between the capitalists and the wage-workers. Russia is the most petty-bourgeois of all European countries.
>
> A gigantic petty-bourgeois wave has swept over everything and overwhelmed the class-conscious proletariat, not only by force of numbers but also ideologically; that is, it has infected and imbued very wide circles of workers with the petty-bourgeois political outlook.'[1]

At the beginning of May Lenin could still write:

> In no other belligerent country in the world is there such freedom as there now is in Russia, or such revolutionary mass organisations as the Soviets of Workers', Soldiers', Peasants', and other Deputies; and that nowhere else in the world, therefore, can the transfer of the entire state power to the actual majority of the people, i.e. to the workers and poor peasants, be achieved so easily and so peacefully.'[2]

By the end of July, however, he is flatly contradicting what he

[1] Ibid., pp. 61–2.
[2] Ibid., p. 165.

wrote in May with regard to the majority principle and the idea of a peaceful transfer of power:

> In times of revolution it is not sufficient to ascertain the 'will of the majority'; nay, one must prove to be the stronger at the decisive moment and in the decisive place; one must be victorious. Beginning with the Peasant War in the Middle Ages in Germany, and throughout all the big revolutionary movements and epochs, including 1848 and 1871, and including 1905, we see innumerable examples of how the better organised, more class-conscious, and better armed minority forces its will upon the majority and vanquishes it'.[1]

In between these polar views there came a significant middle position in late May. Replying to Plekhanov, who criticised the Bolsheviks for being Jacobins, Lenin wrote: 'There are Jacobins and Jacobins. A witty French saying . . . pokes fun at the "Jacobins without the people" (*jacobins moins le peuple*). The historical greatness of the true Jacobins of 1793, is that they were "Jacobins *with* the people", with the revolutionary majority of the nation, with the *revolutionary* advanced classes of *their* time.'[2] He goes on to accuse the Provisional Government of being Jacobins without the people; but of course it is highly disputable whether the Jacobins of 1793 were 'with the people'. Their name is more often associated with centralism in theory and practice. In Robespierre's words, 'They say that terrorism is the resort of despotic government. Is our government then like despotism? Yes, as the sword that flashes in the hand of the hero of liberty is like that with which the satellites of tyranny are armed. . . . The government of the Revolution is the despotism of liberty against tyranny.'[3]

Here is the same ambivalence that we find in Lenin. Between July and September 1917 Lenin completely abandoned the majority principle and dropped the party slogan of 'All Power to the Soviets'. In September the Bolsheviks gained a majority in the Petrograd Soviet, and the slogan reappeared on Bolshevik platforms, but it returned with a narrower meaning. In

[1] Lenin, *Selected Works*, vol. 6 (London, 1936) p. 182.
[2] Lenin, *Collected Works*, p. 534.
[3] *Moniteur universel*, 19 Pluviôse, l'an 2, p. 562. From a speech to the National Convention, 5 February 1794.

May Lenin could refer to 'The majority of the population, i.e. the Soviets',[1] but by the autumn Trotsky and he equated the majority principle with a Bolshevik majority in one Soviet only, the Petrograd Soviet, out of a national total of about nine hundred.[2] The extension of the majority principle to the rest of Russia through the elective system of the local Soviets was deferred until a future time. In the event the vision of government by the whole body of the nation's Soviets proved to be illusory. Lenin's temporary preference for a strong centralised Government became permanent under the onslaught of the civil war and the intervening powers. Quite apart from the subsequent turn of events, it was vain to expect such a politically backward population to set up a system that was virtually unique in history and too unwieldy to work properly in any case.[3]

Thus a centralist policy remained uppermost in Lenin's mind in 1917 after some initial wavering. The policy coincided nicely with favourable conditions for the Bolsheviks in Petrograd. From the practical angle too it was the most sensible strategy. An organised revolution must be sparked off at a particular point or points, and does not burst out spontaneously in all areas. There was no such thing as mass political consciousness in Russia in 1917. The Bolsheviks were a drop in the peasant ocean. In the elections to the Constituent Assembly they got a relatively high vote in the Smolensk guberniia, yet even here there were only 494 party members in 1917 out of a population of about two million.[4] According to Trotsky, a local agitator reported that in the Smolensk guberniia 'Bolsheviks were very rare in the villages. There were very few of them in the counties. There were no Bolshevik papers.'[5]

If the Bolsheviks could seize control in the capital and some other points in the communications network, the provinces might bow to the new rulers. The name of Petrograd exercised a certain magic over the rest of a country accustomed for cen-

[1] Lenin, *Collected Works*, p. 447.   [2] See p. 179 above.
[3] Hannah Arendt considers that once the initial stages of a political revolution are over, it is impossible for 'spontaneous' organs of direct democracy to survive, particularly in a country the size of Russia. See her book *On Revolution* (London, 1963) pp. 268 ff.
[4] M. Fainsod, *Smolensk under Soviet Rule* (New York, 1963) p. 35.
[5] Trotsky, *The History of the Russian Revolution* (New York, 1932) vol. III, pp. 23–4.

turies to look to the centre for guidance. Although some elements in the localities were greatly alarmed by the extremist course adopted in the capital in October, a large part of the nation relapsed easily enough into blind submission to arbitrary control from Petrograd. The political scene, confused since February, became clearer once again, and a tired nation, or most of it, decided for a while to tolerate the new regime. In 1917 the sudden application of great licence to Russia's stifled society led to political extremism and anarchy which had exhausted the broken community.

Even at the fount of Bolshevik power, in Petrograd, it is not possible to speak with any certainty of majority support for Lenin in October. In his history of the revolution, Trotsky pulls out every stop in an attempt to magnify the Bolsheviks' popular support in the city and to minimise the role of force exercised by the Military Revolutionary Committee, but the Bolsheviks' own reports at the time reveal that there was considerable apathy even among their own supporters.[1] The more general attitude of the city proletariat to all politicians, including the Bolsheviks, might be summed up by the reaction of one of their number to the wrangling that went on during the negotiations to form a Socialist Coalition after the armed uprising: 'The devil alone knows who among you is right or wrong. You insult the earth by walking on it. If we could hang all of you on one tree the country would enjoy peace. . . . Let's go, men. We have nothing to gain from talking to this gang.'[2]

THE SPREAD OF THE REVOLUTION: MOSCOW

In February Moscow hailed the Petrograd revolution with joy, as did most of the rest of Russia. The reaction of Moscow to Petrograd politics in 1917 was more anxiously awaited in the capital than any other local reaction. The historical and

[1] See Leonard Schapiro, *The Origin of the Communist Autocracy* (London, 1955) pp. 54–5. These reports were made on 28 October; the successful Bolshevik coup turned the scales, since the elections to the Constituent Assembly which began in Petrograd on 25 November (New Style) resulted in a Bolshevik majority in the capital. As one of the October reports had predicted, 'the masses will follow the Soviet'.

[2] S. Rapoport, *Posle perevorota 25-go oktiabria 1917 goda*, in *Arkhiv russkoi revoliutsii*, vol. VIII (1923) p. 49.

economic importance of Moscow could have had a decisive influence on the course of events in 1917 if this city had taken upon itself to oppose direction from Petrograd.

For various reasons Moscow prior to October was more difficult to win over to the extremist line that was adopted in Petrograd. It lacked the brilliant revolutionary leaders of the capital. It was more insulated from the fronts, from supply troubles, and from the unruliness of soldiers and sailors. No mutinous Finland lay at its gates. Its large proletariat was dispersed round smaller factories than was the case with the Petrograd giants.[1] Moscow workers were better infiltrated by S.R. influence than in the capital. There was an extensive and politically-aware middle class, and far fewer government administrators left over from the old regime. These and many other differences in 1917 tended to set Moscow apart from the city that had succeeded it as the capital of Russia in 1703.

The discrepancy had little or no effect in February, but it helped to account for the widely differing course of the Bolshevik coups in the two cities in October. Whereas in Petrograd the opposition was overcome in two days, it took a week to subdue it in Moscow. The strength of active dissent in Moscow was only half the reason, however. The local Bolsheviks were far less capable and resolute in the way they staged the armed uprising than were their comrades in Petrograd. Trotsky describes Bolshevik preparations for the coup in Moscow, adding that 'the attempt to decide concretely how this seizure should be carried out remained unresolved'. In any case, Trotsky continues, 'the revolution in Petrograd gave Moscow, together with all the rest of the country, a far more imperative motive for insurrection – the necessity of coming promptly to the support of the newly formed Soviet Government'.[2] Subordination to the capital was all-important in Trotsky's eyes. It is significant that the chief organiser of the Moscow coup, V. P. Nogin, was dispatched from Petrograd at the time of the uprising there. Nogin did not take such a resolute line as Lenin expected him to, and anxious Bolshevik telegrams were sent from the capital in an attempt to steel Nogin's nerves.[3]

[1] On this difference between the two cities, see G. S. Ignat'ev, *Oktiabr' 1917 goda v Moskve* (Moscow, 1964) p. 4.
[2] Trotsky, op. cit., p. 413.   [3] Ignat'ev, op. cit., pp. 39–40.

Bolshevik strategy suffered as a result in Moscow. Only vague instructions were issued to the city suburbs. The Military Revolutionary Committee failed to capture the city telephone offices, although they were situated close to the inter-urban telephone building, which was successfully taken. Bolshevik forces went short of arms.[1] To complicate matters, Moscow offered a natural, elevated fortress in the shape of the Kremlin at its very centre. Stiff fighting went on in attempts to take and re-take it. Petrograd was a city on a plain with no obvious stronghold apart from the St Peter and Paul fortress.

THE REVOLUTION BEYOND PETROGRAD AND MOSCOW

In the 1905 revolution, St Petersburg was not the prime originator of many of the new shifts in the political landslide. The first prelude to working-class unrest occurred in Baku on 30 November 1904, and not in some city of European Russia. Later on, the original Soviet of workers was formed in Ivanovo-Voznesensk, and not in the capital. Revolutionary activities in the Navy did not link up with St Petersburg politics through the Baltic Fleet, but were more influential on the Black Sea, as the mutiny on board the battleship *Potemkin* demonstrated. In 1905 Russia was not engaged in a war on her western flank near St Petersburg, but was fighting distant Japan. Trouble from Russian troops occurred far to the east of St Petersburg, on the Trans-Siberian railway. Finally, the liberal movement was centred on the local zemstvos and city councils: in 1905 the liberals counted far more politically than in 1917. In the former revolution they held a niche in the political spectrum that was sufficiently left-wing by the standards of 1905 to ensure wide popularity.

One of the main reasons for the eventual failure to weaken the autocracy effectively in 1905 was the lack of co-ordination between the diffuse revolutionary elements which did not manage to coalesce successfully. The Social Democrats were like isolated guerrilla detachments scattered through the Empire. Their leaders were abroad, and there was no nodal peg inside Russia on which to hang their embryonic organisation. 1917 was very different in this respect. The only major

[1] Ibid., pp. 42–3, 70–1.

political and social movements that owed little or nothing to
Petrograd were the peasant disturbances and the demands of
the national minorities.

Just before the February revolution a young journalist called
Konstantin Paustovsky was sent to a typical provincial town
not far from Moscow in order to report on local reactions to the
war and the political situation. He was lucky enough to be
there when the news of the February revolution in Petrograd
came through. As it took three days for newspapers to come
from Moscow, the news arrived somewhat late, by telegraph in
the first place. This was followed by the telegraphed appeal to
hold up the Tsar's train, wherever it might be located in
European Russia. After the initial shock was over, some local
worthies went off to the printing office to get the Provisional
Government's proclamation published. Before long the news
had spread out of the town by word of mouth to the surrounding countryside. Curious peasants arrived hot-foot to inquire
what would happen to the gentry's land. Self-appointed orators
were soon to be seen on the streets, speculating vaguely on the
turn of events.[1] In this way correct news and distorted rumours
spread down through the social classes and out into the rural
areas.

News of the revolution spread in a very uneven manner
through Russia. For instance, it reached Pskov, a locality com-
paratively near Petrograd, two weeks later than Nikolaevsk, a
town bordering on the Black Sea.[2] Various factors accounted for
this uneven distribution. The new authorities in the capital did
not have the time to inform the whole of Russia's rural population. The task was delegated to local agents: some of them withheld the information or distorted it for political purposes. Thus
in parts of Mogilev guberniia nothing definite was known until
the end of March. The influence of the conservative military
high command at Mogilev was strong in the surrounding area.[3]
Much further south, in Kherson, the governor went so far as to
publish a statement to the effect that Rodzianko, the President
of the Imperial Duma, had suppressed the disorders in Petrograd 'on behalf of the Army, the Tsar and the fatherland'.[4]

[1] Paustovsky, op. cit., pp. 246–50.
[2] Vulliamy, op. cit., p. 231.   [3] Ibid., p. 232.
[4] S. P. Mel'gunov, *Martovskie dni 1917 goda* (Paris, 1961) p. 14.

A second reason for the news delay was technical rather than political. The communications network just did not penetrate into the whole of Russia. Telegrams were sent to the more important population centres. Apart from them, the first places to learn the news were those which lay along the railway lines. Beyond this stage the rest of Russia's millions depended on more haphazard sources of information. Hence the great importance of rumour in the revolution. Through lack of detailed news, many localities adopted a guardedly neutral attitude to the political scene. They decided on a course of wait-and-see, after which they would side with the strongest central faction. This was the natural reaction of large sectors of a population accustomed for centuries to arbitrary rule from the capital. In a few places left-wing groups adopted a bolder line soon after the February revolution. The Soviet of Workers' and Soldiers' Deputies in Kherson laid claim to all the administrative machinery of the Provisional Government, merely offering the Government's commissar a representative post in the Soviet.[1] This sudden swing to the left may have been provoked by the deliberate distortion of news by the governor mentioned above.

'Independent republics' of this kind set themselves up with increasing frequency as the year wore on. By the summer Kerensky was acting rather like a medieval king, trying to use one local baron against another, not having the power or the means to move his own central forces against the offender. On hearing rumours about an 'independent republic' in Tsaritsyn on the lower Volga (now Volgograd), Kerensky ordered a delegation from nearby Saratov to go there and restore order.[2] Internecine local feuds dating back to long before the February revolution often took precedence over discussions on how to adapt to the new conditions at the centre of government. When the Saratov Bolsheviks met the Samara Bolsheviks to co-ordinate their policies in line with Petrograd, 'the meeting was not a great success, because of the "eternal" rivalry between the towns of Saratov and Samara'.[3]

The sheer size of Russia slowed down the transfer of news

[1] Vulliamy, op. cit., p. 239.
[2] V. P. Antonov-Saratovsky. *Pod stiagom proletar'skoi borby* (Moscow, 1925) p. 135.
[3] Ibid., p. 119.

from Petrograd, situated in the north-west corner. The news of
the February revolution travelled the 6,000-odd miles between
the capital and Vladivostok on the Pacific and reached
Vladivostok on 28 February.[1] On the Kamchatka peninsula in
the Far East there was no Dual Government between February
and October because no Soviets existed in the region. Trade
unions were also very slow in getting off the ground in the remote towns of the Far East.[2]

The situation was scarcely any better in Siberia, even on the
Trans-Siberian railway. Returning to Irkutsk on Lake Baikal
from political exile in the north, V. Antonov-Saratovsky
besieged telegraph offices with fellow ex-prisoners for news
about the February revolution. The first information was contained in a cryptically short telegram, which led them to
believe that there had been some kind of military putsch in the
capital.[3] In 1917 short telegrams on the political situation must
often have led to wild speculation. Telegrams are notoriously
subject to misinterpretation. On arrival in Irkutsk, the exiles
held political meetings and demonstrations in the first two
weeks of March despite their scant knowledge of what was
happening in European Russia. The exiles soon split up into
revolutionary factions like so many dim reflections of the
Bolshevik, S.R. and Menshevik parties in Petrograd. Their
vociferousness compensated in part for their unorthodoxy.[4]
Long after Lenin's April Theses denouncing the war, local
Bolshevik cells in Siberia were still upholding a 'defensist'
policy.

The political ignorance of most of Russia as to the details of
the February revolution can hardly be exaggerated, though it is
true that in the course of the succeeding eight months the
country began to wake up out of its torpor and follow events in
the capital more closely. But when Kerensky took it as an important political sign that no social element or region in the
vast Empire rose up against the Petrograd revolution in
February, he was undoubtedly overstressing the significance of

[1] D. I. Boiko-Pavlov and E. P. Sidorchuk, *Tak bylo na dal'nem vostoke*
(Moscow, 1964) p. 31.
[2] Ibid., pp. 55–7.
[3] Antonov-Saratovsky, op. cit., p. 87.
[4] Ibid., p. 89.

the fact. Many people simply did not know what had happened in the capital, and many who were better informed did not care to learn the details. The Tsar had fallen, liberal rule and widespread reforms were just round the corner, and that was good enough for them.

Local reactions to the abortive July armed uprising in Petrograd show more clearly than reactions to the February revolution how unco-ordinated was the revolutionary temper of the country as a whole. The political aims of the sailors and some of the Petrograd workers and garrison in July were too extreme for all other parts of Russia, the local Bolshevik groups included. Also the equivocal nature of Bolshevik participation in the July Days in the capital confused party organs in the provinces, which consequently interpreted events according to their local interests.

News of the disturbances in Petrograd reached Moscow on the evening of 3 July, but in a garbled form only, since normal communications with the capital had collapsed owing to the strike of Petrograd post and telegraph workers. The Provisional Government did not reply for a long time to appeals for information by direct wire from Moscow.[1] The Moscow Bolsheviks at first ordered their followers not to take part in demonstrations, but were thrown into confusion when they heard of the Petrograd processions on the morning of 4 July. The best they could do was to issue the following lame instructions: 'Follow events in Petrograd closely and all of you be ready to act when required at the call of the Moscow Committee.'[2] At a stormy session some members of the Moscow Bolshevik Committee proposed that party supporters should seize the post, telegraph and telephone offices and the press of the main bourgeois newspaper, *Russkoe slovo*.[3] It was almost a dress rehearsal for the October coup, but it came to nothing.

The Moscow Bolsheviks sent off telegrams to local Bolshevik committees in Central European Russia and the Black Earth areas. The telegram dispatched to Ivanovo-Voznesensk, the

---

[1] A. N. Voznesensky, *Moskva v 1917 g.* (Moscow, 1928) p. 64.

[2] *Revoliutsionnoe dvizhenie v Rossii v iule 1917 g., Iul'skii krizis. Dokumenty i materialy* (Moscow, 1959) p. 105.

[3] O. Piatnitsky, *Iz moei raboty v moskovskom komitete*, in the collection of articles entitled *Ot fevralia k oktiabriu* (Moscow, 1923) pp. 51–2.

home of the first Soviet ever, announced that the slogan to be used was still 'All Power to the Soviets', although it was now rejected by Lenin.[1] The use of the same slogan by all Bolshevik groups was one way of trying to co-ordinate their activities in a difficult period. Bolsheviks in Bogorodsko-Glukhovsk, a town not far from Moscow, got the news after the interval of a whole week.[2] A representative of the Moscow regional office travelled specially to Nizhnii Novgorod on 4 July.[3] News of events in Petrograd also reached this industrial city on the Volga the same day via the Moscow newspapers. Left-wing reaction in Nizhnii Novgorod took an independent turn, coloured almost entirely by local conditions. The 62nd regiment, stationed in the city, had just been ordered back to the front, and soldiers from it staged an unarmed demonstration outside the city Soviet on the same day, 4 July. Their initiative was merely strengthened by the news from outside, which had not touched it off in the first place.[4]

Further away from Petrograd and Moscow, local Bolsheviks were even more cut off and therefore more eccentric in their reaction to the news from the capital. Party members in Ekaterinburg in the Urals were reduced to reading between the lines in the bourgeois press so as to glean some information, since they were not in touch with the Petrograd Bolsheviks.[5] In distant Siberian Krasnoiarsk the local Bolsheviks received such an unclear report of what was going on in the capital that they decided to discuss once again the significance of earlier left-wing Petrograd demonstrations staged on 18 June, and then to make a logical deduction as to what might have happened more recently in the July Days.[6]

Once provincial Bolshevik groups had heard the news from Petrograd, they usually adopted a line and carried it through regardless of the sudden halt to the disturbances in the capital itself. Local issues flared up into major disputes, leading to violence in some cases. In Tashkent, the chief town of Central

[1] *Ivanovo-Voznesenskie bol'sheviki v period podgotovki i provedeniia velikoi oktiabr'skoi sotsialisticheskoi revoliutsii, Sbornik dokumenov* (Ivanovo, 1947) p. 77.
[2] *Protokoly shestogo s'ezda RSDRP (b)* (Moscow, 1934) pp. 343–4.
[3] *Sotsial-Demokrat*, 9 July 1917.
[4] O. N. Znamensky, *Iul'skii krizis 1917 goda* (Moscow, 1964) pp. 147–8.
[5] *Revoliutsionnoe dvizhenie v Rossii v iule 1917 g . . .*, p. 121.
[6] Ibid., pp. 128–30.

Asia, the shortage of supplies caused more disturbances at the start of July than the news from Petrograd, which merely served to exacerbate the local quarrel. For the most part the soldiers at the fronts, particularly the south-west and Rumanian fronts, reacted negatively to Bolshevik accounts of the events in the capital. The executive committee of the Soviets of the Rumanian front, the Black Sea Fleet and the Odessa district went so far as to send a telegram to the Petrograd Soviet ordering it to take up arms against the workers and soldiers in the capital.[1] Military units in reserve and garrisons in industrial towns on the other hand often sympathised with their extremist fellow-soldiers in Petrograd. The close links between the soldiers and the peasantry often led to the involvement of the latter in urban politics in July. This was the case in Nizhnii Novgorod. At the time of the July crisis the number of peasant disturbances increased steeply, especially in the vicinity of the towns of European Russia.

The successful Bolshevik coup in October placed Petrograd in a special position once again, but by this time the political climate in the capital was not so estranged from the rest of the country as it had been in July. By the middle of September the Bolsheviks had a majority in the Moscow Soviet; they were strong in some Volga towns, the industrial centres of the Urals, the Donets Basin and towns in the Ukraine. The northern and western fronts provided them with a large following as well as the sailors of the Baltic Fleet. Lenin in October had enough confidence to hope that, if Petrograd were seized by force, the remainder of Russia would not immediately rise up against the Bolshevik victors there.

In 1917 each of the three major thrusts to the left were initiated in the capital. Of these, the fall of the Tsarist regime in February was the most favourably received in the provinces. The abortive July uprising provoked the most hostile reaction, whereas the successful October coup lay somewhere between these two poles. It is interesting to note that the only major set-back to the left-wing avalanche from Petrograd came from outside the capital. It was organised by General Kornilov, whose closest supporters were the Cossacks – a social group who were representative of the outlying areas of provincial Russia. For

[1] Znamensky, op. cit., p. 173.

centuries they had preserved some measure of independence against the inroads of central autocracy.

LIAISON WITH PROVINCIAL ORGANS IN 1917: THE BOLSHEVIKS, THE SOVIETS AND THE PROVISIONAL GOVERNMENT

As far as the Petrograd Bolsheviks were concerned, two of their three chief instruments of liaison with local party cells were identical with the instruments they used in their broader aim of converting the Russian masses to their cause. Economy of means was essential to a numerically small party. Local Bolsheviks throughout the country looked to three sources of guidance from the capital – the organisation centred on *Pravda*, the itinerant party agitators, and the massive correspondence conducted by the party Secretariat in Petrograd. The first two sources have already been discussed in previous essays.

Letters on all kinds of subjects beyond the realm of the press flooded into the offices of *Pravda* and of *Priboi*, the Petrograd store which handled the sale and dispatch of party literature. The Secretariat of the Bolshevik Central Committee worked furiously on the incoming mail from local organs in an attempt to compensate for the lack of personal guidance at the lower levels. Up to 25 October for the year 1917 the understaffed Secretariat sent out 1,700 different letters.[1] It answered requests, gave encouragement, pointed out the existence of other Bolshevik groups in the locality concerned, and tried desperately to keep the whole network thinking and acting in line with the Petrograders. The detail in these letters is amazing. One correspondent is told that his cell owes so many kopecks for party literature received, another is instructed how to address an envelope to headquarters in such a way as to foil the Provisional Government's censor. Examples of this correspondence have been published by the Soviet regime as a tribute to Bolshevik organisational techniques.[2]

The Central Committee was especially intent on keeping in touch with the smaller cells and even with single individuals

---

[1] *Perepiska Sekretariata Tsk RSDRP (b) s mestnymi partiinymi organizatsiiami*, vol. I, p. vi.

[2] Ibid., vols I and II.

working among the Army.[1] No less attention was devoted to that comparative rarity, the Bolshevik peasant who was also a keen party worker. He was given all possible support in the form of party literature, financial funds, and political news from the centre. In return, the peasants were beseeched to write frequently and in detail on the turn of events in the countryside.[2] The eager, naïve letters from the localities to Petrograd reveal a great thirst for information and comradeship.The sense of isolation is easily apparent in their lines.

Very occasionally politically-minded peasants managed to get to Petrograd in 1917 in order to attend meetings like the All-Russian Congress of Peasants' Soviets, which opened on 4 May. One such Bolshevik supporter describes his impressions of the capital: 'So this is Petrograd! To someone from the depths of the provinces who has not seen large towns before, it seems like a giant. The cars, the trams, the droshkys, the carts. People, people everywhere! It's a real ant-hill.'[3] In the corridors of the Congress building, propaganda is handed out. 'Each delegate holds in his hands a packet of newspapers with different viewpoints. Everyone wants to find out what friends and enemies are writing about, what turn the revolution is taking, what perspectives are opening up.'[4] After hearing Lenin speak at the Congress, he returns home full of confidence. 'Back home we'll apply the [Congress] resolutions in our own way, in accordance with Bolshevik slogans. We don't care a hang that the Congress voted for the SRs!'[5]

Despite the valiant efforts of the Petrograd Bolsheviks to keep in close touch with local organs, it is clear from the 1917 correspondence that even by October provincial sympathisers for the most part felt themselves cut off from central policy. This is evident from the tone of their letters. Yet when we come to compare Bolshevik co-ordination with that of the Soviets or the Provisional Government, it is quite obvious that Lenin's party achieved more than the other two political systems. All

---

[1] Ibid., vol. I, documents 72, 77, 93, 102, 116, 119, 121, 126, 145, 162.
[2] Ibid., documents 80, 112, 127, 135, 142, 148, 163.
[3] A. Kuchkin, *Krest'ianskii s"ezd*, in *Letopis' velikogo oktiabria* (Moscow, 1958) p. 37.
[4] Ibid., p. 40.
[5] Ibid., p. 49.

three were struggling against a tide of increasing chaos in the country at large.

The Soviet structure represented enormous social authority in 1917, but it was of a distinctly inchoate kind, and much more poorly organised for action than the Bolshevik hierarchy. The latter was of course part of the former, since the Bolsheviks were a growing minority in the Soviets between February and September. Trotsky stated the relationship in graphic terms:

> It would be an obvious mistake to identify the strength of the Bolshevik party with the strength of the Soviets led by it. The latter was much greater than the former. However, without the former it would have been mere impotence. There is nothing mysterious in this. The relations between the party and the Soviet grew out of the disaccord inevitable in a revolutionary epoch between the colossal political influence of Bolshevism and its narrow organisational grasp. A lever correctly applied makes the human arm capable of lifting a weight many times exceeding its living force, but without the living arm the lever is nothing but a dead stick.[1]

The Petrograd Soviet had several sources of power after February. Through the Soldiers' Deputies it exerted great influence over the military, particularly the rear units. Through the Workers' Deputies it controlled many technical services that were vital to the running of any Government such as the press, to take but one example. It could provoke or dispel demonstrations on the city streets far more easily than could the Provisional Government, but in other ways it was hampered. Political nonentities led it in the early days until the major revolutionary exiles returned. It was plagued by the knowledge, shared by its Menshevik and S.R. members but ignored by the Bolsheviks, that it was merely an ephemeral instrument of authority that would be superseded once a more stable system came into being. As Kerensky told the British Ambassador, Sir George Buchanan, 'The Soviets will die a natural death'.[2]

The large network of local Soviets that imitated in part or in full the unwieldy tripartite structure of the Petrograd Soviet

---

[1] Trotsky, op. cit., p. 417.

[2] Sir George Buchanan, *My Mission to Russia and Other Diplomatic Memories*, vol. II (Boston, 1923) p. 111.

(Workers', Soldiers' and Peasants' Deputies) were an exceedingly motley assortment. At the provincial level political alignments within the Soviets were obscured. They consisted of 'revolutionary' deputies who had been chosen in the main because they were known to the electing body, not because they belonged to a specific party. In some Soviets there were even officers in the Soldiers' Section.[1] As in the capital, so in the provinces the Soviets had to coexist or compete with their 'bourgeois' counterparts, normally the town Duma. Relations with Petrograd were often tenuous or simply non-existent. If the Kronstadt Soviet, a mere twenty miles from the capital, could set itself up as an independent republic, the possibilities open for unilateral activities in remoter parts seemed limitless.

Outside the towns the eccentricities of local Soviets caused by poor contacts between them tended to proliferate. Behind the fronts the soldiers in the Soviets tried to collaborate with the civilian deputies, but along the fronts themselves they set up bodies which excluded civilians and would or could not work with neighbouring Soviets in the rear. The Peasant Soviets, as might be expected, were rather isolated from the rest. At the end of July there were 52 Peasants' Soviets in the 78 guberniia capitals, but only 371 in 813 districts and an even lower ratio in the sub-districts.[2] In the guberniia towns they were represented by non-peasant intellectuals in many cases. Rural Peasant Soviets rarely maintained relations with Workers' and Soldiers' Soviets, and the S.R.s often encouraged this isolation in order to prevent their own support in the rural Soviets from being swamped by Bolshevik workers and soldiers.[3]

In some ways the Soviet structure did possess advantages. The Workers' and Soldiers' Sections voted according to production and military, rather than territorial, units. This made for closer co-operation and faster work in a country suffering from an overloaded communications network. The Soviets also held frequent by-elections and so contrived to keep in better touch with popular opinion. The Provisional Government was far

[1] O. Anweiler, *Die Rätebewegung in Russland 1905–1921* (Leiden, 1958) p. 143.

[2] T. A. Remezova, *Sovety krestianskikh deputatov v 1917 g.*, in *Istoricheskie zapiski*, no. 32 (1950) pp. 15–19.

[3] Anweiler, op. cit., pp. 150–1.

more cut off in this respect, and was eventually forced to collapse and re-form itself in new coalitions in its attempts to reflect the changing political climate.

Local Soviets made some effort after February to link up in an all-Russian system. Guberniia conferences were staged as early as March, and Soldiers' Sections sent off many delegations to the fronts. On the basis of these and other contacts, the first All-Russian Conference of Soviets of Workers' and Soldiers' Deputies was opened in Petrograd on 29 March. It represented approximately 20 million people,[1] – that is, half the number who voted later for the delegates to the ill-fated Constituent Assembly. Unfortunately the Conference did not succeed in co-ordinating the activities of local Soviets after March. The Executive Committee elected by the Conference had no legal or physical authority over them, and if local conditions warranted it, they adopted an independent stance without heeding Petrograd. If they did pay attention to central policy, they looked to the Petrograd Soviet rather than to the Executive Committee, since the former body had more prestige and power.

The Soviet structure was centrifugal by its very nature. Beginning as a series of spontaneous and isolated organs of revolutionary action and order, the local Soviets never bowed to the party system in 1917; their god was the social solidarity of the suppressed classes. After the autumn of 1917 their ideals were submerged, either beneath a Bolshevik majority, or more frequently at the behest of Bolshevik might. Whilst they flourished they were 'spaces of freedom', as Hannah Arendt has called them. 'The common object was the foundation of a new body politic, a new type of republican government which would rest on 'elementary republics' in such a way that its own central power did not deprive the constituent bodies of their original power to constitute.'[2]

The Soviet system collapsed under the blow of the centralist Bolshevik hammer, just as other non-centralist structures and ideals did also. The final spasm occurred in the winter of 1917–1918, when some local Soviets went to extremes in their attempts to release themselves from the clutch of the Bolsheviks. By a resolution of February 1918, the volost Congress of Soviets in

---

[1] This figure is the one calculated by Anweiler, op. cit., p. 152.
[2] Arendt, op. cit., pp. 268, 271.

the Orlov guberniia set up its own independent Government, complete with commissars for finance, agriculture, food, education, and military and internal affairs.[1] By July 1918, however, officials in the guberniia administration were succumbing to Bolshevik pressure. At an All-Russian Congress they admitted: 'In the early period of the October Revolution on account of the spontaneous reaction against the old bureaucratic state there was created at the local level some sort of trend which sought to neglect the All-Russian Soviet centre and to decide all the problems posed by the revolution at their own discretion and led to the formation of independent republics, autonomous oblasts and so on.'[2] The Soviet system was doomed ever after to play a subordinate role under the thumb of the Communist party.

The nation-wide network of Soviets was at least permitted to survive in atrophied form after October 1917, but the local administration of the Provisional Government naturally disappeared with the central organs in the October coup. The efforts of the Provisional Government to co-ordinate its local branches during its short life resulted in small success. Kerensky was speaking from bitter experience when he declared that the Soviet system was bound to disappear; the same was true of the Provisional Government, as its name implied. All its business was tentative, and subject to eventual alteration by the Constituent Assembly. This knowledge, together with the enormous burden of reform, diluted its efficacy. Control over local bodies was extremely difficult for the Provisional Government from the beginning, as Prince Lvov, its first head, told his advisers on 4 March:

'Look what is happening, gentlemen. Since yesterday telegrams like these have been pouring in from all parts of European Russia. These are no longer the messages of support that you have all been reading. These are official reports from all the provincial capitals and from many smaller towns. They all say more or less the same thing: that at the first news

[1] E. G. G. Gimpelson, *Iz istorii stroitel'stva sovetov, noiabr' 1917 g.–iul' 1918 g.* (1958) pp. 68–70.

[2] V. P. Antonov-Saratovsky, *Sovety v periode voennogo kommunizma (sbornik dokumentov)* (Moscow, 1928) p. 189.

H

of the fall of the Monarchy, the local administration has fled, beginning with the governor and ending with the lowliest policeman, and those higher officials, particularly in the police, who either would not or could not get away in time have been arrested by all kinds of self-appointed revolutionary authorities and public committees.'

There was dead silence in the room as each of us wondered what to do. Here we were in the middle of a war, and large areas of the country had passed into the hands of completely unknown people![1]

The commissars who were eventually appointed as the local agents of the Provisional Government also tended to disappear from their posts during 1917, and had to be replaced with depressing regularity.[2] In conjunction with the frequent changes at ministerial level in Petrograd, this made easy contacts with the local administration almost impossible. Matters were made worse by the fact that 'both the position of the commissar and his rights and responsibilities until the introduction of the reform of local and municipal self-government were not sufficiently clear', as was pointed out at a conference of guberniia commissars on 22-24 April.[3] Moreover in the localities 'It was, and is, no unusual occurrence for one institution to obstruct another, to compete with another power',[4] and to do this within the single framework supervised by the Provisional Government.

The crux of the Provisional Government's weakness in the provinces was its almost complete inability to enforce the authority of the commissars. The Tsarist police was discredited, and the military units were politically unreliable. A deputy to the first Congress of Soviets put the problem in a nutshell:

The Government confers authority on the commissars, but you are well aware that the commissars possess no power at all. For example, this was the position in our place: the day

---

[1] *The Kerensky Memoirs*, p. 227.

[2] See *Krasnyi arkhiv*, vol. 15 (1925) pp. 40-1, and *Sbornik tsirkuliarov ministerstva vnutrennikh del za period mart–iun' 1917 goda*, pp. 13-14.

[3] Quoted in Browder and Kerensky, op. cit., p. 251, from a mimeographed copy of the minutes of the conference deposited in the Hoover Institution.

[4] Vulliamy, op. cit., p. 240.

after he was appointed, the commissar came to the Soviet and said: 'Do as you wish; I have been elected – if you support me, I'll do my duty, but if you don't, then I'll give up my job tomorrow.' We told him: 'If you do your job well, we'll support you, but otherwise not!'[1]

The Provisional Government tried to strengthen its ties with local bodies by sending out questionnaires to commissars regarding the political and economic situation in their areas, but in May these requests had to be followed up by this circular:

In many instances it has been observed that the guberniia commissars either fail to answer written queries or telegrams from the Ministry of the Interior, or answer them after considerable delay. I beg you to note that the queries from the Ministry should unfailingly be given an immediate answer; in case it is impossible to give an immediate answer, the causes of the delay should be explained by telegraph.[2]

It was not possible to oil the machinery of central–local contacts by pouring more funds into administrative work, since the Treasury was already strained to the utmost, as the Ministry of the Interior often reminded the provincial commissars.

One final complication was political rather than administrative in nature. As the year went by, and local commissars were replaced more and more often, the composition of local government personnel tended to become increasingly left-wing under pressure from the Soviets and other sources of public opinion in the provinces. At the centre the Provisional Government also progressed through a series of coalitions which included new blood from the left-wing parties, but the landslide was far more marked in the localities. Thus by the summer the Central Land Committee, which undertook a vast programme of agricultural reform, stood a long way to the right of the regional Land Committees that were supposed to implement its recommendations. As a result co-operation broke down, and the local authorities adopted independent programmes of their own. This lack of political co-ordination was never so apparent in the

[1] *Protokoly pervogo vserossiiskogo s"ezda sovetov rabochikh i soldatskikh deputatov 1917*, vol. 1 (Moscow, 1930–1) p. 257.

[2] *Sbornik tsirkuliarov . . .*, p. 35.

Bolshevik hierarchy. Apart from the dangerous gulf that opened up momentarily in the July Days, Lenin's party was much more of one mind than the heterogeneous group of parties which made up the Provisional Government.

Bibliography

Archives and Documents

Archiv russkoi revoliutsii (Berlin, 1921–37).
Archives of the German Foreign Ministry, *Eisenbahnen in Russland.*
Dokumenty velikoi proletarskoi revoliutsii, vol. 1 (Moscow, 1938).
Golder, F. A., *Documents of Russian History 1914–1917* (New York and London, 1927).
Hahlweg, W., *Lenins Rückkehr nach Russland 1917. Die deutschen Akten* (Leiden, 1957).
Ivanovo-Voznesenskie bol'sheviki v period podgotovki i provedeniia velikoi oktiab'rskoi sotsialisticheskoi revoliutsii, Sbornik dokumentov (Ivanovo, 1947).
Krasnyi arkhiv.
Perepiska Sekretariata Tsk RSDRP (b) s mestnymi partiinymi organizatsiiami, 2 vols (Moscow, 1957).
Protocol of the All-Russian Conference of Social Workers (August 1917).
Protokoly pervogo vserossiiskogo s"ezda sovetov rabochikh i soldatskikh deputatov 1917, vol. 1 (Moscow, 1930–1).
Protokoly VI s'ezda RSDRP (b) (Moscow, 1919).
Protokoly tsentral'nogo komiteta RSDRP (b), avgust 1917–fevral' 1918 (Moscow, 1958).
Russkii istoricheskii arkhiv. Publication of the Russian Historical Archive Abroad (Prague, 1929).
Sbornik tsirkuliarov ministerstva vnutrennikh del za period mart–iun' 1917 goda.
Sbornik ukazov i postanovlenii vremennogo pravitel'stva, 2 parts (Petrograd, 1917).
Shchegolev, P. E. (ed.), *Padenie tsarskogo rezhima* (Leningrad and Moscow, 1924–7).
Sidorov, A. L., et al. (eds), *Velikaia oktiabr'skaia sotsialisticheskaia revoliutsiia: Dokumenty i materialy* (Moscow, 1957).
———, *Revoliutsionnoe dvizhenie v rossii posle sverzheniia samoderzhaviia* (1957).
———, *Revoliutsionnoe dvizhenie v rossii v aprele 1917 g.: Aprel'skii krizis* (1958).
———, *Revoliutsionnoe dvizhenie v rossii v mae–iune 1917 g.: Iiun'skaia demonstratsiia* (1959).
———, *Revoliutsionnoe dvizhenie v rossii v iule 1917 g.: Iiul'skii krizis* (1959).
———, *Revoliutsionnoe dvizhenie v rossii v avguste 1917 g.: Razgrom kornilovskogo miatezha* (1959).
———, *Oktiabr'skoe vooruszhennoe vosstanie v Petrograde* (1957).

Vestnik vremennogo pravitel'stva (1917).

Zeman, Z. A. B., *Germany and the Revolution in Russia 1915–1918: Documents from the Archives of the German Foreign Ministry* (London, 1948).

· *Books and Pamphlets*

Alekseev, S. (ed.), *Fevral'skaia revoliutsiia* (Moscow, 1926).

Allilueva, A., *Memoirs* (London, 1946).

Antonov-Saratovsky, V. P., *Pod stiagom proletarskoi bor'by: otryvki iz vospominanii o rabote v Saratove za vremia s 1915 do 1918 g*, vol. 1 (Moscow and Leningrad, 1925).

Anweiler, O., *Die Rätebewegung in Russland 1905–1921* (Leiden, 1958).

Arendt, H., *On Revolution* (London, 1963).

Avdeev, N., *et al.* (eds), *Revoliutsiia 1917 goda (khronika sobytii)* (Moscow, 1923–30).

Belensky, S., and Manuelov, A. (eds.), *Revoliutsiia 1917 goda v Azerbaidzhane (khronika sobytii)* (Baku, 1927).

Bezpalov, V., *Teatri v dni revoliutsii 1917* (Leningrad, 1927).

Blok, A., *Sobranie sochinenii* (Moscow, 1963).

Boiko-Pavlov, D. I., and Sidorchuk, E. P., *Tak bylo na dal'nem vostoke* (Moscow, 1964).

Bol'shevistkie organizatsii Ukrainy v period ustanovleniia i ukrepleniia sovetskoi vlasti; sbornik dokumentov i materialov (Kiev, 1962).

Bonch-Bruevich, V. D., *Na boevykh postakh fevral'skoi i oktiabr'skoi revoliutsii* (Moscow, 1930).

——, *Vospominaniia Lenina* (Moscow, 1965).

Browder, R. P., and Kerensky, A. F. (eds), *The Russian Provisional Government 1917* (Stanford, 1961).

Brown, J. A. C., *Techniques of Persuasion* (London, 1963).

Bryson, L. (ed.), *The Communication of Ideas* (New York, 1948).

Bublikov, A. A., *Russkaia revoliutsiia* (New York, 1918).

Buchanan, Sir George, *My Mission to Russia and Other Diplomatic Memories*, vol. 2 (Boston, 1923).

Budnikov, V. P., *Bolshevistskaia partiinaia pechat' v 1917 godu* (Kharkov, 1959).

Bunyan, J., and Fisher, H. H. (eds), *The Bolshevik Revolution 1917–1918: Documents and Materials* (Stanford, 1961).

Carr, E. H., *A History of Soviet Russia: The Bolshevik Revolution, 1917–1923*, 3 vols (London, 1950–3).

Chamberlin, W., *The Russian Revolution, 1917–1921*, 2 vols (New York, 1935).

Chernov, V., *The Great Russian Revolution* (New Haven, 1936).

Chugaeva, D. A., *Protokoly i postanovlenii tsentral'nogo komiteta baltiiskogo flota, 1917–1918* (Moscow, 1963).

Cobban, A., *Historians and the Causes of the French Revolution* (London, 1946).

——, *The Social Interpretation of the French Revolution* (London, 1964).

Dan, T., *The Origins of Bolshevism* (London, 1964).
Daniels, R. V., *Red October: The Bolshevik Revolution of 1917* (London, 1968).
Danilov, S., *Ekonomika transporta* (Moscow, 1966).
Denikin, General A. I., *La Décomposition de l'Armée et du Pouvoir* (Paris, 1921).
Deutsch, K., *The Nerves of Government: Models of Political Communication and Control* (London, 1963).
Deutscher, I., *The Prophet Armed: Trotsky 1879–1921* (London, 1954).
Dickinson, T., and De La Roche, C., *Soviet Cinema* (London, 1948).
Dimanshtein, S. M. (ed.), *Revoliutsiia i natsional'nyi vopros* (Moscow, 1930).

Egorova, A. G., *Profsoiuzy i fabzavkomy v bor'be za pobedu oktiabria* (Moscow, 1960).
Ehrenburg, I., *Collected Works* (Moscow, 1964).
Ekonomicheskoe polozhenie Rossii nakanune velikoi oktiabr'skoi sotsialisticheskoi revoliutsii (Moscow, 1957).
Engelhardt, N., *Sketch of the History of the Russian Censorship in Connection with the Development of the Press, 1703–1903* (St Petersburg, 1904).
Erykalov, E., *Krasnaia gvardiia v bor'be za vlast' sovetov* (Moscow, 1957).

Fischer, F., *Griff nach der Weltmacht: Die Kriegszielpolitik des Kaiserlichen Deutschland, 1914–1918* (Düsseldorf, 1961).
Fortushenko, A. D., *Piat'desyat' let radio* (Moscow, 1945).
Futrell, M., *Northern Underground: Episodes of Russian Revolutionary Transport and Communications through Scandinavia and Finland, 1863–1917* (London, 1963).

Gaisinski, M., *Bor'ba bol'shevikov za krest'ianstvo v 1917 g.: vserossiiskie s'ezdy sovetov krest'ianskikh deputatov* (Moscow, 1933).
Gankin, O. H., and Fisher, H. H., *The Bolsheviks and the World War: The Origins of the Third International* (Stanford, 1940).
Gimpelson, E. G. G., *Iz istorii stroitel'stva sovetov, noiabr' 1917 g.–iul' 1918 g.* (1958).
The Goebbels Diaries (New York, 1945).
Golovine, N., *The Russian Army in the World War* (New Haven, 1931).
Gordeenko, Ia., *Kurs zheleznykh dorog* (St Petersburg, 1906).
Gorky, M., *V. I. Lenin* (Moscow, 1931).
Goron, I. E., *Radioveshchanie* (Moscow, 1944).
Grachev, E. (ed.), *Kazan'skii oktiabr': Materialy i dokumenty*, pt i: *mart–oktiabr' 1917 goda* (Kazan, 1926).
Gronsky, P. P., and Astrov, N. J. (eds), *The War and the Russian Government* (New Haven, 1929).

Harcave, S. S., *First Blood: The Russian Revolution of 1905* (London, 1965).
Hunter, D., *Soviet Transportation Policy* (Cambridge, Mass., 1957).

Ignat'ev, G. S., *Oktiabr' 1917 goda v Moskve* (Moscow, 1964).
Igritzky, I., *1917 v derevne* (Gosizdat, Moscow, 1929).

Il'in-Genevsky, A. F., *From the February Revolution to the October Revolution 1917* (London, 1931).
Inkeles, A., *Public Opinion in Soviet Russia* (Cambridge, Mass., 1962).
Istpart 1898–1923 (Gosizdat, Moscow, 1923):
  Revoliutsiia na dal'nem vostoke (Moscow, 1923);
  Revoliutsiia v Krimu (Krimksoe gosudarstvennoe izdatel'stvo, 1930);
  Revolutsiia v srednei Azii (Tashkent, 1929);
  Oktiabr' na Kubani i Chernomore (Krasnodar, 1924);
  1905 (Gosizdat, Moscow, 1925);
  Pervii legalnyi Pe-Ka bolshevikov v 1917 g. (Moscow, 1927).

Kaimin', Ia., *Latyshkie strel'by v bor'be za pobedu oktiabr'skoi revoliutsii* (Riga, 1961).
Katkov, G., *Russia 1917: The February Revolution* (London, 1967).
Katzenellenbaum, S., *Russian Currency and Banking 1914–1924* (London, 1925).
Keep, J. L., *The Rise of Social Democracy in Russia* (Oxford, 1963).
Kennan, G. F., *Soviet-American Relations 1917–20*, vol. 1, *Russia Leaves the War* (London, 1956).
Kerensky, A. F., *The Crucifixion of Liberty* (New York, 1934).
——, *The Prelude to Bolshevism* (New York, 1919).
——, *The Catastrophe* (New York, 1927).
The Kerensky Memoirs (London, 1966).
Knorin, V., *Revoliutsiia i kontr-Revoliutsiia v Belorussii (fevral' 1917–fevral' 1918)* (Smolensk, 1920).
Knox, Sir Alfred, *With the Russian Army, 1914–1917*, 2 vols (London, 1921).
Kruglak, T. E., *The Two Faces of TASS* (Minneapolis, 1962).
Krupspkaia, N. K., *Memories of Lenin* (London, 1930).

Lang, D. M., *A Modern History of Soviet Georgia* (London, 1962).
Lasswell, H. D., *Propaganda Technique in the World War* (London, 1938).
——, Casey, R. D., and Smith, B. L., *Propaganda and Promotional Activities* (Minneapolis, 1935).
Lavigin, V. M. (ed.), *1917 god v Voronezhskoi gubernii (Khronika)* (Voronezh, 1928).
Lebedev, N. A., *Ocherk istorii kino SSSR* (Moscow, 1947).
Lefebvre, G., *Documents relatifs à l'histoire des subsistances dans le district de Bergues pendant la révolution (1788–An V)* (Lille, 1914).
Lelevich, L., *Oktiabr' v stavke* (Gomel, 1922).
Lenin, Stalin, partiia o kino (Moscow, 1938).
Lenin, V. I., *Sochineniia*, 4th ed. (Moscow, 1941–52).
——, *Collected Works*, 4th ed. (London, 1960). This edition only, in Russian and English, is used almost exclusively in these essays.
Lenin v oktiabre-vospominaniia (Moscow, 1967).
Letopis' velikogo oktiabria, aprel'–oktiabr' 1917 (Moscow, 1958).
Letters of the Tsar to the Tsaritsa, 1914–1917 (New York, 1929).

Letters of the Tsaritsa to the Tsar, 1914–1916 (London, 1923).

Levitas, I., *et al.*, *Revoliutsionnye podpol'nye tipografii v Rossii (1906–1917)* (Moscow, 1962).

Liashchenko, P. I., *Istoriia narodnogo khoziaistva SSSR*, vol. 2 (Moscow, 1948).

Lomonosov, Iu. V., *Vospominanie o martovskoi revoliutsii 1917 g.* (Berlin, 1921).

Lozinsky, Z., *Ekonomicheskoe polozhenie vremennogo pravitel'stva* (Leningrad, 1929).

Lukomsky, A. *Vospominania* (Berlin, 1922).

Luxemburg, R., *The Russian Revolution* (Ann Arbor, 1961).

Manilov, V. (ed.), *1917 god na Kievshchine: Khronika sobytii* (Kiev, 1928).

Maynard, Sir J., *The Russian Peasant* (New York, 1962).

Mel'gunov, S. P., *Kak bol'sheviki zakhvatili vlast'* (Paris, 1953).

——, *Legenda o separatnom mire* (Paris, 1957).

——, *Martovskie dni 1917 goda* (Paris, 1961).

——, *Na putiakh k dvortsovomu perevorotu* (Paris, 1931).

——, *Sud'ba Imperator Nikolaia II posle otrecheniia* (Paris, 1951).

—— *Zolotoi nemetskii kliuch k bolshevistkoi revoliutsii* (Paris, 1940).

Meller, V. L., and Pankratov, A. M. (eds), *Rabochee dvizhenie v 1917 godu* (Moscow, 1926).

Michelson, A. M., Apostol, P. N., and Bernatzky, M. W., *Russian Public Finance during the War* (New Haven, 1928).

Mikhailov, I., *Evoliutsiia russkogo transporta 1913–25* (Moscow, 1925).

Miliukov, P. N., *Istoriia vtoroi russkoi revoliutsii*, 1 vol. in 3 parts (Sofia, 1921–3).

——, *Vospominaniia, 1859–1917*, 2 vols (New York, 1955).

Miliutin, V. P., *Selsko-khoziaistvennye rabochie i voina* (Petrograd, 1917).

Mitel'man, M., *1917 god na putilovskom zavode* (Leningrad, 1939).

Morgunov, V., and Machulusky, Z. (eds), *1917 god v Khar'kove: Sbornik statei i vospominanii* (Kharkov, 1927).

Muratov, Kh. I., *Revoliutsionnoe dvizhenie v russkoi armii v 1917 g.* (Moscow, 1958).

Narvskaia zastava v 1917 godu v vospominaniiakh i dokumentakh (Leningrad, 1960).

Nevskii, V., *Sovety i vooruzhennoe vosstanie v 1905 godu* (Moscow, 1931).

Nolde, Baron B. E., *Russia in the Economic War* (New Haven, 1928).

Oktiabr' na Odeshchine: Sbornik statei i vospominanii k X-letiiu oktiabria (Odessa, 1927).

Oktiabr'skoe vooruzhennoe vosstanie v Petrograde (Velikaia oktiabr'skaia sotsialisticheskaia revoliutsiia: Dokumenty i materialy) (Moscow, 1957).

Oktiabr'skoe vooruzhennoe vosstanie v Petrograde (Vospominaniia aktivnykh uchastnikov revoliutsiia) (Leningrad, 1956).

O propagande i agitatsii (Leningrad, 1936).

Orlov, N., *Prodovol'stvennaia rabota sovetskoi vlasti* (Moscow, 1918).

H 2

Ovsiannikov, N. (ed.), *Oktiabr'skoe vosstanie v Moskve: sbornik dokumentov, statei i vospominanii* (Moscow, 1922).

Owen, L., *The Russian Peasant Movement 1906–1917* (London, 1937).

Pares, B., *Day by Day with the Russian Army* (London, 1915).

——, *My Russian Memoirs* (London, 1931).

—— *The Fall of the Russian Monarchy* (London, 1939).

Paustovsky, K., *Story of a Life: Slow Approach of Thunder* (London, 1965).

—— *In That Dawn* (London, 1967).

Petrogradskie bol'sheviki v oktiabr'skoi revoliutsii (Leningrad, 1957).

Petropavlovsky, E. S., *Listovki kak istochnik pri izuchenii istorii KPSS* (Moscow, 1966).

Petrova, E. I., *Oktiabr' v zapadnoi Sibiri* (Novosibirsk, 1948).

Piontkovsky, S., *Oktiabr' 1917 g.* (Moscow and Leningrad, 1917).

Pipes, R., *The Formation of the Soviet Union: Communism and Nationalism* (Cambridge, Mass., 1954).

—— (ed.), *Revolutionary Russia* (Cambridge, Mass., 1968).

Pis'ma trudiashchikhsia k Leninu (Moscow, 1960).

Pokrovsky, M. N., and Iakovlev, Ia. A. (eds), *1917 god v dokumentakh i materialakh*, vol. 1: *Petrogradskii sovet rabochikh i soldatskikh deputatov: protokoly zasedanii ispolnitel'nogo komiteta i biuro I.K.* (Moscow, 1925).

——, *Razlozhenie armii v 1917 godu* (Moscow, 1925).

——, *Rabochee dvizhenie v 1917 godu* (Moscow, 1926).

——, *Krest'ianskoe dvizhenie v 1917 godu* (Moscow, 1927).

——, *Vserossiiskoe uchreditel'noe sobranie* (Moscow, 1930).

Polovtsov, General P. A., *Glory and Downfall: Reminiscences of a Russian General Staff Officer* (London, 1935).

Popova, E., *Moskovskaia provintsiia v semnadtsatom godu* (Moscow and Leningrad, 1927).

Pushkareva, I., *Lenin i oktiabr'skoe vooruzhennoe vosstanie v Petrograde* (Moscow, 1964).

Rabinovich, S., *Bor'ba za armiiu v 1917 g.* (Moscow, 1930).

Rabinowitch, A., *Prelude to Revolution: The Petrograd Bolsheviks and the July 1917 Uprising* (Bloomington, Ind., 1968).

Rabochii klass i rabochee dvizhenie v Rossii v 1917 g. (Moscow, 1964).

Rabochii klass Urala v gody voiny i revoliutsii, 3 vols (Sverdlovsk, 1927).

Radkey, O. H., *The Agrarian Foes of Bolshevism: Promise and Default of the Russian Socialist Revolutionaries, February to October 1917* (New York, 1958).

——, *The Election to the Russian Constituent Assembly of 1917* (Cambridge, Mass., 1950).

——, *The Sickle under the Hammer: The Russian Socialist Revolutionaries in the Early Months of Soviet Rule* (New York, 1963).

Raionnye sovety Petrograda v 1917 g. (Moscow, 1965).

Rathauser, Ia., *Revoliutsiia i grazhdanskaia voina v Baku* (Baku, 1927).

Reed, J., *Ten Days That Shook the World* (New York, 1919).

Ross, H. M., *British Railways* (London, 1904).

Rudé, D., *The Crowd in the French Revolution* (Oxford, 1959).

Schapiro, L., *The Communist Party of the Soviet Union* (London, 1960).
——, *The Origin of the Communist Autocracy* (London, 1955).
Seton-Watson, H., *The Decline of Imperial Russia, 1885–1914* (London, 1952).
Shakhanov, N. (ed.), *1917-i god vo vladimirskoi gubernii: Khronika sobytii* (Vladimir, 1927).
Shavel'sky, G., *Vospominaniia poslednego protopresvitera russkoi armii i flota*, 2 vols (New York, 1954).
Shubin, I. A., *Volga i volzhskoe sudokhodstvo* (Moscow, 1927).
Shulgin, V., *Dni* (Leningrad, 1925).
Smith, B. L., Lasswell, H. D., and Casey, R. D., *Propaganda, Communication, and Public Opinion* (Princeton, 1946).
Spiridovich, A. I., *Velikaia voina i fevral'skaia revoliutsiia* (New York, 1962).
Steinberg, I. Z., *Als ich Volkskommissar war: Episoden aus der russischen Oktoberrevolution* (Munich, 1929).
Stepanov, Z. V., *Rabochie Petrograda v period podgotovki i provedeniia oktiabr'skogo vooruzhennogo vosstaniia* (Moscow, 1965).
Struve, P. B., Zaitsev, K. I., Dolinsky, N. V., and Demosthenov, S. S., *Food Supply in Russia during the World War* (New Haven, 1930).
Sukhanov, N. N., *Zapiski o revoliutsii*, 7 vols (Berlin, 1922–3).

Taniaiev, A., *Ocherki po istorii dvizheniia zheleznodorozhnikov v revoliutsii 1917 goda* (Moscow, 1925).
Tekhnika i ekonomika putei soobshchenii (Moscow, 1920).
Trenogova, T., *Bor'ba petrogradskikh bol'shevikov za khrest'ianstvo v 1917* (Leningrad, 1946).
Trotsky, L., *The History of the Russian Revolution*, 3 vols (New York, 1932).
——, *Oktiabr'skaia revoliutsiia* (Moscow and Petrograd, 1918).
Tseretelli, I. G., *Vospominaniia o fevral'skoi revoliutsii*, 2 vols (The Hague, 1963).

Ukazatel' zheleznodorozhnykh, parokhodnykh i drugikh passazhirskikh soobshcheni pod redaktsii zheleznykh dorog: 1916 goda.
Ulam, A., *Lenin and the Bolsheviks* (London, 1966).

Vasiliev, N., *Transport Rossii v voine 1914–18 gg.* (Moscow, 1939).
V bor'be za oktiabr' v Belorussii (Moscow, 1957).
Velikaia oktiabr'skaia sotsialisticheskaia revoliutsiia: khronika sobytii (Moscow, 1957) I. 27 fevralia–6 maia 1917 goda (1957); II. 7 maia–25 iiulia 1917 goda (1959).
Vompe, P., *Dni oktiabr'skoi revoliutsii i shelezhodorozhniki* (Moscow, 1924).
Voznesensky, A. N., *Moskva v 1917 godu* (Moscow and Leningrad, 1928).
Vulliamy, C. E., and Hynes, A. L., *From the Red Archives: Russian State Papers and Other Documents Relating to the Years 1915–1918* (London, 1929).

Warth, R., *The Allies and the Russian Revolution: From the Fall of the Monarchy to the Peace of Brest-Litovsk, March 1918* (Durham, N.C., 1954).
Westwood, J., *A History of Russian Railways* (London, 1964).
Windlesham, Lord, *Communication and Political Power* (London, 1966).

Zaslavsky, B., Sazoaov, I., and Astrakhan, Kh., *Pravda 1917 goda* (Moscow, 1962).

Zeman, Z. A. B., *Nazi Propaganda* (London, 1964).

Zheleznodorozhniki i revoliutsiia: sbornik vospominanii i dokumentov o rabote zhelezno-dorozhnogo raiona Moskovskogo organizatsii R.K.P. sostavlenyi tt. Piatnitskim, Ziminym i Aronshtamom (Moscow, 1923).

Znamensky, O. N., *Iul'skii krisis 1917 goda* (Moscow, 1964).

Newspapers and Journals

The place of issue is Petrograd unless otherwise stated.

Daily Review of the Foreign Press, issued daily by the General Staff, War Office, London, 1917.

Delo naroda, organ of the Central Committee of the Socialist Revolutionary Party, 1917.

Den', 1917.

Golos pravdy, 1917.

Golos zheleznodorozhnika, 1917.

Istoricheskii zhurnal, Moscow, 1936–45.

Izvestiia, organ of the Central Executive Committee of the Workers' and Soldiers' Deputies (subtitle varies), 1917.

Izvestiia ispolnitel'nogo komiteta obshchestvennykh organizatsii g. Irkutska, Irkutsk, 1917.

Izvestiia kronshtadtskogo soveta, Kronstadt, 1917.

Izvestiia moskovskogo soveta rabochikh i soldatskikh deputatov, Moscow, 1917.

Izvestiia revoliutsionnoi nedeli, published by the Committee of Petrograd Journalists, 27 Feb.–5 Mar. 1917.

Letopis' revoliutsii, 1 vol., Berlin–Petrograd–Moscow, 1923.

Moskovskii metallist, Moscow, 1917.

Mysl' zheleznodorozhnika, 1917.

Novaia zhizn', 1917.

Novoe vremia, 1917.

Pravda, organ of the Central Committee of the Bolshevik Party, 5 Mar.–5 July 1917. Published subsequently in 1917 as: *Listok 'Pravdy'*, 6 July; *Rabochii i Soldat*, 23 July–9 Aug.; *Proletarii*, 13 Aug.–24 Aug.; *Rabochii*, 25 Aug.–2 Sep.; *Rabochii Put'.*, 3 Sep.–26 Oct.; *Pravda*, 27 Oct.

Proletarskaia revoliutsiia, journal of the history of the October Revolution and the Russian Communist Party, published by the Central Committee of the Russian Communist Party, Moscow, 1921–36.

Rabochaia gazeta, central organ of the Russian Social Democratic Party (Menshevik), 1917.

Rech', organ of the Constitutional Democratic Party, 1917.

Russkaia volia, 1917.

Russkiia vedomosti, Moscow, 1917.

Russkoe slovo, Moscow, 1917.

Soldatskaia pravda, 1917.

Sotsial-demokrat, Moscow, 1917.

The Times, London, 1917.
Trud, 1917.
Vestnik putei soobshcheniia, organ of the People's Commissariat of Communication, 1918.
Vestnik vremennogo pravitel'stva, daily official newspaper of the Provisional Government, 1917.
Vlast' naroda, Moscow, 1917.
Volia naroda, organ of the right Socialist Revolutionaries, 1917.

Selected Articles

Anisimova-Slesareva, A. G., 'Bor'ba za moskovskuiu telefonnuiu stantsiiu', in *Sviazisty v bor'be za vlast' sovetov* (Moscow, 1964) pp. 62–5.
Augustine, W. R., 'Russia's Railwaymen, July–October 1917', in *Slavic Review* (1965) pp. 666–79.
Avdeev, N., 'Bolshevistkaia rabota vo flote i armii nakanune fevral'skoi revoliutsii', in *Proletarskaia revoliutsiia*, no. 6 (1924).
Baburin, N. N., 'V bor'be roslo nashe revoliutsionnoe samoznanie', in *Sviazisty v bor'be za vlast' sovetov*.
Bilyk, P. (ed.), 'V tsarskoi armii nakanune fevral'skoi burzhuazo-demokraticheskoi revoliutsii', in *Krasnyi arkhiv*, vol. 81 (1937) pp. 105–20.
Bonnin, G., 'Les bolchéviques et l'argent allemand pendant la première guerre mondiale', in *Revue Historique* (Jan.–Mar. 1965) pp. 101–26.
Chernyshev, I. I., 'Pod znamia velikogo oktiabria', in *Sviazisty v bor'be za vlast' sovetov*.
Dando, W. A., 'A Map of the Election to the Russian Constituent Assembly of 1917', in *Slavic Review*, vol. 25, no. 2 (1966) pp. 314–19.
Dewhirst, M., 'L'historiographie soviétique récente et l'histoire de la révolution', in *Cahiers du Monde russe et soviétique* (Oct.–Dec. 1964).
'Fevral'skaia revoliutsiia 1917 goda', in *Krasnyi arkhiv*, vol. 21 (1927) pp. 3–78; vol. 22 (1927) pp. 3–70.
'Fevral'skaia revoliutsiia v Baltiiskom flote (Iz dnevnika I. I. Rengartena)', in *Krasnyi arkhiv*, vol. 32 (1929) pp. 99–124.
'Fevral'skaia revoliutsiia v Petrograde', in *Krasnyi arkhiv*, vol. 41–2 (1930) pp. 62–102.
Genikina, E., 'Pervye dni oktiabr'skoi revoliutsii 1917 g.', in *Proletarskaia revoliutsiia*, no. 3 (1940).
Golubev, I. P., 'Krasnogvardeitsy-zheleznodorozhniki', in *V bor'be za oktiabr' v Belorussii i na zapadnom fronte* (Minsk, 1957).
Grazkin, D., 'Soldatskaia gazeta', in *Letopis' velikogo oktiabria, aprel'–oktiabr' 1917* (Moscow, 1958).
Kadlubovsky, K. Ia., 'Sviazisty Petrograda v bor'be za vlast' sovetov', in *Sviazisty v bor'be za vlast' sovetov*.
Katkov, G. M., 'German Foreign Office Documents on Financial Support to the Bolsheviks in 1917', in *International Affairs*, vol. 32, no. 2 (Apr. 1956) pp. 181–9.

Khodeev, M. V., 'Po puti, ukazannomu Leninym', in *Sviazisty v bor'be za vlast' sovetov.*

'Kommissia po inostrannym delam', in *Byloe*, vol. 6, no. 12 (1918).

Kondratiev, A., 'Vospominaniia o podpolnoi rabote v Petrograde Peterburgskoi organizatsii RSDRP (b) v period 1914-17 gg.', in *Krasnaia Letopis'*, vol. 7 (1923) pp. 30–74.

Kuchkin, A., 'Krest'ianskii s'ezd', in *Letopis' velikogo oktiabria* (Moscow, 1958).

Lasswell, H. D., 'Agitation', in *The Encyclopedia of the Social Sciences*, vol. 1 (New York, 1930).

——, 'Communications Research and Politics', in Douglas Waples (ed.), *Print, Radio and Film in a Democracy* (Chicago, 1942).

——, 'Propaganda', in *The Encyclopedia of the Social Sciences*, vol. 12 (New York, 1934).

Leiberov, I. P., 'Statechnaia bor'ba petrogradskogo proletariata v period pervoi mirovoi voiny', in *Istoriia rabochego klassa Leningrada* (Moscow, 1963).

'Oktiabr' na fronte', in *Krasnyi arkhiv*, vol. 23 (1927) pp. 149–94; vol. 24 (1927) pp. 71–107.

Parsons, T., 'Propaganda and Social Control', in *Psychiatry*, vol. 5, no. 4 (1942).

Piatnitsky, O., 'Iz moei raboty v moskovskom komitete', in the collection of articles entitled *Ot fevralia k oktiabriu* (Moscow, 1923).

Pogrebinsky, A. P., 'Sels'koe khoziaistvo i prodovol'stvennyi vopros v Rossii v gody pervoi mirovoi voiny', in *Istoricheskie zapiski*, vol. 31 (Moscow, 1950).

Pokrovsky, M. N. (ed.), 'Ekonomicheskoe polozhenie rossii pered revoliutsiei', in *Krasnyi arkhiv*, vol. 10 (1925) pp. 69–94.

'Prodovol'stvennoe polozhenie v Moskve v marte–iiune 1917 goda', in *Krasnyi arkhiv*, vol. 81 (1937) pp. 128–46.

Rapoport, S., 'Posle perevorota 25-go oktiabria 1917 goda', in *Arkhiv russkoi revoliutsii*, vol. 8 (1923).

Remezova, T. A., 'Sovety krest'ianskikh deputatov v 1917 g.', in *Istoricheskie zapiski* (1950) pp. 15–19.

Romanov, B. (ed.), 'Finansovoe polozhenie rossii pered oktiabr'skoi revoliutsiei', in *Krasnyi arkhiv*, vol. 25 (1927) pp. 3–33.

'Russkaia armiia nakanune revoliutsii', in *Byloe*, no. 1 (1918) pp. 151–7.

Salzirn, E. M., 'Ot fevralia k oktiabriu', in *Sviazisty v bor'be za vlast' sovetov.*

Selitsky, V. I., 'Nekotorye voprosy bor'by petrogradskikh rabochikh za kontrol' nad proizvodstvom v period mirnogo razvitiia revoliutsii (mart–iun' 1917 g.)', in *Istoriia rabochego klassa Leningrada* (Leningrad, 1963).

Sviridov, A. A., 'Proletariat Petrograda v bor'be za rabochii kontrol' v period organizatsii shturma', in *Uchenye zapiski L.G.P.I. im. A. I. Gertsena*, vol. 102 (Leningrad, 1955).

Tarasov, A. A., 'U provoda Lenina', in *Sviazisty v bor'be za vlast' sovetov.*

Telegin, P. N., 'Sovet piatnadsati revoliutsionnykh sviazistov Kharkova', in *Sviazisty v bor'be za vlast' sovetov.*

Tobolin, I. (ed.), 'Iul'skie dni v Petrograde', in *Krasnyi arkhiv*, vol. 23 (1927) pp. 1–63; vol. 24 (1927) pp. 3–70.

Tseretelli, I., 'Nakanune iiul'skogo vosstaniia', in *Novyi zhurnal*, vol. 50 (1957) pp. 198–219; vol. 51 (1957) pp. 120–46; vol. 52 (1958) pp. 162–98.

Vladimirova, V. (ed.), 'Bol'shevizatsiia fronta v prediiul'skie dni 1917 g.', in *Krasnyi arkhiv*, vol. 58 (1933) pp. 86–100.

Volin, M. N., 'Formirovanie klassovogo soznaniia', in *Sviazisty v bor'be za vlast' sovetov*.

Ziglin, R., 'Radio Broadcasting in the Soviet Union', in *Annals of the American Academy of Political and Social Science*, vol. 177 (1935).

Zubavnikov, N. S., 'V bor'be za vlast' sovetov', in *Sviazisty v bor'be za vlast' sovetov*.

Index

Index